The Far Western Frontier

The Far Western Frontier

Advisory Editor

RAY A. BILLINGTON

Senior Research Associate
at the Henry E. Huntington Library
and Art Gallery

THE CORRESPONDENCE AND JOURNALS OF CAPTAIN

NATHANIEL J. WYETH

1831-6

F[REDERICK] G. YOUNG, EDITOR

ARNO PRESS

A NEW YORK TIMES COMPANY

New York 1973

Reprint Edition 1973 by Arno Press Inc.

Reprinted from a copy in The State
Historical Society of Wisconsin Library

The Far Western Frontier
ISBN for complete set: 0-405-04955-2
See last pages of this volume for titles.

Manufactured in the United States of America

Publisher's Note: This volume was reprinted
from the best available copy.

Library of Congress Cataloging in Publication Data

Wyeth, Nathaniel Jarvis, 1802-1856.
    The correspondence and journals of Captain
Nathaniel J. Wyeth, 1831-6.

    (The Far Western frontier)
    Reprint of the 1899 ed., issued in series:
Sources of the history of Oregon, v. 1.
    1. Oregon--History--To 1859--Sources.
2. Hudson's Bay Company. 3. Overland journeys to
the Pacific. I. Young, Frederick George, 1858-1929,
ed. II. Title. III. Series.
F880.W98 1973   917.95   72-9474
ISBN 0-405-05001-1

SOURCES OF THE HISTORY
OF OREGON

Volume I   *Parts 3 to 6 inclusive*

THE CORRESPONDENCE AND JOURNALS OF CAPTAIN
NATHANIEL J. WYETH
1831-6

**A Record of Two Expeditions for the Occupation of the Oregon
Country, with Maps, Introduction and Index**

CONTINUATION OF THE CONTRIBUTIONS OF THE DEPARTMENT
OF ECONOMICS AND HISTORY OF THE UNIVERSITY
OF OREGON BY THE OREGON
HISTORICAL SOCIETY

Edited by F. G. Young,
Secretary Oregon Historical Society.

PRICE ONE DOLLAR

University Press
Eugene, Ore.
1899

A tribute to the memory of Captain Wyeth by James Russell Lowell, sent to the Portland (Oregon) High School on the occasion of its having a Lowell evening.

ELMWOOD, CAMBRIDGE, MASS.

24th April, 1890.

Dear Miss H * * *

I feel as if I had a kind of birthright in your Portland, for it was a townsman of mine who first led an expedition thither across the plains and tried to establish a settlement there. I well remember his starting sixty years ago, and knew him well in after years. He was a very remarkable person whose conversation I valued highly. A born leader of men, he was fitly called *Captain* Nathaniel Wyeth as long as he lived. It was the weakness of his companions that forced him to let go his hold on that fair possession. I hope he is duly honored in your traditions. * *

I pray you to give my greeting with the warmest assurance of good will to both teachers and pupils. We are I am sure heartily at one in our desire to maintain and perpetuate the better traditions of our local and national life, and it is upon our schools that we must rely in great measure for the fulfilment of that desire.

Wishing for all of you happy and useful lives—and one includes the other

I remain

Very sincerely your friend

J. R. LOWELL.

Editor's Preface

In the traditions of New England Nathaniel Jarvis Wyeth is highly honored as the principal founder of the ice industry. The *Boston Transcript* in its notice of his death, August, 1856, said: "It is not perhaps too much to say that there is not a single tool or machine of real value now employed in the ice harvesting, which was not originally invented by Mr Wyeth They all look to Fresh Pond as the place of their origin". "As one who laid open a new field of honorable industry" he was held "entitled to the rank of a public benefactor."

Among his friends who came under the influence of his strong personality he was regarded as "one of the remarkable men of New England." The tribute to his memory sent to Oregon by Lowell stimulated the search for the record of those wonderful expeditions led by him. Those in quest of it were rewarded not only in finding the manuscripts, nearly complete, but also in getting from the possessor of them a gracious response to the request for permission to publish.

These sources furnish data for making more adequate and instructive the history of the occupation of the continent, and through the publication of them the author will receive due recognition for a conspicuous part in a great national movement and for the possession of a strong spark of heroic spirit like that whose song is,

> "My purpose holds
> To sail beyond the sunset and the baths
> Of all the western stars until I die."

The manuscript is in the possession of Mrs. Mary J. Fish of Taunton, Massachusetts. When sent to be copied for publication it took its third trip westward across the continent, but this time it was not "to be painfully borne by wearisome marches through almost unbroken solitudes for weary months," but now after sixty-three years to be "swiftly carried in a few days, to find no longer at the journey's end the wilderness of Nature but the homes of an enlightened and progressive people."

The editor owes deepest thanks to Mrs. Fish for being entrusted with the honor of publishing this record and for her consent to present it in its integrity.

The plan has been to reproduce the original faithfully to the letter. From the conditions under which the record was made some parts are faint and mutilated but it is hoped that defects arising from this cause and from shortcomings in editing will not seriously impair the historical value of these documents.

Eugene, Oregon,
July 1, 1899.

ERRATA

Page 12,	"circumsnances"	in line 39	should read	"circumstances"
" 38,	"enongh"	" " 44	" "	"enough"
" 49,	"Tnesday"	" " 32	" "	"Tuesday"
" 62,	"Vadcouver"	" " 5	" "	"Vancouver"
" 79,	"Haying"	" " 4	" "	"Having"
" 126,	"dot"	" " 8	" "	"not"
" 157,	"fiowers"	" " 4	" "	"flowers"
" 212,	"Savvages"	" " 6	" "	"Sauvages"
" 236,	"contardictory"	" " 38	" "	"contradictory"

CONTENTS

CORRESPONDENCE

	Persons addressed	Page

CONTENTS

xii   CONTENTS

JOURNALS

Introduction

The American people are just experiencing some startling disclosures of the depth of significance to them in their destiny springing from the fact that they have a territorial basis continental in its proportions. Their facing of the two oceans through so much of the north temperate zone of itself affords a mighty leverage among the nations of the earth.

The main story of the making of this nation holds two fairly equal interwoven threads—one follows the development of a new order of national institutions; the other shows the lead of that instinctive craving of a progressive people for a territorial basis adequate for their destiny. Who will say which national motive inspired the larger measure of the heroic? The victories of arms have been more resounding where issues of freedom and equality were at stake. There is, however, no brighter page of American history than that which records the victory of American diplomacy when in 1783 against the greatest odds the "father of waters" was secured for our western boundary. And what could have been more sagacious than the stroke of 1803 through which our national domain was more than doubled?

Thrilling were the achievements of George Rogers Clark in the winter of 1778-9 and grand the work of the American commissioners at Paris in 1783, still our expansion to the Pacific is a tale of pioneering. The ensigns of an axe on the shoulder of a pioneer, a pack horse, and a "prairie schooner" with a household as occupants—all facing westward –tipify our rise to a world power.

Our national progress towards the occupation of the continent assumed an especially interesting phase in the thirties. During this decade all conditions were maturing for that grand migratory on-sweep across the plains in the forties and fifties. The vanguard of the pioneers had reached the western limits of Iowa, Missouri and Arkansas. Settlement of the plains beyond before the age o railroads was out of the question. The next move then must be as it were a flight to the Pacific coast where communication with the civilized world would again be open by the sea. But it was a move the difficulties and dangers of which were appalling. All the previous history of the world had enforced the principle that broad belts of uninhabitable country and high mountain ranges constituted the natural limits of national territory. To overturn this god Terminus and lead the way to a wider and higher national destiny called for effort that was heroic. Wyeth and Whitman will always stand as representative American heroes because of their resolute initiative and achievement in connection with this American problem of expansion to continental proportions.

Let us note the elements of the situation at the opening of the year 1832, when Nathaniel J. Wyeth had first matured his plans for an expedition to the Oregon Territory. A quarter of a century had elapsed since Lewis and Clark had threaded the valleys of the upper Missouri and followed the waters of the Columbia to the western ocean. An accurate account of the character of the country and its inhabitants had been immediately given to the world. The Winships in 1809 and then Astor in 1811 made attempts at occupation with trading posts. Nearly twenty years had now gone since these ventures had suffered dismal discomfiture. These failures had not provoked renewed efforts for the conquest of the difficulties involved in the occupation of the Columbia basin. True, there had been immediately a considerable development of fur-trading activities with St. Louis as a base. Annual expeditions by two or three companies were made to the headwaters of the rivers flowing to the Pacific. Now and then American trapping and trading parties would penetrate to California and far down the tributaries of the Columbia. But American enterprise seemed to quail before the difficulties confronting any project for securing such a foothold in the Pacific Northwest as could become the nucleus of a colony. There was no promise in the posts of the fur companies scattered sporadically through the Rocky mountains.

The English were our only persistent rivals for the possession of the Columbia basin. Our claim to it was fortified by priority in discovery, exploration and occupation. Quite different, however, was the outcome of their ventures for joint occupation from the disasters which befell ours. In 1813 the British Northwest Company purchased what was little more than the wreck of Astor's outfit at Astoria. A few months later an English man of war arrived there to formally seize what was already British in sympathy. By the terms of Article I of the treaty of Ghent, 1815, all places "taken by either party from the other during the war" were to be restored, and accordingly in October of 1818 an American agent, a Mr. Prevost, received the nominal restitution of what had been Astoria, renamed Fort George. The American occupation of the Columbia basin had dwindled to what was represented in the ceremony of hauling down the British flag and running up

the Stars and Stripes in the presence of the post of a British fur
company, the crew of a British man of war, and a solitary agent
of the American government. This lone American, further, "signed a receipt for the delivery of Fort George, and accepted a re-
monstrance from the British against the delivery until the final
decision of the right of sovereignty to the country between the
two governments." A few days later he was hustled away and
the British colors were again floated for nearly a generation above
the parapets of the fort.

With the consolidation of the Northwest and Hudson's Bay
Companies in 1821, the establishment of headquarters at Fort
Vancouver, and the effective administration of Dr. John McLoughlin as Chief Factor west of the Rocky mountains British interests
developed at a wonderful rate. It was claimed on the floor of
congress that "shares in the Hudson's Bay Compay, which origii -
ally were of the value of 20 pounds each, were now selling in the
market at the enormous price of 200 pounds sterling." And again
"that shares of that company have risen from sixty to two-hund-
red and forty pounds sterling." With the growth of English interests on the Columbia English claims to sovereignty grew
apace. American operations were confined to irregular incursions
by fur-trading parties and to traffic carried on with natives from
the decks of vessels brought into the inlets of the coast. The
British were establishing posts and extending a well-organized,
lucrative and strongly supported trade.

American enterprise pitted against English on the Columbia in
the line of fur trading operations was clearly worsted. It is not
difficult to see the reasons why this was so. The Oregon country
lay much more accessible to British activity than to ours. Judging merely from the map it seemed almost equally contiguous to
British and to American possessions. The forty-ninth parallel
had deen extended to the Rocky mountains in 1818 as the dividing line between the United States and British America. The
southern limit of the Oregon territory was the forty-second parallel, the northern boundary was fifty-four degrees and forty minutes, hence it abutted on the United States through the length of
seven degrees and on English territory through nearly six. But
considered with reference to actual conditions in this border country the advantage of the English is patent.

The "Great American Desert" was never represented as extending into the region lying between Lake Superior and the
Hudson Bay on the one side and Rocky mountains on the other.
A vast expanse of arid plains lay as a barrier between St. Louis,
the base of operations of the American companies, and the game
preserves of the Rockies and Oregon. This region had to be
traversed with the more expensive pack-horse transit. Before the
British company with bases on Lake Superior and the Hudson Bay there lay stretched an uninterrupted game preserve to the

headwaters of the Columbia. For traversing this there were
wonderfully convenient natural facilities of reticulated water
courses making easy water transits. English occupation of the
Columbia basin was but a slight extension of a long-established
chain of posts. American occupation as contemplated by the Winships, by Astor and again by Wyeth depended mainly upon communication by sea over a route of 16,000 miles. Formidable as
was the advantage of the English in relation to contiguity, her
measure of advantage as represented in the organization, resources,
personnel, and experience of the Hudson's Bay Company was simply
stupendous. How could American companies, newly organized
with raw recruits and small capital, hope to cope
with a corporation possessing in sole right an im-
perial domain enormously rich in just what suited its
aims, a capital of two millions and available assets of many millions more, the stability that activity of one hundred and fifty
years along the same lines gives, and as its working force a race
bred, adapted and trained to its purposes of exploiting this
vast region with its unnumbered tribes to its profit? I am re-
ferring now to occupation for purposes of trade with the Indians
and exploitation of the region for furs and not to occupation for
purposes of agriculture. When conditions were matured for the
pioneer movement the very influences that had made so strongly
for England in the lower form of occupation told against her quite
as effectively as before they had wrought in her favor.

For the time, however, the agreement between the English and
American governments to a joint occupation resulted in an exclusive occupation by the English company. And immediately
Floyd in the House (1820) and Benton in the Senate were sound-
ing the alarm that we were in danger of losing Oregon. They
urged, further, that with the English fortified there holding influence
over the Indians our northwestern frontier would be exposed to
depredations like those suffered during the English occupation of
the "Old Northwest." These leaders proposed measures to protect and support American interests on the Columbia. The matter was kept before Congress almost continuously during this decade. President Monroe in his annual message in 1824 also urged the establishment of a military post at the mouth of the
Columbia with the view of protecting and promoting our interests
there. Expansion to the Pacific, however, was an idea that did
not in the twenties recommend itself to a majority of the two
houses of congress.

The expense of the proposed undertaking and the possibility
that the step would be viewed by England as a violation of the
terms of the existing treaty and thus lead to war were deterring
considerations with the law-makers. An Oregon community as a
state of the Union was generally held as a chimera in that day before ocean steamships and railway locomotion. Those constitution-

ally conservative without the gift of prophetic vision or the index of manifest destiny could not but regard it in that light. Under such conditions to lend further inducement to the westward movement of a people already possessed of a perverse bent in that direction seemed to invite a future separation into Atlantic and Pacific nations.

The termination of the ten-year agreement in 1828 made some diplomatic action on the matter necessary. England's interests on the Columbia were now too substantial and preponderant for her to recede in deference to any claim of title based on discovery and exploration. And, further, deceived as to the character of the country she could see no reason for doubting her ability to maintain her supremacy there. The cause of the United States could hardly develop a weaker aspect than it presented at that time. Both were, therefore, willing to bide their time and continue the status of so-called joint occupation indefinitely subject to termination on a year's notice.

Our chain of right to Oregon had snapped in our failure to hold our own against the strongly organized English trade. But we might easily forego that form of occupation if we could only forge the link of occupation by home-builders. The other links to the chain of our title had been so gloriously welded to fail at this point would be a national disgrace. So thought many. The idea was soon to warm a host of pioneers. It had already set one mind aflame.

Hall J. Kelley, a Boston school teacher, became in 1815 an enthusiast for saving the Oregon country to the Union through colonization. From 1824 on he gave himself up to the work of agitation. In 1828 an emigration society with a large membership was organized. This was incorporated in 1831, and the spring of 1832 was fixed upon as the time for setting out on an overland expedition to Oregon. But something more than enthusiasm was needed to get an expedition even mustered, equipped and started for Oregon, to say nothing of conducting it successfully through two thousand miles of wilderness.

While preparations for the expedition by the Boston Colonization Society were in progress Nathaniel J. Wyeth, then twenty-nine years old and superintending a flourshing business with some separate interests of his own, became impressed with the idea there was a role for him in executing one of his country's trusts for civilzation. There was in the Oregon territory a remnant of the continent still to be subdued to man's higher uses and he felt his fitness for the work. He says, "I cannot divest myself of the opinion that I shall compete better with my fellow men in new and untried paths than in those to pursue which requires only patience and attention." He partially engaged to attach himself with a company to the expedition planned by the Society of which Kelley was the secretary.

Kelley, the moving spirit of this undertaking, wished to transplant a Massachusetts town to Oregon and make it the nucleus of a new state. He hoped to repeat with appropriate variations the history of the Puritan colony of Massachusetts Bay. The New Englander of the nineteenth century, however, was not so ready to sacrifice himself for an idea as had been his progenitors of the seventeenth. Unless Kelley could organize conditions so that success seemed certain, he could not expect the enthusiasm of his followers to bear them on. Such conditions he could not organize. His colony failed to muster.

Wyeth had proposed, to incorporate his company with Kelley's colony solely for the strength there is in union. When Kelley began to falter with his plans, shift dates and change conditions, Wyeth swung clear of the Oregon Colonization Society and organized his expedition independently.

The motive that impelled Wyeth to undertake his expeditions to the Oregon country was that same primal instinct that has been the predominant influence in producing the westward movement of the Aryan peoples since their first promptings of might. The suggestion was received by Adam in the Garden of Eden when he was told to subdue the earth and have dominion over its creatures.

There was much at this time in a Boston environment to bring the Columbia basin very close to the consciousness of natures endowed as were Kelley and ·Wyeth. Boston traders had so far monopolized the American trade with the Indians on the Pacific coast that these had no other name for Americans than "Boston men." The Columbia river had been discovered by a captain in the employ of a company of Boston merchants. Wyeth was cognizant of at least half-a-dozen Boston houses that had grown wealthy in prosecuting the fur trade of the North Pacific coast.

Even before starting Wyeth had appreciated the fact that the American activities beyond the Rockies were of a nomadic order and that the British company with its established posts was supreme. He knew that it represented a higher economic organization and was impregnable against such forms of assault as the Americans had so far brought against it. He, however, believed that the region from the Columbia river south to the forty-second parallel and from the Rocky mountains west to the ocean, a country three hundred by six hunred miles in extent, was still fairly open for occupation. He proposed to occupy it. He expected the status of joint occupation to last but a few years longer. By the time of its termination the American trade from vessels would have wholly disappeared before the more economic methods of the Hudson's Bay Company and his own and he would be left in sole possession of the region above described.

Wyeth as a New Englander is hardly to be blamed for not having foreseen the impending pioneer movement. It came from the western frontier. So precipitately did this sweep on and constitute an occupation by an agricultural population that there could

not have been successful a occupation by American traders organized under the higher form with established posts. Moreover, he un-
derestimated the overwhelming strength of the Hudson's Bay
Company and its grim determination not to brook competition.

His was not to be a hide-bound fur trading enterprise. He began that which has been developed into the great salmon industry
of the North Pacific coast. He located a farm in the Willamette
valley. It was his purpose to select those branches of business
for which he deemed his company most competent and which appeared to hold out the best prospects. Had he been able to get
his enterprise fairly on its feet his keen business sagacity would
have found and developed those lines for which the time and
country were waiting.

With high American spirit he scorned monopoly privileges. Difference of nationality and the bitter clash of business interests did
not act as a bar to the good fellowship and mutual regard of
Nathaniel J. Wyeth and Dr. John McLoughlin. A life-long friend-
ship was cemented between them. Fortunate, indeed, it was for
the English and the American peoples that in this crisis they
were represented by men of such depth of character and largeness
of humanity. The restoration of the correspondence that passed
between them would no doubt give much insight into the moving
forces of this period of the history of the Pacific Northwest.

In a summary of his views on the Oregon question submitted to
a Congressional committee in 1839, three years after his return
from his second expedition, Wyeth says: "In conclusion, I will
observe that the measures of this [Hudson's Bay] Company have
been conceived with wisdom, steadily pursued, and have been well
seconded by their government, and the success has been complete;
and without being able charge on them any very gross violations
of the existing treaties, a few years will make the country west
of the mountains as English as they can desire. Already the
Americans are unknown as a nation, and, as individuals, their
power is despised by the natives of the land. A population is
growing out of the occupancy of the country, whose prejudices
are not with us; and before many years they will decide to whom
the country shall belong, unless in the meantime the American
government make their power felt and seen to a greater degree
than has yet been the case."

Not yet had he discerned the rising of that human tide on the
western frontier that was so soon to overleap the two-thousand
mile barrier of arid plains, deserts and mountains steeps. Still as
Bancroft says, "He it was who, more directly than any other man,
marked the way for the ox-teams which were so shortly to bring
the Americanized civilization of Europe across the roadless
continent."

CORRESPONDENCE FROM THE LETTER BOOK OF

CAPTAIN NATHANIEL J. WYETH,

Referring to His Expeditions to Oregon.

I.

Philad   Augt 30th   1831

Hall J Kelley Esq. (Genl Agent for the Oregon Colonization
    Society Boston)

Dear Sir   I write to inform you that I shall
not return as soon as I expected having been detained here on
buisness.   I shall be in Boston about the 6th of next month, and
will see you as soon thereafter as practicable in regard to my application for a scituation in the first expedition to the Oregon
Country.

Doct Jacob Wyeth a brother of mine now practicing Medicine
and Surgery in N. Jersey at Howell Furnace, wishes me to enter
his name as an applicant for the birth of Surgeon in one of the
companies of the first expedition, which scituation he is desirous
of obtaining only in the event of a scituation being offered me
which I shall accept, he not wishing to remove to that Country
without me.   He is thirty three years old or thereabout was educated at Harvd. University studied medicine with Mr Revere of
Baltimore and Doct Shattuck of Boston and attended Lectures in
Boston was regularly graduated as a Phisician, he is unmarried.

I am yr obt Servt   Nathl. J. Wyeth

II.

Cambridge   Oct 5th   1831

Bro Charles   (Baltimore)

I have received your favour in reply to a former one
of mine.   The expression of good feelings that it contains you
may be assured are gratifying to my feelings, p[a]rticularly under present circumstances.

All earthly things are uncertain and none more so than those,
the accomplishment of which depend upon others and this is the
case in regard to the expedition to Oregon, there is no other
doubt of my going except the failure of the whole concern but as

this is possible I do not wish you to take the trouble to come here to utter your last speech and dying confessions at present. The moment I find there is any certainty of their going I will write you.

My plan is to go out there and carry with me what property I can spare after leaving a support for my wife, and do what I can with it. It will perhaps not much more than get me there, and after finding what can be done in the fur trade, or other buisness, write to friends, whom I shall prepare before hand, to send me the means of doing buisness, of these friends I mean you to be one, Leond. another, and a third here. More I can have if wanted but would rather confine myself to these, and what money I can make for myself or those in whom I have an interest

N J W

III.

Cambridge   Oct 5th   1831
Bro. Jacob   (Howell Furnace N. J.)
                    Yours of the 22nd ulto is at hand.   Many women are going, but for my own part I would not carry one in the first expedition they will of course ride, the route is practicable for horses.   I will make riding provision for your wife   I fear no difficulty on the route for any one, but some for the first year after getting there.   Would it not be better to defer marrying until your wife can get out there by means of the second expedition? The amt. of salary which you will receive is not worth the trouble of asking about.   If the expedition is successfull you will reap a rich harvest from the buisness of the country if otherwise you will loose your time, the salary which Kelley refers to will be paid you for services as an appendage to an army and the duties of your place will not admit of general practice because your corps will be moveable.   I will pay over the $20 for your acc.

The expedition does propose to leave this the 1st Jany. but most of such appointments are delayed beyond the time set, all you have to do is to close your accounts as fast as you can, and I will inform you as soon as I know myself the time when it is necessary to start from your place to meet us. All the preparation I will make for you.   Surgical instruments clothing &c we will purchase on the route in the cities through which we pass, and if requisite and with your leave draw on Leond for what is necessary for your fixtures.   The route will take in Boston, N York, Philad. Balto. Cincin[n]ati St Louis, thence in a right line acrost to the Rocky Mountains overland to near Santa Fee where there is a pass in the mountains thence a N. W. course to meet Lewis river down which we go to the Columbia river, the place of our destination distance from St Louis about 2000 miles.   The b[e]st manner you can invest your property except what is requi-

site to equip you for the Journey is to leave it at interest as a resort in case of failure in your objects out there. Books are too
cumbersome to carry out, the knowledge must go in your head
the books can be got by the second expedition, and the instruments we can purchase in five minutes when I meet you in New
York. The first expedition are all to be soldiers, as much land
as wanted can be bought of the Co.   200 acres is to be a privates
portion what the officers are to have I have not enquired.

N. J. W.

IV.

Cambridge   Oct 17th   1831
To Col J W Neil   Boston
          Dear Sir   In the absence of the Genl.
Agent for the Oregon Colonization Society I take the liberty of
addressing to you the following queries viz Whether any persons
which I may induce to join the first expedition will be attached
to my Company.   Whether it is expected that a person receiving
the appointment of a Surgeon is expected to pay the Society $20
mentioned in their 3rd Circular as a loan and whether there will
be a surgeon appointed to each Company and if so whether a
brother of mine who has received an assurance from Mr Kelley
of an appointment will be connected with my company.

An answer to these particulars and also any information which
you may be disposed to communicate in regard to the certainty
of an expedition at all, the numbers which may be expected to go
in the first expedition the route to be taken after leaving St.
Louis, the time when to be commenced &c &c, and also when I
may call on you to confer upon these subjects will be thankfully
received by

Yr. obt. Servt.   Nathl. J. Wyeth

V.

Cambridge   Nov 11th   1831
Brother Charles (Baltimore)
          Will you have the goodness to collect
the information required for answering the questions below and
as soon as practicable forward me answers to them.   This information I have no doubt you will easily obtain from many of your
neighbors and customers who are in the tobacco buisness either
as planters or venders of the same, be pleased to give your answers as definite as possible and be certain that it is correct as it
is required in order to the raising the article as one of trade beyond the Rocky Mountains and a mistake would be bad buisness.

1st Should it be planted as early in the season as to be entirely
out of the reach of Frost, or will it bear a slight degree of it.

2nd How should the seed be planted in the field where it is
intended to grow? or in beds to be transplanted?

3rd In what scituations and soil? with manure or without? in a dry or wet place?

4th How thick will it thrive

5th what mode of culture is required weeding? training, gathering at what time

6th [What] method is used to cure it and how kept after it is cured

7th How is the seed obtained at what time gathered How treated and kept and what is the ordinary quantity required per cwt. of the product usually

Beside these queries be good enough to make any remark which you think will be usefull in the culture of the plant.

As time passes on the project of emigration assumes form and shape, and a nearer approach toward certainty. I think there is little doubt of my going, for I find that I can get good men who will follow me on a trading project, on the basis of division of profits, and this thing I will do (if I can) if the emigration fails. I believe I can find other men who will for a certain other share of profits furnish all the money wanted which will not be great, for I mean to have a cargo ready there, before a vessell leaves here and the investment will be only the trading articles sent out, the return cargo will pay the freight, and possibly be in time to meet the notes given for the articles sent me.   It is about 10 months voyage there and back. It appears to me that if I can find means to get the men out there with articles of trade suf[f]icient with their exertions as hunters, smiths &c to obtain a cargo, that finding persons to send out a vessell and cargo of trading articles on the strength of it will not be dif[f]icult. This I have no doubt I can accomplish to the extent of 50 men with equipments, and articles of trade as many as they can carry with some iron and steel for our smiths to work up, and traps for catching furs, and with them I have no doubt I can scrape together a cargo for a vessell of 150 Tons in the course of a year. After having done this of [or?] so nearly done it as to be sure of doing it I shall write home for the vessell and an invoice of articles of trade, which from my then acquired knowledge I shall be competent to do.

Present my respects to all your folks wife and little one, tell Charlie I am going where I can catch him a wild horse to play with I think the Idea will take his fancy much

N. J. W.

P. S. Will you have the goodness to send me what information you can respecting the route from your City to Pitsburg, and thence to St. Louis by way of the river. Name the distance, fare, and mode of conveyance from Balto. to Pitsburg the fare down the river whether the boats will take Horses and Wagons whether they will reduce the fare in consideration of our number sle[e]ping on deck &c or not, with the times required to make the different routes with any other information you may be able to add. I wish to know also if the boats go in the night.

VI.

Cambridge Nov 12th 1831

Brother Jacob (Howell Furnace Monmouth County New Jersey)
In case the contemplated colonization project should fail it is still our intention to go to the new Country in which case we shall form ourselves into a Trading Company in furs. It is the object of the present letter to ascertain whether in such case you will follow us in your capacity as surgeon your compensation will be a certain share of the profits of the concern and your exertions in forwarding the interests of the concern will be required not only in administering to our own men but also to the Indians the payment for which will go into the common stock your answer is wanted immediately if in the affirmative I will take care that an equitable share of the profits is obtained for you in the contract and other requisite provisions made for you

I am &c   N J Wyeth

VII.

Cambridge   Nov 14th   1831

Brother Leonard (New York)
I write to request you to collect what information you can in respect to the route up the Hudson and through the Canal to Buffaloe thence by the Lake to Erie on Lake Erie and thence by the Canal to Pitsburg thence down the Ohio to the Missouri Branch and up to St Louis

Any information you can gather respecting these routes will be valuable and is wanted in order to the fixing of a route for our troops   We wish to know if any deduction will be made in consideration of our numbers say 50, what are the rates of passages usualy paid a person and per Ton for Baggage up the Hudson to the Canal   what are the rates on the Canal for person and Baggage at what rate they travel on it   whether they travel all night whether any saving could be made by marching during the day and taking passage during the night,   and whether their rate of traveling is faster than the march of men, what the expence of toll is on the Canal for a Boat with 50 men and their Baggage, what is the facility of going from Buffaloe to Erie and by what means and what rates of fare and what distance and the time required for the voyage, what the Length of the Canal from Erie to Pitsburg and the other queries relative to the Hudson and the Erie Canal as above, also what information you can obtain in regard to the river route from Pitsburg to St Louis. If in your way you can also give me some information concerning the route from N York to Pitsburg by way [of] Philad and Baltimore making as little Land traveling on said route as possible also bear in mind in our travel we cook for and lodge ourselves and will for suitable compensation or reduction of Fare do any work that will not retard our passage and require nothing but the uper deck if these things would lessen the expence.

If the Colonization Society go through with their project I shall go out in their service if not I shall get up a Joint Stock Trading Concern (if I can) and go on with a similar plan but on a smaller scale the details of which I will give you as far as settled when you come this way which I hope will be before the 1st Jny we shall not probably start before 1st April from this place provided we go out on the last maned [named?] plan   [No signature.]

VIII.

Cambridge Nov 28, 1831

Saml S. Hamilton Esq (Washington)
      Chief clerk of Bureau of Indian affairs
            Sir
                  Having in contemplation to undertake an expedition to the west of the Rocky Mountains for the purpose of trade, and to that section of the coast claimed by the American Govt. I am desirous of obtaining information in regard to the Laws regulating Indian trade. In the course of the contemplated expedition transactions may be had with tribes this side of the Mountains.

It is the object of the present communication to request of you the favor of pointing out to me the best mode of obtaining this information, or if it is embodied in a Pamphlet form at your office to forward the same to my direction. In case I have applied to the wrong person for this information will you have the goodness to send this letter to the proper person and much oblige

Yr Obt Servt N. J. W.

IX.

Cambridge Dec 4th 1831

Brother Charles (Baltimore)
                  Your favour of 28 Nov is at hand and contains all the information that is wanted and for which I am much obliged to you, but as one good turn deserves another I will trouble you to be on the lookout for a man who is competent to rearing Tobacco and who will Join our expedition on the terms hereinafter mentioned as the foundation upon which all the others are to go for the terms are to be all alike with the exception of myself and the surgeon. The plan now proposed by me is to have nothing to do with the Oregon Society, but to form a Joint Stock Concern composed of 50 persons who are to be bound to each other for the term of 5 years for the purpose of following under my direction the trade and buisness of that Country in all its branches selecting those for which we deem ourselves most competent and which appear to us to hold out the best prospects and to be determined upon on the spot all expenses are a charge against the

amount of proceeds, Freight Charter party Cost of goods and all disbursements of every description the residue after this deduction is to be divided into 50 equal parts 8 of which are to be mine 2 are for the Surgeon and Doctor and the remaining 40 are divided equally among the men.   I am to procure all credits wanted for the expedition and all disbursements necessary for their fitting out with the exception of their personal equipments and expences as far as Franklin Missouri.

This plan I have adopted in preference to hiring all the men and taking Capital at the halves, for which I have many offers, because I think that hired men would not effect so much as those who have a share of the profits, and probably could not be kept together at all, in consequence of which Half profits would not amount to as much as my present plan gives me, also the scituation I would be in would be more difficult and attended with more risque as pay of men would amount to a large sum and would have to be paid profits or no profits.   This plan obliges me to raise some 5000$ for articles of trade, munitions of hunting, stock for manufacturing and the like including horses from St. Louis to carry baggage, and a few provisions $2000 to $2500   I shall have to borrow of you and Leonard, for I will not ask it of any one else even if I go without it and if you agree to lend it to me you will get it again if I ever return if not charge it to my acc. in the next world this money will be wanted on my draft from N. Orleans or St Louis given about the 20th April.   Will you write we whether you can lend me this sum or half of it as soon as convenient The residue say 2500 to 3000$ I shall have of my own that I can spare from the support of my wife.   With regard to the vessell and cargo of Trading articles I cannot order them to advantage until I know the trade which will not be until I have remained in the country a short time, and I *shall* not order anything until I have on hand a return cargo of the results of our exertions, and of the first stock taken with us, as a pledge to offer those persons who charter me a vessell and which being insured on their passage home will answer as a remittance to pay for the articles sent out by the vessell whichif purchased at a credit of a year they will be in good season to pay for, and this buisness too I am in hopes to manage between you and Leonard, and I do not see as you need run any risque in this last matter except of my good faith, as the operation will be predicated on the amount of avails which we have at the moment of our ordering actually on hand and to which may be also added all that will be collected between the time of ordering the vessell and her arrival.   When you answer this letter which do soon answer what you are able to do in this matter also.   In addition to the offer Mr. Jarvis made me of assistance in New York last summer, he has again offered me by letter any assistance which I may want. This is very good in him and will be duly remembered, but I do not wish to avail myself of it if I can avoid it which I am confident that I shall be able to do. Something however depends upon your answer. The reason why I wish not to accept of Mr. Js offer is that I have no claim upon his kindness and I can offer him no prospect of profit as for the first five years at least all the profit which *I can spare* must go to those who earn them, but after the expiration of the first term my acquired knowledge will be such as to warrant me in taking charge of a buisness in which it would be safe and profitable to invest money to a large amount and then those who assist me now will receive their reward, but at present men have not confidence enough in the enterprise to embark their persons in it unless they can have a large share of the profits.

I think you had best abandon the idea of coming on here this fall or winter at least until further news. It is most probable I shall pass through your city on my route to Pitsburg. As far as I now know a packet from this to your place will be the best plan.

My best respects to wife and remember his uncle to the little Boys.

I am afftly yrs   Nathl J. Wyeth

X.

Cambridge Dec 5th 1831.

Brother Leonard (N. York)

Since writing you last I have received from Jacob an order on you at sight for $600. This I obtained from him on account of his outfit which I can make to more advantage for him than he can for himself $100 is the extent of what I shall spend for him on this account, and this sum will be wanted about 1st April certainly not before, and can probably be taken up in Baltimore of Charles for in all probability our route will be by packett from this to Balto. direct and thence to Pitsburg. The residue of the Draft please retain in your hands in the same manner as though it had been accepted by you, this in order that he may not make a pretext of the expedition for spending the little remaining money he has and which if given to his order will be entirely useless to him and to the expedition.

The colonization Society have so far altered their plan as to join the first and second expeditions into one and both go by the way of St. Louis, Platte River Lewis River Lake Timpanagos,* Columbia &c. This plan I do not like as women and children can not get started from St Louis before the 1st July. They do not propose to set out before the 1st June and there will be at least one months falling off from the time set. This with the unavoidable delay of such a cavalcade will make the 1st Sept. before reaching the pass of the Rocky Mountains at the head of the

---

*"A map of the Internal Provinces of New Spain" given with Coues'"Expedition of Z. M. Pike" practically identifies this with the Great Salt Lake of Utah.

Platte River and this is but half way and it is necessary to reach
the place of Destination a sufficient time before the 1st Nov to
make provision for the winter as about that time a great part of
the Indians from whom supplies might be had as well as the greater part of the Birds and Beasts leave the country for southern
quarters and the fish leave the River for the Sea, and a party so
composed and so large will call for all the exertions of all the men
attached to them, and then leave much undone that might conduce to the comfort of the party, and in this way it will be at
least a year, and I fear longer, before we shall get any time to devote to the purposes for which we go out viz. making money, and
for this they offer only the poor advantage of 200 acres of land,
which is hardly a quid pro quo, beside which there is some danger that they may get into so much dificulty as to be obliged to
return, which would be an entire defeat of our enterprise, for it
would be hard to get men to travel over the same ground twice.
It is quite as much as I can do to get good men the first time and
after one failure it will not be possible to get them to start again.

These considerations have induced me to delay entering into
any agreement with them until the last moment, and not then
unless I am better satisfied with their arrangement than I am now.
If the advantages appertaining to the Society can be obtained
without a material sacrifice of my own objects I will join them
but not otherwise.

My plan (in which I have proceeded so far as to raise 26
men) is to raise 50 men to go out to that country so early
as to leave St. Louis on the 1st May 1832 for the purpose
of following the trade of that country in all its branches
for which we deem ourselves competent. Many of these
men are manufacturers in the various branches of iron work man-
facturing of arms and ammunition and a few to cultivate such articles as are of use to ourselves and in the Indian trade such for instance as tobacco. The proceeds of the exertions of these men
are to be divided into 50 equal parts, 2 of which are to belong to
Jacob if he goes out as surgeon or to whoever is surgeon 8 to myself and 40 to the 48 remaining men or at the same ratios for a
diferent number of men. I am to furnish all the camp equipage
and trading articles necessary for our first outfit to the extent
of 5000$, and to procure credit for the Co. for a vessell and an
Invoice of trading articles to be ordered to that country when a
quantity of avails suffiicient to secure the payment for the same
has been collected. The first disbursement of 5000$ as well as
the freight and cost of articles sent out and all other disbursements of every description are to be deducted from the gross proceeds before the division mentioned above in other words for furnishing the use of 5000$ in cash, and the required credit for ves-
sell and Invoice of articles for which I have the goods to pledge I
am to have the exertions of 7 men beside myself. This though

not a large share of gross profits is a good share of nett profits, and I shall have to strain some to accomplish my part of the contract. 2500 or 3000$ of the cash I have on hand the residue I must borrow and I hope to be able to get it between you and Charles. I also hope to get you or Charles to manage the getting me a vessell to bring the articles I send for and bring home those I have collected. The vessell may be taken up and the freight to be paid on the delivery of the home cargo and thus far managed without money, and probably the goods sent for might be purchased on an obligation to pay at the end of the year or on the return of the vessell and the consideration for length of credit made in the price, and for security the home bound cargo insured, an invoice of which I will send you when the order is sent for the vessell and the goods. If you feel disposed to favor me so far as to lend me on 1st April next the whole or half of the cash wanted over and above what I have say 2000$ or 2500 if the whole and 1000 to 1500$ if you can furnish but half and take upon yourself to manage the sending out of the vessell, you would favor me by answering in the affirmative. I know it will be inconvenient for you but at some rate or other I must accomplish it and I at present know of no other means without I resort to Mr. Jarvis who has recently made me an offer of assistance by letter but I feel an almost insuperable objection to using him or puting myself under any obligations to him. I have offers of plenty of cash for half profits but in this case so small a share of profits can be offered the men that good ones cannot be induced to go and hiring must be resorted to and I apprehend that a set of hired men would make my scituation very difficult. They would desert me, would be idle while in the employment and if not their pay alone would take a large share of the profits and render my then half profits a smaller sum than my present 16 per cent. besides the greater dificulty of getting up an expedition on such a foundation.

Please write me what time I may expect you this month or when I may think of seeing you if you cannot come this month. It is quite requisite that I should see you before I to and I apprehend if I see you at all it must be here for unless your information is more favorable than I expect in regard to the Canal and Lake Erie route I shall take packett from here direct to Baltimore.

The country looks like the spirit of Winter had passed over it in tempest and frost leaving a legacy of a foot of snow behind him and a gale of wind from the N. W. I hope the cold will continue until I am done icing which will be with good luck about in time for a move. I am now all in heaps having just moved into my new house and things are not yet put to rights.

Be pleased to give my affectionate regards to your good wife and kiss the little ones for their uncle Nat. and believe that I remain   Y Afte Bro.   N. J. W.

XI.

Dec. 8th 1831

Brother Jacob
   (Howell Furnace Monmouth Cy. N. Jersey)
   Yours of the 25th ulto. is at hand containing your answer in
the affirmative to my query "of whether in case the Oregon Colonization fail in their objects" you would join a trading expedition to the same parts. I have entered your name as one of
the Co. The formation of a Trading Co. on a similar plan
to the Hudson Bay and North West is the ultimate object of
my going to that country, and *this* new plan is no farther new
than so far as to form the Co. here in stead of after getting out
to the place of destination, and to this alteration I am induced
by a fear of the failure of their plans, and a desire that mine may
be carried into effect in any case. The first plan would be the
best in-as-much as men tied in the toils of such expeditions,
might be picked out, the second is best in that it enables me to
go on in case the Company do not, and also to go on independently of them if their arrangements are such as do not meet my
approbation. Now in the first place I think they will fail entirely of going, but supposing they do not, they have so far
changed their plans as to unite their 2 expeditions into one,
comprising a host of men who are merely cultivators of the earth,
unused to any hardships, and unwilling to meet any, women and
children and to start on the 1st June. You have seen how true
my predictions were in regard to their first start, and they will
be equally true in regard to this. If they propose the 1st
June they will not *certainly* go before the 1st July, and after that,
allowing the best luck they will not reach any of the passes of
the Mountains before the 1st September, and that is the latest
month of their proper arrival at their place of destination, and is
only half the way from St Louis. You may judge yourself how
much such a host must suffer by arriving at their Destination at
the Commencement of winter, when the natives (of whom supplies may be had), leave the country, as well as beasts, Birds and
fishes, and also that it is a sacrifice of one years time in our buisness and for which we gain nothing but *such a tittle* as they can
give us of 200 acres of land each. This is not a "quid pro quo"
and if they manage their buisness as I apprehend they mean to
do I shall wash my hands clean of them, at least if I can get
along without my plan without them.
   In this state of the case I have not paid to them the 20$ on
your account, but have made an arrangement by which if *I choose*
I can with all my Co. be exempt from paying the same by being
answerable for all the disbursements of my Co. after leaving St.
Louis and still retain the ordinary priviledges of emigrants. I
shall not make my election until I find what their arrangements
are in order to see whether it is worth while.

The foundation of the division of profits in this concern will be, myself for furnishing the requisite capital and leading the same 8 parts   The surgeon 2 parts 4& men 40 parts, the whole profits being divided into 50 parts; division at the end of the contract viz 5 years.

Your Draft has been duly received and please notify Leonard that it has been given, all arrangements I will notify to you in season   only one suit of clothes will be required for you and this one suitable to appear like a gentleman in the places through which we go.   A uniform dress will be provided for you and arms.   Keep all your surgical instruments but buy no more   We will buy them in Philad. or Balto. as we go on, which will be about the 1st April next whether the Society go or not.   *I shall delay* no longer.   In the mean time continue your buisness or if you must come this way before you go close it and quit it and go [o]n with us.   The chief cost of the journey will be coming this way for I shall travel cheaply on the route outwards.

Yrs   N. J. W.

XII.

Cambridge   Dec. 19th   1831.

To the Hon. E. Everett
Sir

Enclosed you have a letter from Mr. Nuttall containing in part my views in regard to this application to the executive.   I have to repeat that no view of emolument induces it but only a desire to serve the views of the Govt. in regard to that Country.   It has occured to me that the Govt. might avail itself of my services to obtain information concerning that Country which in time would be useful to them.   I would willingly devote a portion of my time to their service without other compensation than the respectability attached to all those who serve their country, and the advantage of having some employment for the mind, in a buisness that will afford much Leisure.

In order to the better understanding [of] my advantages for collecting information I will detail to you my plan of operations, which is the formation of a Joint Stock Trading Company of about 50 mèn to proceed to the Country, without positively settling the particular buisness in which they will engage but to be dictated by circumstances when there (probably the fur buisness will be selected).   This company will leave this vicinity some time from the 1st March to the 1st April next.   31 persons have already entered their names.   This· body will go out in company with the Oregon Colonization Society provided that society do go at about that time, but will go without them in case they do not move near the time above named, and are to be no otherwise connected with them, than may be dictated by convenience on the route as far as the sources of the Columbia.   The contract by which this Co. is bound together is to continue during 5 years, and if successfull is to be extended through an indefinite time.

I have to ask that you will communicate this offer to the Government in case you deem proper, or if you think it better that I make application personally (with refference to you) I will do so, but I have to request you in such case to inform me what department of I should apply to for this purpose. In conclusion I must ask you to excuse the liberty I have taken in troubling an entire stranger witn my affairs but I am induced to do so by your well known re[a]diness to serve your constituents and your ability to do so.

　　　　I am Respectfully Yr. Obt. Servt.　　Nathl J. Wyeth

P. S. In case you should answer this, it would much oblige me if ycu would indicate some method by which I can obtain copies of two treaties in regard to the Country claimed by the U. S. on the Pacific Ocean, and made with G. B. somewhere about the years 1817 & 1828.

XIII.

　　　　　　　　　　　　Cambridge　　Dec 26th　　1831

Bro Jacob
　　　　　(Howell Furnace Monmouth Cy. N. Jersey)

Yours of the 16 inst. at hand. I wrote you on the 8th Dec. an answer to your letter of 25th of Nov. last the following is a summary of my letter of the 8th inst. That I considered your letter as an engagement on your part to go to that Country as a member of a trading Co. in case the Society do not go. That the Society have so far altered their plans as to join their two expeditions into one. That I considered this joining of the two expeditions as very objectionable in-as-much as it encumbers us with a heavy mass or women and children and other helpless persons whereby great delay and probable failure will ensue. That I have not paid in the 20$ on your account but have made an arrangement by which with all my Co. I can be exempt from paying the same by being answerable for all our expenses after leaving St. Louis, and still retain the ordinary priviledges as emigrants. That I should not make my election whether to be answerable for the said expence or pay in the 20$ until the last moment. That the foundation of the division of profits would be 8 parts to myself for leading and furnishing the required capital, 2 parts to the surgeon 40 parts to be diveded among the men, contract to last 5 years. That your draft had been received and requested you to inform Leonard that the same had been drawn. That one suit of clothes will be requisite for you and this one suitable to appear as a gentleman in, a uniform dress will be provided for you. To keep all your surgical instruments but to buy no more, they are to be got in Balto. We go about the 1st April next certainly not later.

The above is a short summary of my last letter to you this letter you have probably received before this time. I have to request that you will continue your buisness to the last moment. I will notify you in season of our movement from this place, and as far as I can see this will be the 1st March from here in a vessell to Balto. to which place you can then transfer your person and baggage, all of which, not suitable to carry can be packed and left for a future conveyance by water. Your request in regard to the Centinel shall be attended to. Your request to obtain guarantee and commission from the Society, I will also attend to under the limitations contained in my last. The speculations at the close of your letter are those of all who look at the map but neither your or my days will see them verified, but our enterprise may lay a foundation. Leonard has just left here and informs me that your funds are in the hands of Charles and therefore he could not accept your draft. This draft I will keep and return when I see you and please send me a similar one on Charles.

N. J. W

XIV.

Charleston   Dec 27th   1831

Cap Dixie Wild (Boston)

Sir

In putting into writing the verbal proposition which I made you this morning, I do not wish to be understood that it is the only shape in which it would be acceptable, but only that this form is one that is readily understood by the parties, and I should conceive that in this way each would sooner come to an understanding of the others views on the subject. That those who furnish the vessell and articles of trade would better understand what they are to gain by such risk and trouble, and that those so furnished would know at one view what they are to pay for the same. If this view meets your approbation you have only to say for what per ct. you will enter into the requisite engagements. If any other form of compact suits you better, you will oblige by proposing the same. That a party is to proceed to the Country near the sources of the Columbia to De Fuca streights as may be decided, to leave here between the 1st March and 1st April next, and from whence as soon as may be send home an account of the valuable articles which they have collected. and a schedule of such articles as are wanted for that trade, and for the substantial correctness of the account of such collections of articles the agent of such Co. will be bound in the sum of 2000$ to be used as an indemnity for loss occasioned by intentionally false information on the subject. That you are not bound to disburse any sum or moneys for any purpose until information has been received of the collection of such quantity of articles as will according to ordinary judgement and under usual circumstances pay the cost and charges of a voyage out and home.

That after such information has been received you are as soon as can be to fit out a vessell or vessells such as are required, one certainly and more if you deem proper, and put on board the same at your cost such an invoice of articles as may be required by the agent of said Co. That interest at the rate of ten per cent on the cost of the vessell including insurance and repairs, and the actual disbursements of the voyage for men, provisions &c, cost of articles sent out and 8 per cent int. including insurance, shall be considered the cost of the voyage and that you are to agree to furnish as above and for your profit in the buisness are to have — per cent and that this agreement is to last as long as the party continue together under their first contract viz 5 years, or until they dissolve the contract by unanimous vote of said party, which shall in no case be done with a view to evade this agreement, but will remain in force against me personally so long as I shall continue in any way engaged in that trade, until the expiration of the said 5 years.

If you or your friends wish to make any enquiries concerning me I beg leave to refer you and them to Mr David Devan of this place who knows more of my buisness character than any other person.

I am &c.   N. J. W.

XV.

Cambridge   Jany 3d   1832

Brother Charles (Baltimore)

Your favour of the 17th ulto. is at hand. I write in haste to request you to place the note of 888 25-100 against Morton Brown & Co in the hands of Judah Touro Esq. of New Orleans and at my disposal. If the note is good some goods can be purchased there as well as elsewhere for our buisness please advise him to look to me for instructions on the subject. Please make what exertion you can to procure the tobacco man, more than one if convenient and they are suitable men. I shall leave here about the 1st March for your place by vessell and shall see you there and thank you personally for your kindness in thus assisting me in my projects. I shall endeavour that you do not suffer by it. Jacob some time since gave me an order for 600$ on Leonard this order being improperly drawn on L I have written Jacob to exchange for one on you This I had done with a view to preventing him from spending it on his outfits for which purpose now nothing is necessary. This sum I shall not draw from you in any case further than the small amt. requisite for J outfits, but wish to know if in case of unexpected need of money at St. Louis for indispensible articles and the want of which I cannot provide against or obtain in any other way if I can draw it from you   any need of so doing I shall avoid if there is any power in me to do so but it is possible that I may so far miscalculate as to be under the necessity of a little more money than I may happen to have left at that place.   Please answer this question in your next. With this last assurance and with the note and what L. will do and my own cash I shall make out to do. As it regards vessells and goods to be sent me I apprehend I have made an arrangement that will provide for all this of this I am not certain but the negotiation· has proceeded so far that I think it will be closed and on quite as good terms as I could expect. The other particulars of your letter I have not time to answer but will talk over matters when I see you on my journey out.   Jacob is not yet married and in his recent letters to me he has not mentioned the subject and I hope he will go without for the reasons you name.   I hope your children are now recovered.   Give your wife my respects and remind little Charles and Nathaniel of their Uncle Nathaniel

Affcty Yr Bro   Nath. J. Wyeth

XVI.

Cambridge   Jany 3d   1832

Solomon K. Livermore Esq

(Milford New Hampshire)

Dear Sir   I have an unexpected visit from your son who has left his school of which I suppose he has apprised you. He seems to me to have arrived to that time of life at which a young man should have chosen some buisness to meet the wants of existence, and done something to fit himself for it.   In this line he appears to have done nothing effectual, and he to me seems mortified at the fact.   The pride which produces this feeling is laudable and denotes at bottom a well toned mind, and it will certainly eventuate in something either for his weal or for woe.   To humour and direct rather than repress this feeling it appears to me is the best policy. He talks of the sea and other things, but has no settled determination except to do something. This determination ought to be indulged.   He wishes to join our expedition to the Country west of the Rocky Mountains and I think that it would be well for him to do so, his share of the profits will be large: ⅞ of an equal division.   He can there spend nothing, all that his division comes to will be in his hands when he comes home, and judging from the course of that trade heretofore it would be no small sum.   The country is entirely healthy, the Indians mild in their natures, and entirely peacible.   Vessells are to be in our employ to run between this place and that, to insure the requirements of trade, of life and means of returning if requisite.   The contract will give me 8 parts for taking charge of the buisness and furnishing capital, the surgeon will have two parts the residue of 50 persons will have 40 parts to divide among them contract to last 5 years. I think his turn of mind quite suitable to this buisness and I should be glad to have him to go with me, and will endeavour to do well by him. I shall give him no encouragement to go on this or any other scheme without your consent, but think you would do well to give it. He will return home in a few days.

Excuse the liberty I have taken in thus intruding my ideas upon you but the similarity of his scituation to my own at about his time of life induces me to speak freely in regard to him and to say what he cannot as well say for himself.

Be pleased to give my respects and love to all your family and be assured I remain   Yr   Af.   Nephew
                                        N. J. W.

P. S. His equipment and expences as far as St. Louis are paid by himself in all 50$ this if you determine to let him go you can give him or I will furnish him with it and take it from his share of the profits. We are to leave about the 1st March.

XVII.

Cambridge   Jany 6th   1832
Hon. E. Everett (Washington)

Dear Sir   Your favour of 24 ulto. has been received. From what I can learn Genl. Cass is of the right stamp of character to make application to in this matter, but I cannot spare time for a personal interview, being very much engaged in preparation for moving which I intend to do by the 1st March. If the matter could be opened to Genl. Cass and his views in some measure ascertained to be favorable I would come to your city and finish the buisness during the time that it would require for my men to march from Balto. to Pitsburg. I cannot think of delaying my movements for an object for which I ask no other compensation than the honor of conveying to the Govt. information which will soon be of great value to them. I will request you if consistent with your view of the case to broach the matter to either of the Departments as you deem most suitable and then to advise me whether it is worth my while to come to your city in my way out to Pitsburg.

I believe that it is not lawful for armed bodies of men to pass through the Country. I would beg leave to enquire of you whether any permission is required to be had for so doing and if so to obtain the same for me, and also what sort of licence or permission if any is requisite for trading with the Indians beyond the Rocky Mountains.

I herewith enclose a petition which was handed me by Mr. Kelley and signed by some of those who propose to go with me in this enterprise. We have no connection with Mr. Kelleys enterprise further than accident and circumstances may indicate. and only wish that something should be done as an inducement for

Americans *generally* to go out to that Country in order to form a preponderating interest there to counteract that of the British already established. Govt. would poorly serve our interests in granting to the Oregon Society any exclusive priviledges there. Nothing on our part is desirable excepting aid to get *men* out there and the enacting of some laws for their regulation when there and then leave us to ourselves. I should be sorry if these petitions should have any other effect than to call the attention of Congress to the subject in such manner as to induce them to act as their wisdom may dictate, in aiding good men to form a settlement in that region and to assume the government of the Colony when there, and not as the petition may possibly be construed to mean to throw the trade or government of the Country into the hands of this or any other society, neither is it our intention to follow our trade in connection or under the patronage of that Society. I wish you to understand that it is at your option to present this petition or not. If you conceive that it will forward our interests as above explained, present it, if it is to serve the purpose of throwing the controul and trade of that Country into the hands of a society, whose buisness should be to aid men in getting there, and then leave them to form their own mode of society, withhold it.

I have to thank you for your kindness in regard to the treaties, and ask you to excuse the liberties I take in thus troubling you.

I am &c &c   N. J. W.

XVIII.

Cambridge, Jany 11   1832

Brother Leonard
(N. York)
Not having heard from you since you were here I have been fearfull you had writen and the letter miscarried. If this is the case please send me a duplicate as I am in want of the names of the persons whose address you proposed to get for me at St. Louis. This is a matter that demands immediate attention. Since you were here I have had letters from Charles. What he can do with what you proposed will answer my purpose. Please, let me know definitely and as soon as possible what and when you can do. Upon further investigation I find that there will be no dificulty as regards vessells, as they always leave that coast but partly filled, consequently remittances to meet the exigences of the buisness may be made in them at reasonable rates, beside which I have nearly closed with one, already in the trade, who will send out vessell and goods as soon as I leave here and to arrive there about the time that I may be expected.

&c   N. J. W.

XIX.

Cambridge   Jany 16th   1832

Brother Leonard (N York)

Yours of the 10th inst. is at hand. The sums which you mention may be available to me in some shape and if so they will be used of which due notice will be given you. The draft of the furnace altho common I should like to have if convenient as it will be as good in any other and I have no small one. It can be sent to me in care of Chas. in Baltimore. You have done well to say nothing to Mr. Osgood as he could not do enough to help me, and one great credit is easier gotten than twenty small ones.

Give my thanks to Mr. Osgood for his kindness in regard to the letter but inform him that it will not be used unless the present negotiation fails and I do not wish to broach the matter to any but those who are to be eventualy concerned if possible to avoid it.

The object which I propose to accomplish through an acquaintance at St. Louis is to have my drafts cashed on Judah Touro a person well known in that section of country and residing at N. Orleans in whose hands I shall place funds and obtain a letter of credit for the amount from him to them. I have money at N. Orleans of my own and some which Chas. has lent me, which I may or may not use as circumstances may indicate. The drafts may be at sight and the money is wanted to purchase goods for the Indian trade. Letters of introduction to as many different people as possible are desirable in order to get information concerning Indian trade and other matters connected with the pursuit of it. I am happy to hear that your loss is all insured I presume you mean with the exception of what you might have made from them and the loss you sustained by not having them, which is or is not a loss as the case may be.

This day received a request by letter from Mr. C. your partner to join the expedition. I presume he means *if indeed he means anything* as a partner. As this cannot be, I shall after considering the matter with due attention answer in the disuasive. He must be very ignorant of his capabilities. As no one knows the extent of his ignorance of himself all we have to do is to pray that *we* are not in the same darkness of which we accuse others. Be so good if the fact was not known to you before as to keep it to yourself to save appearances both for him and me as I do not wish to be an informer on the actions of any one however much I may think that he needs a guardian.

Y &c   N. J. W

XX.

Cambridge   Jany 18th   1832

Mr The. Bache
        (N York)   Dear Sir
                    Your favour of 14th inst is at
hand I think you have done well to remain where you are
until you set out to meet us at Balto. I have no idea of whom the
person could have been who called on Mr. S. Swartnoute. It
could hardly have been any one who had a knowledge of our enterprise but must have been some one desirous of joining the emigration to the same country under the auspices of the Society
formed in Boston for that purpose and with whom I do not propose any connection. As you wish to shew this letter I shall
omit answering in it some parts of yours. The subjects to which
I allude are satisfactorily to me at least settled. According to
request I shall detail the plan of the expedition and also the proportion of profits which will accrue to each person engaged in the
enterprise. We are to cross the Continent to the shores of the
Pacific between 42 and 49 degrees N. Latt. and engage in the Fur
buisness. Vessells will ply from Boston or N. York to supply us
with articles of trade and bring home or carry elsewhere what
articles are collected, and by means of posts established there save
the great delay of vessells on that coast which in the present
mode of conducting the buisness amounts frequently to 30 months
and will average two years. This item alone would with the
ordinary profit of the trade give all the success which we look
for beside the great advantage which residents there have over
those who can be there but about once in 4 years for the collection
of furs and other articles of value. As to our route across the continent I can only say that we shall be governed by circumstances
On the spot my general idea is that our course will [be] from this
place to Baltimore by vessell thence by land to Pitsburg thence
down to the confluence of the Mississippi and Missouri rivers and
up the latter river to Franklin from that place strike for the Platte
River and follow the same to its source in the Rocky Mountains,
near which is the southern pass by which we shall make the transit of the mounts which done we strike for Lewis River or the
Multnomah which we follow to their junction with the Columbia which we follow to the sea and locate our posts on this river
or near De Fucas Streights as may then be deemed proper. Our
compact is to last 5 years. The profits are to be divided in
such manner that if the number concerned was 50 and the
whole nett profits were divided into that number of parts, I
should get 8 the surgeon 2 and the remaining 40 parts would be
divided among the remaining 48 persons. The 8 parts which I
take is consideration for my services as head of the concern and
furnishing the requisite capital and credit for the buisness and

which is to be invested in goods to a small amount to take with us by land, camp equipage, wagons, horses, &c, and in vessells and goods to be sent out to us so as to arrive there within a few months after us. Each man will be required to furnish his own equipments and pay his passage as far as Franklin in Missouri which will amount to 40$ and the surplus to be paid for him from the capital if it amts. to more. In case any very good men apply to you you can engage them on these terms especially Coopers, Blacksmiths, Founders, and ingenious persons of any trade but having nothing to do with any persons who are not industrious and temperate men and of good constitutions and peacible dispositions, and in case you engage any their equipments will be brough[t] on with me to Balto. where they can meet us at the same time as yourself by equipments I mean arms and clothing They may therefore come as scantily provided for clothes as possible with the exception of a great coat which should be ample in order to sleep in it. We may be expected to arrive in Balto. by the 10th March but when I leave Boston I will advise you more particularly In the mean time please write and give me any particulars which may transpire.

I remain &c N. J. W.

XXI.

Cambridge Jany 18th 1832

Broth. Jacob

Your favor of 6th inst. is at hand enc[l]osing a draft on C. Wyeth for $600. Of this sum so much will be spent as is requisite for surgical instruments, medicines, your own equipments and cloths and travelling expences as far as St. Louis. The residue will be left in Charles hands at interest and for your benefit or if used by me int. at 6 per ct will be paid you. Your 2 shares are for your professional services and also for all other services which you may render the Co. in any shape for you will be required to do all and everything for the common benefit. If you persist in returning befor[e] the 5 years expire there will be ample opportunity by means of our vessells but you will loose your share of profits during the time that you are absent from duty

Ys. &c N. J. W.

XXII.

Cambridge Jany 23d 1832

Capt Dixie Wildes

(Boston)

Dear Sir Having examined your proposition I have satisfied myself that to enter into an arrangement on these terms would be to ruin myself and injure every one concerned in the undertaking and to deprive you of that eventual profit to which you should look as the reward for engaging in the undertaking and incurring

its risques. In regard to risks I have to say that all you incur is merely the risk that the goods which you send out to me
to be used on a *particular* part of the coast may be unsuitable
for the *general* trade of the Coast. So far as this is likely to
happen you run some risk, but this is the only risk you incur
as all the other risques are insured against at our cost. Even if
we should never arrive on that coast your vessell would have the
same chance of making a good voyage that she would have if expressly fitted out for a N. W. Coast voyage with the exception of
the risk above stated whiĉh as you have the selection of the
cargo need not be great.

With regard to the items of proposition I have to say that it is
not my wish to assume specific sums as the cost of the voyage
and then cast you[r] per centage on them. For instance you assume that the vessell will cost 8000$. Now altho. this is
about what a vessell of 160 Tons might cost yet it is probably
not the exact sum. Insurance at 4 per cent may or may not be
the exact sum paid and 18 months will not be the exact length
of the voyage and thus of all the other items. My intention was
to propose to you to find vessell and cargo and to agree upon a
certain per cent upon their actual cost as your profits in the buisness. And as far as goods and cost of sailing are concerned including insurance and interest at the legal rate there would be no
dificulty but for the vessell some other arrangement must be made.
I would propose that a certain per cent on her *actual* cost be agreed
upon and the amt. of this per ct. be considered as the cost of
her use or charter and on this sum your per centage of profit
cast, and making the per ct. on her cost sufficiently great to
cover insurance wear &c. In short my object is to arrive at the
actual cost of everything and pay a certain per cent of profit on
it to those who will furnish me with the accommodations which I
am in need of to carry on this buisness. There is a natural impos-
sibility in my complying with the terms of your proposition, you
ask at least 12000$ profit for the first voyage which is in itself as
much nett profit as the best voyages have given when no larger
an amount of capital was used. In your recent voyage 2 vessels
and 12000$ worth of available goods and 2½ years time was
consumed and about 18000$ made whether including int. and
insurance or not I do not know but supposing that that amt.
was including these items there would have been not a dollar remaining after paying you 50 per cent on 18 mos. The expences of the voyage were about 18000$ as I understood you and
would have been 20000$ had you not bought your vessells when
they were low and sold them when they were high if you had
had 50 per cent on the disbursements of that voyage for 18 mos
and in proportion for the extra time it would have amounted to
16000$ and more.

You have estimated that the product of our first voyage would
be 40000$. This would be more than I think would be be real-
ized but allowing that this sum should be realized from the
4000$ worth of goods which I shall take with me. The arming
and equiping of 28 men and their time and the disbursements contained in your proposition and your 50 per ct. Let us cast all
these up and see what each one would get. In doing this we
will take first those items which must be paid in any event viz.

The estimates of your proposition and 50 per ct..........	29885$
Disbursements by myself....................................	4000
Int. on same 18 months...................................	360
Arms and traveling expenses out for 28 men a 75$.....	2100
Wages for men a 5$ per month............................	2520
Which deduct from 40000$	$38865

There remains profit to us................................... 1135
To be divided among 28 persons which would leave me who
have 16 pr ct of the nett profits about 200$ for 18 months.

In your first proposition your estimates of the disbursements of
the voyage were about the same, and of the product about the
same and according to that the profit would have been 20000$ on
which you asked 25 per cent as your profit this would be 5000$.
In this you ask almost 10000$.

It is undoubtedly the interest of both parties to give the other
a good chance. If you have all the profits, I should very
soon be unwilling or unable to carry on the buisness. If I should
get more than my due proportion you would not continue the
buisness and whether the one or the other happened both parties
would be the loosers by it in as much as the buisness must be
discontinued whereas if the profit should be more equally divided
the buisness would be carried on for a long time to a mutual advantage. I think that you would do well to consider that in
case the buisness is good to all concerned it may be extended to
almost any amount and your profits 5 years hence may possibly be cast on 200000$[?] yearly. To the great increase of the
buisness I think that you may fairly look for your increased profits. I do not think that in employing only one vessell you could
make as much as in the ordinary course of the trade but in the
common method it is dificult to extend with advantage in this
way an unlimited extension of the buisness may be safely
attempted.

I am in hopes that you will alter your proposition as it is absolutely impossible for me to accept this. It would be far better
for me to go out without any arrangement. I could in that case
in one year gain the required experience, and product of the
goods which I carried out would if shipped home as well might be
done in almost any of the vessells which go there, for they return

but partly filled, produce the requisite capital. At the end of the first voyage I should have collected here all the capital which I should want and should have gained all the requisite experience for directing it. You cannot but see how much better this would be for us than to make an arrangement on your terms which would bind us during the whole 5 years to pay for the capital and experience which we only want for the first voyage almost the whole of all the profits we could make even in case of the greatest success.

I am however very desirous of coming to an agreement with some one previous to going out and think that I shall be able to do it on terms which will offer a fair chance to all concerned. I am particularly desirous of making it with some one already in the trade. I beg that you will reconsider this ground carefully and soon for the time grows short with me and I do not wish to apply to any other persons until all hope of an arrangement with you is at an end.

Wednesday or Thursday next I will call and see you.

Respy &c   N. J. W.

XXIII.

Cambridge Jany 23d 1832

Brother Charles (Baltimore)

Your favour of the 16th inst. is at hand. I note what you say of the note of Morton and Co. nevertheless please forward it as at first proposed. Most of my goods must be purchased at St. Louis, which is the great mart of the Indian trade at which I can not only get what articles are wanted but the knowledge requisite for selecting them and there I shall make all my purchases with the exception of a little Iron and Steel which will be got at N. Orleans and the residue of this and other money I shall draw for from St Louis.

If you cannot get a tobacco man please put me up some tobacco seed sufficient for a considerable crop and have it well dried and soldered up in tin cans. Would it not be well to advertise in some country papers for a man stating generally that he is wanted for a foreign voyage. In this matter do as you think best.

As it regards Jacobs affair it is only requisite that I bring on with me an order from father to pay the ballance of account to me, and I will then take what I have expended for Jacob say 100$, and leave the residue in your hands subject to my draft in case of accident as proposed in my last or to remain as the case may be. The draft as you say can be examined when I am there.

I am well aware of what you say in respect to the number of men I think however there is no danger of being troubled with too many. All the other matters contained in your letter either will or have been attended to. Please in your next write me the names of some of the best mercantile house[s] at St.

Louis and if possible procure me letters to them these letters keep but the names send me as soon as possible.

The reveries at the end of your letter are proof that you let that liar and thief "hope" cheat your better senses with idle dreams, the sober truth of life is that man was made to mourn to fight and die at last disapointed and broken hearted

Yr. Aff. Bro.   N. J. Wyeth

XXIV.

Cambridge   Jany 23d   1832

S. K. Livermore Esq. (Milford N. H.)

Dear Sir

Your letter of the 20th inst is before me. I beg you to believe that I have used no means to induce Thomas to engage in this undertaking with the exception of the letter which I wrote you on the subject and which I read to him. He heard of the expedition elsewhere and came to me for information. I should conceive it very dishonorable in me to interfere in his plans of life otherwise than through his natural guardians. I have in this instance rather held forth to his view the dificulties of the enterprise than its inducements. I shall not even now write him on the subject being content to leave the matter to you and him. If he goes he should be here by the 20th Feb. He wants nothing to bring with him but one good suit of cloths which are decent to appear in in the cities through which we pass. The company dress will be made her[e] as also his arms and equipments. No chest is necessary as our baggage wagon will answer that purpose as far as to Franklin, where we take horses and then bags must be used. As few articles of baggage will be carried with us as possible their transportation costs more than their value and they can be purchased any time before leaving the settlements at one of the last of which St. Louis our final arrangements will be made. The bugle of which I spoke to him should be of the plainest kind and the most simple to use and the least liable to get out of repair or broken. It will be used chiefly as a signal for parties at a distance, and sometimes in marching a little music will enliven us. We propose that one should learn it well and then teach all the rest. We shall have as much as ten and to be used alternately so as not to be tedious to any one. I am ut[t]erly ignorant of all kinds and uses of music but have thought that we could march by a number of bugles but if we cannot they will at least do for signals which is in fact their only es[s]ential use. If Thomas will make himself master of the bugle and determines to go please write immediately on the receipt of this, as in case that he does not I must engage some other person to do it. In addition to what I stated to you in my last I will only observe that in case the undertaking should prove unsuccesfull it would be abandoned by mutual consent in a much

shorter period than 5 years and in this case Thomas would
come home having a good knowledge of the hardships of life and
consequently more willing to put up with its unavoidable privations and disappointments than he now is, and I question whether it would not be as profitable knowledge as he could acquire,
for as you say, "there is plenty of buisneas here for which he is
suitable" if he can only bring down his mind to its dull routine.
But I should be sorry to have him go against the inclinations of
his parents not to say their *positive* disapprobation in which lat-
[t]er case he certainly should not go with me.   In case he should
go I will comply with your desire in regard to religion.   It is a
subject which in a peculiar sense rests with each one and his ma-
ker, and if I have sometimes agitated the subject with you, it has
been more to test and correct if possible my own views of the
matter, than any hope of proselitism for which I am not desirous.

    I beg to be remembered to your good lady and children and
wish them all kinds of happiness.

Yr Aff. Neph.   N. J. Wyeth

XXV.

Cambridge   Jany. 27th   1832

Mr. I. P. Hughs
                Sir Your letter of 19th inst. is at hand.   As
to dificulties in the undertaking each man must judge for
himself and also what his prospect of gain.   What my own opinion is
on the subject may be judged of by my giving up for it a salary of
1200 per year and a buisness that brought me as much more.   My
own opinion of this thing must be good or I am an arrant fool.
To say more on this head would be useless.   Examine for yourself, look about in Boston and see how many independent fortunes
have been made in this buisness.   As to giving you every particular of this buisness it is quite impossible.   Two days would not
suffice to write such a letter.   The outlines I have given you.   As
to Capital as much will be invested as I deem requisite and no
more and what is invested will be in outfits say 4000$, these we
will take with us across the land, then a vessell to leave here and
arrive there near the time that we do   Cost of sailing there and
back 5000$, goods sent out by her $8000 these amts. are the
smallest sums that will be invested.   And I shall increase them
as I think proper in the course of buisness.   The conditions of
my furnishing this and all capital which I deem requisite are my
receiving 16 per cent of the nett profits.   The surgeon will have 4
per cent and each person will have 1¾ per cent or nearly these
different shares make 102 per cent and as there can be but
100 the 2 per ct will come out of the 48 shares which amts. to
less than 1-50 of 1 per cent deduction from each mans share.   The
amt. of all is that each man gets as near as possible of 8-10 of a
full and equal division of the profits and the other 2-10 go to pay

me for my services as head of the Co. and to furnish Capital
and Surgeon.   I am to be sole director of the movements of the
Co. and its agent in all transactions of buisness.   I will come under no bonds to the Co.   Conceiving that the fact of my carrying
out with us 4000$ is bond enough because if I do not send the
rest this would be all lost.   The reason of the case will shew that
if a bond is necessary anywhere it is from the men to me, that
they shall not after my property is invested in this thing desert
me which would occasion a sacrifice of all I am worth but I ask
no other than that of expending in the buisness 40$ which they
will loose if they do not pursue the plan.   I think you said that
T. A. Livermore mentioned this thing to you.   His father writes
me that he may go and the young man is determined to go and is
learning the bugle.   I hope that this will also be your determination.

Yr Obt Servt   N. J. W.

XXVI.

Cambridge   Jany 28th   1832

Mr. Geo. Cripps (New York)
                    Dear Sir   Your   fav. of the 12th
inst was received in due course of mail.   The receipt should have
been acknowledged before but the pressure of buisness and the
want of a little time to think the matter over induced me to wait.
I should be extremely happy to have you join us if it were only
for the benefit of your society, for in an expedition of this sort
most of the persons must be not of the same class with ourselves
the society therefore of even a very few well informed persons is an
object.   You are undoubtedly as fit for the enterprise as most
men but do you wish to place yourself upon a par with such men
as must form the bulk of our band?   It appears to me that it
would be unwise in you but in this judge for yourself.   I can
offer you no better terms than the rest have viz 8-10 parts of a
full and equal division of profits.   We leave here about 1st
March next for Baltimore.   I refer you to your partner for
further information on this subject.

And Remain &c   N. J. W.

XXVII.

Cambridge   Jany 28th   1832

Brother Leonard, (New York)
                    Your favour of the 24th inst. is at
hand.   The arrangements which you have made as to letters are
well.   The goods you name are used in indian trade but whether
on that part of the coast to which we go is the question.   All indian marketts are not the same any more than other marketts.
Traps, guns, and amunition are all the articles which I should at
present meddle with.   I wish you would ascertain if Beaver traps

can be had in your city. Those wanted should weigh 5 lbs.
double springs, Jaws without teeth and chain 6 feet long with
two swivells in it. Of these I want about 40 Doz. If you can
find the article please write me as soon as possible. Also find
if you can get the kind of gun used by the Amer. Fur Co. and
at what price. There is also a certain kind of beads which
is a kind of a cur[r]ency among the Indians and therefore an
article in demand among all Indians. Please write me what you
could do in all these articles. I can then tell better whether I
will purchase in your place. My cash at N. Orleans I can transfer to this place at any moment through Mr. F. T. who is paying
freights there all this spring.

I have not yet closed with any person for vessells and
goods but have raked up security enough with what you
named to charter a vessell on as fair terms as could be
done for cash. Have at command 4000$ in cash and have remain-
ing from 2 or 3 M of security to give to those who will credit me
for the goods which I want to send out by her. Amt. from 5 to
8000$. I think I could pay on account of goods to send by this
vessell 1000$ down, and 2000$ security of one good name beside
mine and to be paid in default at the end of the voyage say 14
mos. Would your firm for a certain per cent profit over and above
their cost furnish this amt. Your partner being in England would
furnish great facilities in procuring the goods. If I can get this
done by competent persons my difficulties would be much diminished, and I shall save giving away during the whole 5 years 25
per cent of profits to pay for assistance which I only want during
one voyage. I shall work hard before I will give up so much.
Is there no person in N. York who would do this if you cannot.
I have some hope of getting it done here but have no certain offer
better than the 25 per cent as above. Write me as often as you
can

Yr. Aff. Bro.   N. J. W.

XXVIII.

Cambridge Jany 27th   1832

Bro. Charles (Baltimore)
                    Since my last of 23d inst. I have been buisy
trying to make arrangements with some men already in the
N. W. trade for such vessells and goods as I shall want in
the course of this buisness. The best offer is 25 per ct of
profits to be paid them on my whole buisness for five years. Now
if successfull in this buisness I should want neither information or
capital at the end of the first voyage and even in furnishing me
the first voyage they run no risque because if I never arrive there
they have only to continue the voyage as an ordinary N. W.
Coast voyage with just as good chance of profit as if expressly
fitted out for that purpose. Under these circumstances I cannot

think of committing myself in such an arrangement if there is any possible way of avoiding it. Mr. Tudor agrees to assist me in a certain amt. If you would obligate yourself to pay 1000$ as an indemnity to those of whom I might take up a vesell to be paid in my default at the expiration of the first voyage say 14 months from the 1 July next I think there is a chance that I can procure vessell and goods to be sent out to me on my own acc. and thus save loading my buisness with a nightmare. As all losses are to be insured against there will be no other risk in this matter than what appertains to me personally, of whether I get there and whether I collect articles enough to pay for the goods and vessell. If I get there it must be a hard buisness if all my own property and the full amt. of the securities are sunk. If you agree to do this I understand that all the accommodations that you have promised are to stand as settled. Please answer soon.

Yr aff　N. J. W.

XXIX.

Cambridge　Jany 31st　1832

Robt. H. Gardner Esq.

Dear Sir　Having in contemplation a voyage to the Columbia where salmon are abundant I am desirous of information in regard to them. None of these fish being taken in our waters I am at a loss where to apply for this information. Your scituation near where they are found induces me to apply to you and your uniform politeness toward me induces me to hope that you will convey what information may be in your power or if not too inconvenient to collect what may not be within your own knowiedge or indicate to me where I may obtain the same and of whom. What I wish to know is how salmon are pickled and how smoked and how taken. Any information on these heads will confer an obligation on

Yr obt. servt.　Nathl. J. Wyeth

(Inserted)　How to keep and when they go up and down the rivers.

XXX.

Cambridge　Feb 5th　1832

Mr. Seymour Whiting (New York)

Dear Sir　Your letter of 31th ulto. came in due time to hand proposing certain inquiries concerning my expedition to the country claimed by the U. S. on the Pacific Ocean, which I answer as follows. This Company go out for trade in such branches as may be found expedient the terms of agreement to last 5 years and to be rendered a permanent settlement if found practicable and agreeable. No families or other helpless people will be taken until this question is decided, which will not be until w[e] have been some time there and can judge from a better knowledge of facts. Young, active and industrious men are wanted and any number will be received that will comply with the conditions of the association. The precise conditions are not fixed the proposition has been that the capital and myself shall draw 8 parts in fifty of the whole profits the surgeon 2 and the remaining 40 parts to be divided among 48 persons. This will give 8-10 parts of a full and equal division of profits to each man. This proposition supposes that I shall furnish a suitable outfit from St. Louis for crossing the country and procure a vessell and cargo to go out to meet us on the coast and pay all the expenses for the arming and equiping and transporting the company to St. Louis which shall be incurred over and above 40$ There are here now 23 men who have paid in their first assessment toward the 40$ as above, and there is no doubt of our going before the 1st April, the 1st March is however the time set for starting. Our camp equipage is now almost finished and our arms and equipments are partly in the armory and the residue contracted for to be delivered 20th inst. We deem 25 men enough for the enterprise but are willing to extend the number to any amt.

What you say of Mr. Kelley I think will prove true. As yet he has no means of moving a step in the buisness and in my opinion never will move. For further particulars I beg leave to refer you to Mr. Leonard I. Wyeth of the firm of Cripps and Wyeth Pearl St. of your city. What you may decide upon in the matter please make known to me as soon as possible, for the time is short.

You will be required to pay into the treasury 20$ for your arms and equipments when you meet us on our way out at Baltimore. The arms &c will be brought with us. The remaining 20$ may be paid in when voted by the company prior to reaching St. Louis.

As soon after you make known to me your acceptance of propositions, not differing materially from the above, as practicable notice will be sent you of the time of our moving, place of meeting and other particulars.

Yrs &c N. J. W.

XXXI.

Cambridge Feb 6th 1832

S. K. Livermore Esq. (Milford N. H.)

Dear Sir I have a letter from your son Thomas intimating that you wish to know what authority I have obtained from Government to trade in the country about the Columbia. In answer to which it is to be observed that the Government has not extended its Laws over that country and claims over it only a right of preemption. There can be no infraction of law where none exists, and beside which the right to trade there is inferred from the public acts of the Government, first in protecting by its public armed ships vessells engaged in that trade. 2dly in the demanding the restoration of a trading post taken by the British during the last war. 3dly by a stipulation of the convention between the U. S. and Great Britain that citizens of each shall have a right to trade in any country there claimed by either. That the Govt. would have a right to impose a licence to trade with the indians there in the same manner as they have done in the Territories has never been assumed and I think will not be until territorial governments are erected by them there. I have written to the secretaries of War and State on this subject but have yet received no answer.

Thomas mentions preferences and dificulties concerning the two kinds of bugles. These are matters I know absolutely nothing of. You will oblige me by directing him which kind to get. Only keep in mind that the capability for using as marching music is subordinate to that of being used for signals, and that economy, durability and use are before shew and noise. Nevertheless good marching music has its use in keeping up the spirits of the company and exciting the attention of the natives objects by no means to be overlooked, but to be obtained if possible without sacrificing the other.

Please present my compliments to your family.

I remain Yr. Aff. Neph   N. J. W.

XXXII.

Camb.   Feb 6th

Mr. Leon. Jarvis (Baltimore)

Dear Sir   Circumstances impel me to apply to you for assistance in my projected expedition. Having no claim for your favorable consideration on this subject and knowing you to be averse to the plan I have avoided making this request until the last moment, and to very near the time when I must either close with very disadvantageous terms or commence a hazardous enterprise without adequate means. In the beginning of this thing I was induced to believe that certain persons here would furnish me the small amount of capital of which I was in want on decent terms but in this I find myself mistaken for after finding me fully committed to the buisness they have enhanced their demands, and think to use me for their advantage. This they shall never do.

I am at present trying to make arrangements to furnish the whole outfits both by sea and land and have raised what I think will procure me the land outfits and a vessell and perhaps $1000 toward a cargo for her. The amount of goods requisite for this cargo is from 5 to 10000$ which if I had $3000 in cash or good security I believe I could get on good terms here. If you are disposed to assist me in any shape in this buisness I would beg leave to suggest the following as to me the most desirable and as giving to you some chance of profit as well as loss while at the same time you are conferring a great favour on me. It is this, that you furnish all the goods wanted by us during the 5 years of our present contract at a certain per cent over and above their actual cost including interest and Insurance and to make sale of the product of our trade on a certain per cent commission to have on the first investment sent out 1000$ in cash from me as security for the goods and an equal lien with the owners of the vessell on the goods sent home the said owners to be secured in the sum of 5000$ which must first be consumed before they have any claim on the return cargo and by contract to be debarred any claim on the outward cargo in any case. This, as a considerable amount of goods are carried out with me would put out of the question any very great loss. At the end of the first voyage if the buisness is found not to be practicable, it must be abandoned. If otherwise it will be continued and the proceeds of the buisness will be accumulated here to answer as security for the debts of the Co.

This proposition I should not have made to you if Mr. Tudor had not offered me such assistance as would nearly enable me to keep clear of very hard terms, and having so nearly accomplished the object was a strong inducement to ask a thing from you to which I have not the slightest claim, and if the thing is disagreeable to you, I ask you to excuse the liberty I have taken.

A strong inducement to this enterprise has been the peculiar state of the trade of the country in question. The American Govt. with ideas of reciprocity in their head made a convention, which after having been once extended will terminate in 1838 with G. B. by which the citizens of either power have a common right of trade in the whole territory claimed by both on that coast. I think this convention will not be renewed because it virtually destroys our trade there by opening it to the competition of the British Co. whose capital and facilities are so great that vessells cannot trade to a profit on that coast they being subject to a long delay on the coast whereas the British trade is effected by posts and their vessells have nothing to do but to discharge and re-load. If at the expiration of this convention it should not be renewed and I do not think that it can be some part of that coast will be an unencumbered field to whoever may then be there, because in the mean time the present American trade in vessells will disappear before the more economical methods of the British and mine so far as that has any effect. And I do not think that any other person will think of establishing posts in that country if I succeed in so doing. Of the goodness of this trade if I can get it free from other competition than that of vessells there can be no doubt and I think I may do well in it even under present circumstances. Another inducement with [me] has been the being obliged to leave one half of my buisness and the insufficiency of the other to secure me employment more than half of the year, or give me the amt. of income which at this time of life I ought to be getting. Altho I am well aware that you do not approve of the direction my mind has taken yet your conversation with me at New York convinces me that you think I should make a move of some kind. Now in the kind of move which I have taken I have been guided I think by a sound judgement in regard to my capabilities whether experience will justify this judgement remains to be proved but in the mean time I cannot divest myself of the opinion that I shall compete better with my fellow men in new and untried paths than in those to pursue which requires only patience and attention. You have accused me of want of patience and the world will readily believe you but I think both you and them blend the want of patience and the want or perseverance in one idea whereas I believe them to be quite separate and not at all incompatible. In raising means I beg you to believe that I have not availed myself of my position in the family to borrow money or credit of those who it is a duty in me to keep from risque of damage or of any person who is not in a scituation to judge for himself of the danger and to sustain the damage that may accrue and that no extremity will tempt me to do so. I mention this to put your mind at ease on a subject upon which you might naturally feel solicitude. I will conclude this letter by asking of you as a favour that you will answer it as soon as possible as my time is very short.

I am &c   N. J. W.

XXXIII.

Cambridge   Feb 8th   1832

Mess A. Norris & Co
Gent   Will you have the goodness to ascertain if Traps suitable for the N.West trade can be purchased in your city and if so at what price. They should weigh 5 lbs each have double springs Jaws without teeth with a chain 6 feet long having two swivells in it. Of these I want about 20 doz. If you will attend immediately to this buisness you will oblige me as they are wanted to start almost immediately on their destination.

(P. S. Please direct me at this place)   Yr Obt Sevt N. J. W.

XXXIV.

Cambridge Feb 7th 1832

Judah Touro (N Orleans)
Dear Sir   Some time since I directed Mr. Charles Wyeth of Baltimore to place in your hands a note against Morton Brown & Co. for 888.25. Will you please get it discounted without recourse to the original endorser and after taking out your commissions transmit the proceeds to Baltimore to my direction to the care of Mess Wyeth and Norris in a U. S.

Bank check on St. Louis or Baltimore. You are authorized to pay as high as ten per cent for discounting this note, but please present it to the giver in the first place. The reason of getting this note cashed at so high a rate is not want of faith in it, but an immediate want of money on my part.

N. J. W.

XXXV.

Cambridge   Feb 7th   1832

Robt. H. Gardner Esq

Dear Sir   Your very polite and useful favour of 4th inst. came duly to hand. As I have carefully examined the mode of taking all the fish caught in your rivers with the exception of salmon the modes described by you were readily understood and are every thing I wished on the subject. It is impossible for me to visit your vicinity at this time. Mr. Tudor's ice must be shipped and that done I must leave immediately.

In asking you to ascertain from Mr. Palmer the modes of curing salmon, I fear to trespass on good nature and nothing but my inability to get the information elsewhere induces me to trouble one whose time I know to be so much occupied. If you will admit this as an excuse I will ask the favour.

The kind wish expressed at the end of your letter I value much, in as much as it is highly creditable to have the wishes of the good in ones favour. The older writers affirm that such prayers avail much and this supposition is so consonant to human feelings that I am not disposed to doubt it. Will you accept my thanks for your good wishes and assistance in this matter. Should you have buisness in any part of the world where I am I should esteem it a favor to be able to make a return for these favours.   I am &c   N J W

XXXVI.

Cambridge   Feb 8th   1832

Brother Charles

Your letter in answer to mine of the 23 and 29th ult. is at hand. Your proposition of purchasing at N. York has been adopted and all goods except a few staple articles will be purchased in accordance to it. Letters to Mr. Johnson will be highly acceptable and usefull.

The request which I made you was to give your name for security for any contract which I may make for a vessel in the sum of 1000$ and is independent of the 888.25. The 800$ you name will do, and the earliest liability on this will be at the expiration of a voyage commenced at 1st July next to last at least 14 months that is 17 months hence. The offer of 25 per ct. of profits for furnishing me goods and vessel was never a good offer, but such as it was they backed out of it, by adding commissions for buying and selling fixing prices of articles, and charter of vessell, to such an amount as would have been ruinous and was no part of the original understanding. I have therefore rejected any further overtures with them, and consider that they have broken faith with me and attempted to use me like a fool. I am offered room for shipping home goods on board of 3 vessells now on that coast on good terms and I think of closing the agreement, and taking with me such goods as I know will do and sending home my collections by one of them with directions to forward me such goods and vessells as are wanted which I will then be able to determine and the 1000$ for which I asked you to bind yourself will probably be used to enable me to obtain the credit of a vessell the arrangements for which I must make before I leave here, so as to be sure that there shall be no fail when it is wanted. I have written to you Mr. Jarvis and Leonard in the same manner as though I were to fit out this thing immediately on my own acc. and Risk because it is possible that I may be obliged to do so, but I would by no means do it if the arrangement above stated can be made, for if the buisness is fit to be pursued I shall when such vessell arrives here have an amt. of property in Boston which with $5000 in security in good names (which the 1000$ I ask of you will complete) will enable me to purchase the goods and the vessell on ordinary commissions. It is very important that I do not bind myself to throw the commissions of this buisness into the hands of strangers for the whole 5 years of our contract altho. I may be obliged to do so at first as an inducement for giving for me the accommodations which I want. If this buisness should prove successfull the commissions alone would amt. to 4000$ per annum and the control of them I mean to keep if I can to repay those who may now help me of my own family and who may again be in want of something of the sort to keep them up in the world as has happened in days past. If you speak with Mr. Jarvis on the subject you can name to him my reasons for not accepting the offer of 25 per cent.

I have hinted the nature of my objections to it in a letter to him. I shall be careful not to name what you propose to do to any one, there is no advantage in talking of these matters. I shall probably be in Baltimure by the 15th March and may then see you. Please write me whether Mr. Jarvis is angry that I have undertaken this thing. I wish to know on what terms I am to stand with him and how to meet him. He told L. that he though[t] that you had advised me to it. I will undeceive him in this matter.

Will you please to look in the city for Beaver traps. They should weigh 5 lbs. have double springs, Jaws without teeth and chain 6 feet long with 2 swivells in it. Of them I want 40 doz and write me the price for which they can be had cash. If such are not to be found write me the nearest thing you can get and the price.

If you agree to be responsible for me in any similar sum to the one asked, please write me a letter containing (nothing else) stating that when called on to do so you will be bound for me in 800$ or 1000$ as the sum may be, for any debt or engagement my merchant here may make for me, payable as an indemnity for my default, on three months notice, at any time after Sept 15th 1833. This letter with others I shall place in the hands of my merchant here, and when I order him to send me out a vessell or goods he will call on you to give said bond as secnrity for the fulfilment of my engagement. If you are willing to do this, please forward the letter as above as soon as possible.

And oblige

Yr aff. N. J. Wyeth

P. S. When I arrive at Baltimore I shall want about 6 horses to carry my goods and wagons to Pitsburg or Wheeling please write me in what manner they can be hired and for what sum probably. The horses only are wanted harness I have complete. They will be wanted from the 15th to 20th March. At New York I will send you specimens of some small articles which I want if I do not get them before you go there.

XXXVII.

Cambridge Feb 10th 1832

Mr. John Ball (New York)

Dear Sir

Your favor of 8th inst is at hand. The letter to Mr Bache dated 18 ulto. contains all the information which I can at present communicate in regard to the plan of the expedition. What Mr. Kelley tells you is not the truth. It is true that I once proposed to join this expedition of his, but I relinquished that idea when they joined their two expeditions into one, for I consider it impracticable to and inhuman to attempt a passage across the continent with a party composed of men women and children. The undertaking is enough for men. Your observation in regard to the salmon fishing is good, and a strong effort will be made to arrive in season to avail ourselves of it to procure food for the winter. I see no probability that Mr. Kelleys party will move at present. They have made no preparation as yet, nor do I believe that they can ever make provision for moving such a mass as they propose.

My party will leave Boston early in March and may be expected to arrive in Baltimore by the 15th of the month. We have now nearly enough men but any number of suitable persons will be received on the conditions named in my letter to Mr. Bache. Please use this letter as one of introduction to Mr. Charles Wyeth of the firm of Wyeth and Norris Merchants Baltimore who is my Brother and has some general knowledge of my plans. This gentleman will leave Balto. for New York about the 25th inst. after which time he may be found at Mess. Cripps and Wyeth in Pearl St. Mr. Leonard I. Wyeth of the last named firm will also give you any information on this subject which he may possess. He is also a brother of mine. If you conclude to join our expedition please give me early notice and bear in mind that there will be no avoidable delay in setting out.

I am Yr Obt Servt   Nathaniel J. Wyeth.

XXXVIII.

Cambridge Feb 1oth 1832

Brother Leonard (New York)

Yr favor of 3d. has been received I have been fearfull for some time that some things would turn out as appears to be the case   Nevertheless be of good cheer patience overcometh all things.   I have found a master of a vessell just from the N.W. who will furnish me with the requisite information as to goods and I have written A Norris & Co of your city to procure some of them.   I have closed all except drawing bonds with a substantial commission merchant here an agreement which is entirely satisfactory.   He agrees for ordinary commissions to bind himself to execute my order in regard to goods on the strength of furs collected and deposited on the N W Coast and will furnish at my order at any time within two years at a certain agreed rate of charter a vessell or vessells as many as are wanted to fetch and carry on my furnishing names as security in indemnity for loss by my fault to the amt. of 5000$ payable three months after loss ascertained.   The first voyage cannot be terminated before July 1834 because it will not be commenced until a year from the time I leave here and the voyage will take one year and delay four months and the 3 months above added will bring the earliest responsibility to the 1st Oct 1834 within a few months of the time which you proposed in your letter of Jany 1oth for the last payt.   Will you agree to indemnify in my default to the amt. of 1500$ 3 months after damage is settled. If so please write me a letter containing nothing else in definite terms what you are willing to do.   This letter I will place in the hands of my merchant here and when I order goods and vessells he will call on you for a bond of indemnity for the amt.   A copy of my agreement with him I will furnish you before leaving. Mr. Tudor of his own accord offered to give his name for 2500.   This with yours, and a similar one for 1000$ of another person enables me to make this arrangement.   This arrangement is all that I want in as much as there will be next summer on that coast 3 vessells by which I can make shipments home in all probability and at any rate can send information home of what I have collected and what I want which will do just as well.   I have been requested to take letters to all these vessells with orders to let me have what freight I want on reasonable terms if they are not full of which there is no great danger as vessells never fill up entirely in this trade. Finding how inconvenient this thing might prove to you I have written to Mr. J. to ask him for cash or name to a small amt. if he agrees I shall relieve you of any trouble.

Yr Afte &   N. J. W.

XXXIX.

Cambridge   Feb 13th   1832

Sol. K Livermore Esq. (Milford N. H.)

Dear Sir   Your favor of the 9th is but this moment received. We may leave Boston the 1st Teuy of next month and shall not be here the 7th day.   If Thomas is to go he must be here very near the 20th inst as some little time is required to organize.   The bugle buisness is well.   I never went to Washington for anything relating to this buisness not having been there this four years.   I have notified the Government by letter of the expedition and asked information of them in regard to the laws relating to Indian trade, and offered to communicate to them any information which I might obtain while there.   My letters have been answered as I expected conveying information in regard to the laws of the trade and notifying that the Department of War would receive and avail itself of any information which I might communicate.   The information which you have received that a party left Boston for that country is not fact no party has left any part of the U. S. within several years for that country and there is now no American trading posts or Americans there except what may be in vessells on the coast.   There are in the space from the Rocky Mountains to the sea and between the 42 and 49th deg. N.Latt. three British trading posts there may be more but this is all that I know of, but between the Columbia River in 46 deg. 15 min. and the Spanish line in 42 deg. and extending back 600 miles to the Rocky Mounts. there is no establishment of any kind.   Smith, Pilcher, Ashly, Soublette, Jackson, of the western states are all said to have made money in this buisness. J. Baker and Son, the two Boardmans, Josiah Marshall, Dixie[?] Wilde, the Perkins of Boston have made money in this buisness, which proves that the buisness must be carried on, which is as much as to prove that those who may become practicably acquainted with the buisness and are found capable and intelligent can always have good buisness as agents for others, for all of these men must have agents, none of them go out themselves. Thomas is young and 5 years hence would be early enongh for him to undertake buisnes seriously, and he would then be fit if he pays attention to it to conduct any fur buisness and in my

estimation there is as fine an opening in this as any he could undertake especially as in this trade knowledge will stand in lieu of
capital in a greater degree than in most kinds of buisness for who
had not if he was about sending out an expedition rather give $\frac{1}{4}$
profits to an experienced man with no capital than to a man with
capital and without experience.

I beg you to bear in mind that I do not urge his going.   If he
does go let it be at his own instance and not mine.   All I can say
is that if he exerts himself he shall have a chance in proportion
in any arrangement that shall be made after the five years are ex-
pired and that during that time he shall have the same prop.
of profits as the other men and be used as well in all respects and
receive from me every kindness and attention in my power to
bestow.   I am Yr. obt. Servt.

                                            Nath. J. Wyeth

                         XL.

                         Cambridge   Feb 13th   1832
Hall J. Kelley Esq (Washington)
                    Dear Sir
                              Your favor of the 7th inst
is at hand.   However well affairs are going on at Washington
matters little to me Anything they can do will come too late for
my purposes.   My arrangements are made to leave here 1st
March and I shall not alter them, neither can I delay on my
route.

I wish you well in your undertaking but regret that you could
not have moved at the time and in the manner first proposed.
When you adopted the plan of taking across the continent in the
1st expedition women and children I gave up all hope that you
would go at all and all intention of going with you if you did.
The delays inseparable from a convoy of this kind are so great
that you could not keep the mass together and if you could the
delay would ruin my projects.   I am much obliged to you for the
information concerning licenses and Remain
                    Yr. obt. servt.   Nath. J. Wyeth

                         XLI.

                         Cambridge   Feb 13th   1832
Mess Davenport & Byron (N York)
                         Gent   Your fav. of 10th
inst is at hand.   Please order 20 Doz of the traps such as you
name and such as used by Mr. Astor to be done as soon as
possible and sent to Baltimore so as to arrive there certainly by
the 7th March.   Concerning chains I will advise you farther
and also of what other goods are wanted and cannot be obtained
in this place.

Please inform me whether you wish me to send the funds to you or whether you will draw on me. If the latter let it be at 5 days sight and so as to reach here not later than 1st March.

I am yr obt. servt   Nathl. J. Wyeth

XLII.

Cambridge   Feb 17th   1832

Broth. Leonard (New York)

Your favor of the 13th is at hand and as you do not acknowledge mine of the 10th I fear it has miscarried. In lieu of the proposition contained in it I will ask you to place your guarantee on the back of the agreement which I have made with Mess Hall and Williams which will be the same thing to you and save future trouble if loss should arise. You cannot be called upon for indemnity short of 30 months which will be Sept 1834 but a short time prior to the last sum named in your letter of 10th Jany. and differs so little from your own proposal that I have proceeded on the presumption that you would do it and sha.   ^   ¬ the document to your place before the 25th. You will percei.   y the agreement with Tucker Hall & Williams that the first shipment that will be made (and of course the first responsibility which you will incur) will be predicated on on orders sent home by me which cannot be short of a year. One year more at least for the shipment to return and loss ascertained and unavoidable delays will bring your liability to as distant a time as the one I have named but if you think advisable you can name the time at which you do bind yourself to indemnify in the entry on back of the agreement.

The agreement I have made is precisely what Mr. Osgood though[t] could be procured of Mess. J. Baker and son. I called on them but they would make me no offer, but after having closed with Hall and Co. they were anxious to do it, and expressed themselves disappointed that it was too late. I would have liked an arrangement with them better because they are in the trade. The others otherwise are as good men as they can be. I am afraid I closed rather hastily but I had been bandied much by those in the trade and I expected the same thing with them. My time was short and the offer I got as good as could possibly be made by good men.

Say to Mr. Osgood that I am much obliged to him for his kindness and that his letter will yet do me service probably in enabling me to make arrangement with Mr. Baker to take any surplus of goods which his vessells are liable to have when leaving that coast.

Please answer soon.   Yr aff Bro. Nathl. J. Wyeth.

XLIII.

Cambridge   Feb. 21   1832

Mess Davenport & Byron (N York)

Gent.   The Bond of A. Nor-
ris & Co mentioned in your letter of 16th inst I will take up, and
transmit the same to you with funds to meet the balance of disbursements in a Branch check at which time I will advise you
further.   I am &c y   N. J. W.

XLIV.

Cambridge   Feb 22d, 1832

Bro. Leonard N. York

Your letter of 18 inst is at hand.   I
shall send to New York a copy of the agreement with Hall and Williams and Mr Tucker as soon as the same is signed by them which
cannot be until the 1st March because the stile of their firm is then
to be changed.   I am pleased that you are suited with these men.
I have been long acquainted with them and esteem them highly
as honest and upright men.   The surplus funds are subject to my
order so far as to cover all the disbursements made by me and
any surplus funds after said deduction are subject to the order of
the Co. so far as placing them where they please in trust for the
said Co and as a fund to secure the debts of the Co and to be so
kept in trust until the expiration of the 5 years.   My agreement
with Hall and Williams binds them to deposit in bank any surplus fund that may arise in default of orders on the subject.

I shall forward to you the agreement to be signed by the Company which will explain to the persons you name the nature of
their duties and proportion of profits.   In the mean time assure
any that call that we are really going to start by or before
1st March.   When I forward this document I shall give information concerning the hopes and prospects of the Co &c. and speci-
fy how many are then wanted to fill up and of what trades.   For
this purpose I shall then request you or some other person to advertise in your city.   Persons thus engaged will arrive in Balto.
as soon as we shall and there join us.   This must serve instead of
your proposition of coming on by land.   Policy forbids sending
on the men alone.

The offer which you make of a letter of credit for 500$ relieves
me much, if you could give me one for 1300$ and in case I draw
for more than the 500$ you could draw on Jas. Brown for the sur-
plus it would accomodate me much.   B will answer drafts for the
800$ at ten days sight and in such case pledge property of mine
in his hands to raise it.

The guarantee which I wish you to make I have placed on the
back of my agreement with H & Williams made payabl e in default 27 months from date.

[No signature.]

XLV.

Cambridge   Feb 26th   1832

Brother Jacob (Howel Furnace N Jersey)

I write to inform you that on Thursday March 1st we shall form our camp on Long Island in Boston Harbour and that within 6 days thereafter we shall sail for Baltimore. I write thus early that you may loose no time in making preparations for a moove to—

[This letter breaks off because a leaf of the letter-book has been torn out at this point.]

XLVI.

Cambridge   Feb 28th   1832

Mess. Davenport & Byron (N York)

Gent. Enclosed you [will find] the bond of Mess. A. Norris and Co. which please pass to my credit, and after making the small purch[as]es below named forward to me an acc. of your disbursements with ballance due you said ballance I will then forward to you in a Branch check. These papers must arrive here by the 6th March as I may leave Boston as soon as that time. Let them be directed to me in Boston to the care of Frederic Tudor Esq. If you find it impossible to get these accounts here by the time named present them to Mess Cripps and Wyeth Pearl St. whom I will request to settle them. I wish you to send the goods to me to the care of Mess Wyeth & Norris Baltimore and by the steam-boat line if possible to avoid the risk of their not arriving in season. Nearly all the goods wanted have been obtained here. The chains I have obtained. What I now want is 3 doz. Spanish knives of best quality for personal arms 5 ½ inch blade with a set to prevent its shutting when open, 60 to 8[o] yds of red cloth such as is used in the Indian trade to cost not more than 1.75 per yard of a bright scarlet 6–4 wide. Purchase none unless of the kind you know to be used in the Indian trade, about 50$ worth of beads of the size of the large ones which are enclosed ¾ of the blue of the same shade as nearly as can be of the small ones. Of the small ones I have purchased an assortment.

[No signature.]

XLVII.

Long Island Boston Harbor March 3d   1832

Mr Seymour Whiting (New York)

Dear Sir Your fav. of 27 ulto. came in course to hand and would have been answered before this but for my being extremely buisy in forming my camp at this place which was done on the 1st inst. We shall sail during all the time to the 8th inst [?] for Baltimore per Bg. Ida with a fair complement of men.

This expedition employs so nearly all my means that I find it impossible to comply with your proposal but were my means more extended I would with pleasure do it to ensure the benefit of your company.   Say to Mess Ball and Sinclair that we have commenced in the work and shall go on with spirit.   They have probably ere this had a note from my brother of the firm of Cripps and Wyeth in whose hand a copy of the compact has been placed.

I am yr obt servt   N. J. W

XLVIII.

Camp Long Island Boston Harbour   March 3d   1832
Mr. H. J. Kelley (Washington)
Dear Sir

Your fav. of 24th ulto. was received on the 2nd inst. being the day after I formed my camp at this place.   I have not and shall not call on Genl. Mc Neil having written him once and received no answer.   I sail per Bg. Ida within 5 days for Baltimore and may be expected there from the 15 to the 20th inst. but shall remain there no longer than I can possibly heip.

I am perpectly well aware of the importance of cooperation of all the Americans who may go to that country but I am well convinced that this thing has been delayed too long already and that further delay will defeat my enterprise beside not being in the habit of setting two times to do one thing.   I am quite willing to join your emigration but will not delay here or at St. Louis.   You very much mistake if you think I wish to desert your party, but you must recollect that last 1st Jany was set at first as the time of starting.

I am yr Obt Servt. N. J. W.

XLIX.

Cambridge Camp Long Island March 4 1832
[This part of the head of the letter and the date are written with the ink used in writing the first portion of the following letter.   All excepting the date is crossed out with ink used in writing second portion.]

Bg. Ida at Sea
[With ink used in second portion.]
Bro. Perry (Newbury Vt.)

Your letter of Dec 22 was received in due time.   I have defered answering to this time that I might speak as one on the verge of a great event.   Yr letter to Mess. Clark and Grau shall be delivered if opportunity serves.   Perhaps it is a *dead* letter.   What you write in regard to myself I presume is the truth and that I am not ashamed of, altho. it may be sealed "Cordiality and kindness is what I always presume on" feeling as tho. I deserve it from the hands of all men in-as-much as they deserve it from me.

The though[t] of leaving N. England *forever* has never entered my mind. As to the hazard of it there can be no hazard greater than death (in my crede) and that all must meet at some time and if there were I should not much regret leaving the land of religious freedom as you call it but it is not so to me finding in it [Across the above portion of the copy of this letter is written "continued on the next page." Copies of letters L. and LI. are interposed between the preceding and the following portions.] none of that freedom of religious opinion of which you speak, by freedom of opinion I mean the exercise and avowal of ones ideas without harm accruing therefrom. Can any one say that my opinions have been exercised in freedom and that no harm has accrued to me. Can one any assert that I have not been lowered in the estimation of my fellows thereby? Yet they are as honest opinions and as conscientiously believed in and perhaps as much pains and investigation used in their formation as in those of most men. Have I not been told that those who believed not in the bible were not fit to be argued with and that too by men who hold themselves especially called to preach forth the religion of love and charity to all men. Are not men of one denomination of opinion avoided in all the relations of life by those of another does not the orthodox man employ the orthodox in most buisness that he may have the disposal of does not the temperance society man often say that he will employ none but his own class whereby damage accrues to the other and for merely taking the liberty to exercise his own opinions. And yet you call this a land of civil and religious liberty. I repeat I have not found it such.

I doubt not brother Perry but you have much at heart my welfare both *temporal* and *eternal* a difference of opinion has never in me created any hardness of opinion toward you I have always though[t] you sincere in your professions and have respected you accordingly as one who being convinced that he was in the right path and only path was anxious that all should walk therein for their good. I cannot but respect such disinterested and arduous exertions for the good of others altho. I think them mistaken. I do not ridicule nor would I persecute altho I do not believe but am willing that all should enjoy their own opinions and am convinced that all honest opinions will be tolerated elsewhere if not—[Across the copy of this second portion of the letter is written "continued on the 3rd following page from last page." About half of the page designated is cut out. This mutilation of the book was caused evidently by the desire to suppress the remainder of the letter—at least two other letters were sacrificed as the two following remnants indicate:]

Camp Long Island Head Boston Harbor　　March 6th　　1832
Mr E. E. Lansing (New York)

　　　　　　　　　　Dear Sir　　Your favor of 2nd inst is
at hand I have instructed my brother of the firm of Cripps & Wyeth
Pearl St. your city—[Half leaf removed.]
—advised if I had given any on such a subject.　You can communicate at least twice a year, and if the expedition is fortunate you
will be able on your return to live in the stile you like, if otherwise
the thing will be abandoned within two years and you will return
just as well off as you are now.　Please consider this my last letter
from this place..　　　　　　I am yr afte Bro.　N. J. Wyeth

[Copies of six letters at least were inserted between 2nd and 3rd
(which is missing) portions of letter XLIX.　This indicates un-
unusual deliberation in writing that letter if not hesitation in copy-
ing it into his book.
　　The irregularity in the order of appearance of the letters in this
part of the book is most likely due to a failure to have the letter
book always at hand in passing back and forth between Cambridge,
Camp Long Island, and Boston.]

L.

　　　　　　　　　Boston　　March 9th　　1832
Brother Leonard (New York)
　　　　　　　　　Enclosed you have a check in fav. of
Mess. Davenport and Byron for 450$ with which please settle
the balance due the above gentlemen of 525.79.　The above is all
the money that I can spare at this place.　The surplus you will
oblige me by considering as in part of what I am allowed to draw
on you for.　If you cannot do this draw on me in Baltimore and
it shall be refunded.
　　　　　　　　I am &c　N. J. Wyeth.

LI.

　　　　　　　　　Boston　　March 9th, 1832
Mess. Davenport and Byron(N York)
　　　　　　　　　Gent　Your fav. of 3d inst.
is but just received and is very satisfactory.　Please accept my
thanks for the promptness with which you have attended to this
buisness.
　　By this mail I have made remittance to Mr. Leond. I. Wyeth
of the firm of Mess. Cripps & Wyeth Pearl St. your city on
whom please call for settlement.　I go hence by water therefore
cannot have the pleasure of seeing you in N. York as you are polite enough to hope.
　　　　　　　I am yr obt servt.　N. J. Wyeth.

LII.

Cambridge   March 5th   1832
Bro. Leond. (New York)
Mess. Tucker and Williams will for-
ward to you the agreements between them, Henry Hall and myself on both of which you will please place your guarantee for
$1500 and request Charles to do the same for 1000$ and in case
he is not in your city send them to him to execute and in either
case have one returned whence it came and the other sent to me
at Baltimore, also all letters of credit which you have for me to
arrive there from the 17th to the 20th inst. Please take a copy
for your own satisfaction and request Charles to do the same. I
shall not write to you again from this place but will endeavour to
do it from Baltimore if I do not see you there which if buisness
permits would gratify me much.
All well here and in haste.
Yr afte. Bro. N. J. W.

LIII.

Cambridge March 6th 1832.
Bro. Leond (N. York)
Your fav. of 3d inst. is at hand. My let-
ter book is at Long Island therefore cannot give you a duplicate
of my letter of the 27th inst. I think it contained some agreements between myself and men and instructions to engage 15
who would comply with the same, and write notes to all those
had seen you on the subject. This letter was enveloped in a
newspaper covering post paid to the care of your firm. Please
on the receipt of this write notes to The. Bache, care of Mr.
Swartwort the collector and to E. E. Lansing care of Mess Whit-
ney and Mc.Farlan 91 Maiden Lane stating that such a letter has
miscarried. A duplicate I will send to-morrow. We sail in the
Bg. Ida for Baltimore on the 10th inst. The letter to E. E. March
is received for which I thank you.
I am Yr Afte Bro N. J. W.

LIV.

Camp Long Island Head Boston Harbor Mr. 5th 1832
Mr Theo. Bache (New York)
Dear Sir
Your fav. of the 1st inst. is at
hand. Our camp was formed at this place on the 1st inst. We
sail for Baltimore in the brig Ida on the 10th inst. and should we
have a good passage we may be expected to arrive in that
city by the 18th by which time please be in that city.
Ere this I suppose you have received a note from my brother
of your city in whose possession you will find a copy of the contract to be signed and which will be done when you meet us.

The letter from Mr. Lansing is at hand and is answered by this mail.   I am &c N. J. W.

[Half leaf of letter book is here cut out. This mutilation destroyed the 3rd portion of letter XLIX. and the main parts of two letters remnants of which are given in connection with letter XLIX.]

LV.

Boston   March 10th   1832
Mr John Ball   N. York
            Dear Sir   This is to inform you of our sailing this day in the Baltimore Packett Ida and to request you to meet us at Baltimore as soon as the 18th near which time we may be expected to arrive in the city.   When there enquire of me of Mess. Wyeth & Norris Markett St. Baltimore.
            Yr Obt Servt N. J. W

LVI.

Boston March 10th 1832
Mr. John Sinclair (N. York)
            Dear Sir   This is to inform you of our sailing this day in the Baltimore Packett Ida and to request you to meet us at Baltimore as soon as the 18th near which time we may be expected to arrive in that city.   When there enquire of Mess Wyeth & Norris Market St. Baltimore for me.
            I am yr. &c   N. J. Wyeth

LVII.

Bg. Ida at Sea   March 15th 1832
Bro. Leonard (New York)
            Fearing I may not see you on my arrival at Baltimore I employ my leisure in writing to you.   I have given Mr Brown a power of at[t]orney to act in my behalf.   This I did because he is on the spot and also more intimate with my affairs than any other person.   Another reason was that there is a bank getting up in Cambridge of which he cannot fail of being a director, and through him if I wish I shall have the power of raising money provided I make him sufficiently intimate with my affairs.   If successfull my operations will require a large sum of money and a bank in Camb. will be the one to raise it from and by placing my unavailable property at his disposal it may be used through his endorsement at a bank that will always want customers.   I have not yet made up my mind whom I shall commission to examine the acc. of Mess. Tucker and Williams and I think I shall not at present commission any one to do it inasmuch as nothing will be required until the shipments are made nor do I know that any examination will be requisite until the expiration of five years. If you think otherwise and are willing to at-

tend to it I will request them to forward their accounts to you.
I shall send you certified accounts of my disbursements in behalf
of the Co.   These are available according to the agreement as
soon as the amt. can be spared from the operations of the concern
without interest, as also all private loans to the different members
on account of their outfits and traveling expenses and notes or
due bills for the latter I will forward you from St.Louis or Franklin in order that I may send you all at once.   As to the commissions of this buisness they are all mortgaged for the 5 years and
must go to Tucker and Williams.   I should have been better
pleased to have kept them at my own disposal but I could not do
it and perhaps during the 5 years it would be no object.   I have
obtained letters from J. Baker and Son which will enable me to
send home goods and information by their vessells also to purchase any surplus goods that their vessells may have when leaving that coast.   This may be an advantage to both saving them
the loss of carrying home a few useless goods and enabling me to
purchase what I want without paying freight.   They also if they
continue the salmon [trade] wish to make arrangement with
me to put up their cargoes which I may do provided it does not
interfere with my own trade in this article.   I like the men much
and if it lays in my way to do them a favor it certainly will be
done.   Letters will reach me through Tucker and Williams Boston and I enjoin upon you to write me as often as you have an
opportunity and you may rest assured that I will do the same.
My journal I shall send one copy to Mr. Brown and one to
you and Charles jointly.   These you must preserve with care as
it will be intended for publication if on finishing it is found
worth it, and as the character of the expedition will depend much
on this care must be used that it be not lost or divulged, as publication would destroy one half of its value and it may be that I
would not wish all the facts of the trade divulged before I have
done with it.

As I am leaving all reasonable vicinity I must bid adieu
to all my friends among which I number your good wife.
Say to her that her life has been checkered with heavy afflictions
but still there have been other misfortunes more difficult to bear,
that there is comfort in some sorts of affliction but in others there
is naught but bitterness and that as we advance in life we are
gradually weaned from our love of life until we pass naturally
from this to another existence and that death which in early life
we dread so much I doubt not may come a welcome visitor to
the weary and worn in misfortune and to those whose dearest
treasures have gone before them.   Say to the little girls that
their uncle Nat has gone far from them but that in the wilderness he stil[l] remembers them while probably in a few months he
will be forgotten, all but the name by them and this I have no

doubt you will keep in their minds, life is too full of pleasures for them to remember their distant friends long.

My health is pretty good and hope and excitement has made another man of me. I am determined to give up no more to melancholy feelings but rouse myself up to exertion and enterprise and forget the things that have been and all but what is before me. If I am successful there will be some comfort in it if otherwise I will have some serious and present misfortunes to keep me from brooding over more distant and metaphysical ones. If I fail in my enterprise it will be an undertaking that few men could even look at if successful it will be fame and wealth enough to keep me on a par and in standing with the best other circumstances to the contrary notwithstanding. The present which Mr. Tudor made me on settlement is as fair an offset to Mr. J. . . conduct that in a civil way he shall know it, it is too good an encomium on my character to keep from him. You need not be alarmed for my temper, for I will keep the advantage of coolness over him and he shall find that I have more patience than he imagined and too much pride to shew that he can hurt my feelings even if it is really the case. I expect a little spleen from him but he shall keep it all to himself he shall not infect me with it, it would gratify him too much.

I left our parents all well and also the other members of the family some scolding and some crying, and both to equally little purpose, altho they have their effect and show who values us.

I am &c   N. J. W.

P. S.   Baltimore   March 24th   1832
     I arrived here on the 23d inst. and received your fav. of the 15th enclosing a letter to Tiffany Shaw & Co. and check for 424.21 which is very timely, as Charley had even forgot to forward Mortons note which he had been twice directed to do. I shall leave this on Tuesday and shall wish to receive an answer to this at Pitsburg.

LVIII.

                                   Baltimore March 24th 1832
Judah Touro Esq. (N. Orleans)
     Dear Sir   I write to apprise you that on my arrival at this place on my way out to the Columbia River I found that my brother Mr C. Wyeth had neglected to forward to you the note against Morton Brown & Co. referred to in my letter of the 7th of Feb. last. The note will be disposed of here or left behind or sent to you, in the last of which cases please look for advices to Mr. C. Wyeth.
     Please excuse my troubling you in this matter.
                                   I am &c N. J. W.

LIX.

Baltimore   March 24th   1832

Mr. H. J. Kelley (Washington City)

Dear Sir   I arr[i]ved here on the 23d at midnight and have received your favor of same day. I will take charge of any of the emigrants who will defray their own expenses at any part of the route provided no delay will be occasioned to my party.   I leave this on Tuesday next for Pitsburg and should be pleased to receive from you a copy of the map referred to in your letter.

N. J. W.

LX.

Baltimore March 24th 1832

Mr Jas Brown (Cambridge)

Dear Sir   I arrived here on the 23d inst. after a severe passage.   Please fix in your mind some means of mortgaging my house for about $800— and pledging the note of F. Tudor for its amt. in order that when drawn as I possibly may you may not be put to inconvenience.   I shall be obliged to draw at short sight if at all, on acc. of the scarcity of money at the West.   If you feel able to do it, forward to Leond. I. Wyeth another letter similar in tenor to the first, allowing him to draw at what sight you are able and for what further amt. you think yourself safe in doing. I hope and think that I shall [not] call for more than $200 but wish to be on the safe side.   On board the Brig Ida you will find a bundle of nine Buffaloes which are I. Reads please pay freight and hand them to him and pay the damage and give him my thanks.

Give my love to your good wife and boys.

Yr friend   N. J. W.

LXI.

Brownsville   April 6th   1832

Brother Charles (Baltimore)

I write to apprise you that I shall have to draw on you in accordance with your letter of Cr. given me by Mr. Norris for 300$ from Wheeling and in case I should not be able to dispose of such draft I shall from that place request you to forward me a Branch Check for the same.   I write this knowing the state of the money markett and in order that you may be prepared.

N. J. Wyeth.

LXII.

Pitsburg   April 8th   1832

Bro. Leonard (New York)

Your fav. of 28th ulto. is at hand.   I shall in case I fail to obtain money on a letter of Cr. from Charles

for 300$ draw on you for the 1100 provided I want so much and
if I want more I shall presume to draw on you for the full amt.
of 1300 and presume that Charles will meet the same,as I relieved
him from doing so at Baltimore, and Mr. Brown can certainly
avail himself of sufficient from my property in his hands to meet
any thing that I will draw.

Jacob says his trunk is worth $100 you may therefore calcu-
late it $25. It can be of no importance to me nor do I believe to
himself. Leave this morning direct for St. Louis. I will request Jacob to write to you.

There is a balance of a draft of Jacobs for 150$ with father's
endorsement thereon in my favor on Charles, and this amt.I shall
not use and from this you can reimburse yourself if you deem advisable and I will retain the draft for your advantage. As Charles
has seen it he cannot refuse to pay it. The draft is for 600$ and
is in my hands. $450 was consumed by a little cash and the
letter of credit above referred to. I will send it to you on Charles
if you direct me so to do, at St. Louis where I wish to receive an
answer to this.

N. J. W.

LXIII.

Pitsburg April 8th 1832
Bro. Charles (Baltimore)
　　　　　　　　Being Sunday cannot sell a draft on you.
Please pay the amt. of your letter of Cr. to Leond. I. Wyeth and
oblige　　　　　　　　Yr Afte Bro N. J. Wyeth.

LXIV.

Pitsburg April 8th 1832
Mr H. J. Kelley (Washington)
　　　　　　　　Dear Sir Your fav. of 29th ulto. is
at hand. I will in conformity with my first assurance given in
my letter of 23d ulto. take charge of ten of your emigrants.
Any further arrangement must be with the persons who are
disposed to go out. My reason for this is that I am bound
by my engagements to my Company and must consult them in
regard to any arrangements on the subject but you need not by
this understand me positively to refuse it as I do not know how
the Co. will be disposed to act.

I shall at all times be disposed to further an emigration to the
Columbia as far as I deem, on actual knowledge of the country,
that it will be for the advantage of the emigrants, but before I
am better acquainted with the facts I will not lend my aid in inducing ignorant persons to render their scituation worse rather
than better.

[No signature.]

LXV.

Cincinati   April 10th   1832

Leond. Jarvis Esq. (Baltimore)

Dear Sir Your fav. of the 5th inst. came safe to hand, enclosing the very acceptable letters to Mess Pilcher & Sanford, also authority to draw on you for $500 if my necessitys required and if such happens to be the case I shall advise you of it. You have my thanks for the kindness and you—

LXVI.

[Letter LXV breaks off abruptly. Letter LXVI. opens without date or superscription. As they appear on pages numbered as consecutive the inference would be that occasion suddenly arose to pack the letter book at Cincinnati and not again use it until Ft. Vancouver was reached. The words "Probably to F Tudor Esq." are in Mr. Wyeth's hand.]

Probably to F. Tudor Esq.

On the 4th of Jany inst.the wind vered to the N.E.and immediately the weather which to that time had been rainy and warm set in clear and cold, like that you have when the wind is N. W.but not so cold, the Ther. varying from 12 deg.to 20 deg. above zero. The Columbia as near as I can find freezes up about half the years. Last winter and this it has frozen. The ice when it freezes smooth is good. It is now about 6 inches, but the surface is a complete chaos, but as this trade will not soon thrive in this quarter it ceases to be a subject of interest.

In an agricultural view there are many advantages in this country the most prominent of which is that the operation of plowing need never be suspended more than one month, and one half of the years not at all, (thereby giving much more time for the farmer's work,) and the facility of feeding stock in winter for the snow seldom falls here and the horses and cattle feed out all the year. When the wind comes from the land it is cool and dry, when from the ocean it rains incessantly. There appears to me to be but a small proportion of the country fit for cultivation. Near the sea the country is mountainous and rough so much so that I believe 9-10 of the land could not be ploughed. Farther in the interior the nights are frosty all summer the earth excessively barren producing but a scanty portion of very nutritive grass, and I presume there are few parts of the earth where less moisture is found than in the interior of this country. The best part of this country that I have seen is on the Wallemet but I am informed that there is a good section of country near Pugets Sound and on the Cowliskie River. On the Columbia itself there is little or no valuable land. Of the Salmon and Fur buisness I can inform you nothing as no buisness letters can go out of this country by this conveyance. When I arrived at the British posts my men what were then left being determined to wander no more I was left to myself in this dilemma. I was invited by Dr J. McGlaucland (Gov. in behalf of the H. B. Co. in this country) to make this post my habitation until I returned. I have been treated in the most hospitable and kind manner by all the gentlemen of this country. There are far more of the comforts of life enjoyed here by the residents than is imagined in the states.

Respectfully yr. obt. Servt.   Nathl. J. Wyeth

LXVII.

Fort Vancouver   Jany 16th   1833

Dear Parents (Camb)

After much delay and some difficulty in the shape of long marches on foot I am at last here and now am as much in haste to get back again. From hunger I have suffered not much. This climate proves to be warm and agreeable but in winter rather too much rain. You may expect me home in October next.

Jacob could go no farther than the mountains. His heart looked back to the things of home and he could not see the return convoy depart alone. Livermore deserted me twelve days out from the settlements. Both are I hope safe with their friends but the latter behaved very dishonorably. I do not write much at the present as I hope to be so soon with you beside I cannot by this conveyance touch on matters of buisness all I can say is that the first of it looks bad enough. If I should be longer in returning than above stated do not be alarmed for in the way I shall travell there is no danger except of my health and that is now pretty good. My party have now all left me and I have hired two men who are to return with me. I have in time of need found (in this land of strangers) kind friends who have alleviated all my sufferings with the exception of that one which arises from a consciousness that I shall never be able to repay to them those civilities that I have received but I am sure that the opportunity of assisting me has afforded them pleasure. You can have but little idea how much men improve in some points of character in scituations like these. If polite carriage and shrewd intellect are best acquired in more populous parts of the earth, generous feelings are fostered by the wilds, and amid savages the civilized man seems to uphold his character better than among his fellows.   Yr. afte son,   Nathl. J. Wyeth

LXVIII.

Fort Vancouver   Jany 16th   1833

Mess. Tucker & Williams (Boston)

Gent I am not at liberty by this conveyance to send you any information touching matters of buisness. I can say to you nothing farther than that no orders will come to you from me at present. My party have all left me and I am about returning across the mountains with two men that I have hired for the purpose. The small amt. of goods which I took with me are deposited in the interior as well as some furs. Of these I shall endeavor to avail myself on my return route but their value is not sufficient to fit out a sufficient party expressly for them and unless I meet a party going very near my deposits I shall dispose of them or leave them as may happen. Perhaps so much as the above may be allowed to pass by this conveyance. We have not suffered much owing to the politeness and attention which I have received from the Traders of this country both English and American. They have always given me all the information and assistance in their power.

I am Yr. Obt. Servt. Nathl. J. Wyeth

LXIX.

Fort Vancouver Jany 16th 1833

Brother Leond.

I write you this which will reach you near the same time as myself provided I meet with no accident, but write for fear that this should be the case. My route will be across the land to about Latt 43 deg. in the Rocky Mountains and so down the Platte to the Missouri. This letter will reach you by the favor of the H. B. Co. to whose agents in this quarter I am much indebted for assistance and information but for obvious reasons I cannot touch upon matters of buisness in a letter conveyed by them further than to say that I shall draw on you or Charles for a very small amt. due them for supplies and please consider this as notice for the same. My journey hither has been attended with much less difficulty than I expected but it appears the hardships of the undertaking are much greater than those with me anticipated as they have as they fell in with chances deserted, so that I now have but two men whom I have hired to go back with me. I think I may reach home in Oct. or Nov. next but it need occasion no alarm if I am detained a year longer. My object in returning by a different route from that by which this will reach you is to avail myself of some deposits of valuables which I have in the mountains. If I am so unfortunate as to meet no American party going to the states I will not be able to come for it is too dangerous to cross the mountains with but three men and those not the best for such a purpose. My health is pretty good and I enjoy myself as well as I can while dependent on the hospitality of others. I make this letter short expecting soon to be with you.

You will give my respects to your good wife and love to the little nieces. My respects also to Mr Osgood.

Yr. afte. Bro. Nathl. J. Wyeth.

LXX.

Fort Vancouver   Jany 16th   1833

Brother Charles (Baltimore)

This will be short and I hope sweet. It comes to you by the politeness of the Hudsons Bay Co. and as a matter of consequence cannot contain matters of buisness. From the agents of this Co. I have received all manner of attention and assistance rendered in such a way as to make it palatable. I expect to be with you about the time that you receive this but if I should be a year later do not be alarmed for it is entirely a chance if I meet with an American party in the upper country and if I do not, I must remain on this side of the Mts. I have now with me two hired men only, all my party having left me, and with only three men I will not undertake to cross the mountains beside when I am in a country where I can get horses to ride, Buffaloe to eat, and Deer skin to wear I am as well off as I can be anywhere and if I make no money, I shall loose none and so much of life will be gone, all the trouble of life will be all the same a hundred years hence. From the Hudsons Bay Co. I have drawn some supplies and for these I shall draw a small draft on you or Leond. and please receive this advise of the same. Our journey out was attended with few of the difficulties anticipated as also with less of the romance and adventure. I expect soon to be with you and therefore do not write so much in full as otherwise I would. Please present my best respects to your good lady and to the little nephews. My name sake is by this time a famous fellow and I hope he is as much like him he is named for, as little Charley, that is much more quiet and tractable than the latter.   Yr. Afte. Bror   Nathl. J. Wyeth.

LXXI.

Fort Vancouver   Jany 16th   1833

Leond. Jarvis Esq.(Baltimore)

Dear Uncle   I write you, because it would be unpardonably in me not to do so whenever I have an opportunity rather than because I have much to communicate. Matters of buisness cannot pass by this conveyance which is through the Hudsons Bay Co. I am about returning to the states by the same route by which I came which I do to obtain some deposits of valuables which for want of horses I left in the interior. In this I shall probably fail but the chance is worth trying for. In case I am successfull I may arrive in your city about Oct. next but if any disappointment occurs in meeting some American party I may be a year later. My party have all followed suite—

[The removal of a leaf from the letter book at this point makes the copies of letters LXXI and LXXII fragmentary and probably caused the entire loss of several other letters.]

LXXII.

—the Bg Sultana bound to the Columbia owned by Joseph Baker and Son to the master and supercargo of which I had letters of Cr. to enable me to take any supplies from her that were wanted at certain regulated prices settled in Boston 6th [a]s to abandoning the enterprise it was by their desire to a man. If the above does not justify me from all reproach except ignorance I must bear it but at the same time with a consciousness of not deserving it.

The enclosed proposition I have forwarded to the Gov. through Mr Herron by whom I was induced to make it. While with you I had no idea that any arrangement of the kind could be made otherwise should have handed it to you. I do not ask you to put in a good word for me because I know you will do it if consistent with your judgment and not otherwise. If you remain in the country I shall have the pleasure of seeing you again as I am determined, at the present moment, to revisit it and endeavor to improve by past experience. Of this letter you are at liberty to make what use you think proper. It is intended to meet any strictures that may be made on my conduct (for where there has been suffering there is usually crimination) and to explain anything that to anyone may appear misterious. I cannot close this without expressing to you how much I am indebted to Mr. Pam-brun Mr. Herron and Mr. Hermatinger for the attention they have shown me.

Should any American vessell come to the Columbia there will probably be on board and I think to be delivered to any British post some articles for me. The order which I gave if I recollect right comprised Books, seeds and clothing. Should such come to hand the seed you will consider for the benefit of the Country, and should be used to prevent loss. Books you will take for yourself and all other articles after one year from receipt if not otherwise ordered sell for the benefit of such persons as you deem most worthy of it. Will you allow me the priviledge of writing you from home.   N J Wyeth

LXXIII.

Inclosing copy of proposal contained in next letter.

Fort Colville   March 12th   1833

Sir

I am induced by gentlemen in this country to suppose that you would enter into some arrangement for a supply of goods and therefore send the enclosed proposal. I left the Boston in March last with 32 men with the intention of forming on the Columbia or south of it [a post] for collecting furs and salmon to be sent to the States by vessells ordered therefrom such vessells to bring out the goods required for the trade. My plan was based on the following grounds viz. that Salmon (worth in the States 16$ per Bbl. of 30 gallons) would pay all the expenses that goods introduced by this route would be entitled to the drawback and this would be a consideration as they are nearly all foreign to the States and being coarse pay a heavy duty, that the saving made in the purchase of horses here instead of at St. Louis is at least 25$ per head, that the danger of transporting this side of the mountains is infinitely less than on the other and the distance to the Fur country much less. In the first part of said undertaking I have completely failed. All my men have left me and what goods and valuables I had with me have been expended or deposited where they will probably be lost to me. I am now on my return to the States for the purpose of forming new arrangements to carry my original plan into execution. In case I make no arrangement with the Co. I shall if I arrive in Boston by the 1st Nov. next come to the Columbia the following summer, if I arrive later I shall be delayed until the next.

It appears to me that as an American I posses some advantage that an Englishman would not inasmuch as I can visit parts of the country from which he is excluded and still not so remote in point of distance difficulty or expense as from St. Louis.

I have already lost largely from a capital at first small and am therefore desirous to proceed on a more secure plan even if it should offer less prospect of profit. I have to observe that in case of agreement being made I will give surety satisfactory to the Co. for fulfilling any part of the same or if required will deposit in their hands a sufficient sum for the same purpose. The only objection to the latter would be the difference in the rate of interest in the states and with you.

In case of an agreement for supply of goods the supply of men would still be a consideration. If men could come to this side of the Ry. Mts. as early as July a fall hunt might be made which is all that can be done from St. Louis. Canadians are to be had cheaper than Americans and are for some purposes better men. Their conveyance would not be so expensive as horses would be saved which cost 30$ at St. Louis and the same set of animals are fit for a full hunt. I would not wish more than 15 Canadians. These might be procured by myself or agent or furnished me by the Co. as they might elect and the residue of the men required might be procured in the Mts. without the expense of bringing them into the country or learning them the ways of it. If no political dificulty exists there must be some advantage in using a few Canadians. Should you deem it for the interest of the Co. to close with me an agreement not essentially different from the enclosed proposal you would much oblige me by for-

warding to my address care of Mess. Jarvis & Brown Merchants
Baltimore Maryland a contract to the purpose which I will execute and immediately proceed to fulfill. I request this mode of
proceedure because I will have but one month after my arrival at
Boston to prepare for a voyage to the Columbia, in case of failure of this negotiation with the Co.

  To Geo Simson Esq Gov. H. B. C.   York Factory
                          Yrs &c   N J W

  Copy of the proposal enclosed in the two foregoing letters.
  1st The Hon. H.B. C. to furnish at their store at Vancouver to
N.J .W. such goods as he may select at the same rate that the
clerks of the said Co pay for the goods supplied them viz 50 pr ct
on their original cost
  2d The said Co to lay no obstruction in the way of the said
Wyeths trading at any post or place for provisions or animals to
be used in his buisness or to his trading furs anywhere south of
the Columbia and not within a 100 miles of their posts and generally in matters indifferent to their interest to forward his views
and operations and to give him such information as may be in
their power and not inconsistent with their immediate interest
  3d The said Co to Cr the acc. of said Wyeth at the rate of $5
for full Beavers and in proportion for kittens and yearlings and for
all other furs and skins usually secured by the said Co. as mer-
chandise at the same prop. to their markett value in London or
wherever that Co. dispose of their furs as 5$ is to the markett
value of the Beaver skin.
  4th The said Wyeth to deliver all Furs and skins of every description of which he may get possession to the Co.
  5th Said Wyeth to continue the arrangement for five years
and in case of his not doing so to be bound not to do a Fur buisness in any country to which the H. B. Co. have access.
  6th In case said Wyeth faithfully performs this said agreement,
then the H. B. Co. at the end of the time agreed on is to pay over
to him any balance that may be due him in cash or goods as the
said W. may elect and at all times he is entitled to claim from
them in cash any balance which may be due him over and above
$1000.

                        LXXIV.

  To Captain Bonneville of Salmon River   June 22d   1833.
Sir
  I send you the following proposition for a mutual hunt in the
country south of the Columbia river which I visited last autumn
and winter. As to the prospect of Beaver there I will only say
that I have no doubt of taking 300 skins fall and spring. As
much sign as would give me this I have seen. I have little doubt
much more might be found, but in that country a hunt cannot be

made with horses alone, boats must be used. I have obtained some maps of the country beside my own observations in it, and I have little doubt but I can make my way through it without guides, who cannot be procured. As this country is distant an immediate answer is required. As it regards the mules[?] Horses would do but are by no means so good for grass in some places is very bad. If the number required is a very great objection 9 would do but goods enough to buy 3 more must be given in their stead. The men that are wanted must be good, peaceable and industrious, but need not be trappers. I would prefer good men who have not been more than one year in the country. In case of agreement being made you are to engage to deliver what letters I wish to send home, a boy about 13 years old and about 25 lbs. sundrys. The expenses of the boy in the States my brother in N. York will pay to whom he is to be delivered. The boy will have a mule to carry him. With so many animals as I have and so few men I cannot come to the forks and I think these Indians will go no further than where in your route to Green River you strike the plain of the Three Butes. There I hope to see you and in case you acceed to the proposal, with all the things required in it, this hunt to be for one year to meet you at your rendezvous of next year the furs to be equally divided between us and I to have the right to take mine at any time during the year yourself to have the right to send a man to see to your interests—

PROPOSITION.

To be furnished by Mr B.	To be furnished by Mr. Wyeth.
9 men, armed, clothed for the year with saddles &c	19 horses
12 mules	3 mules
9 skins dressed for making boats	20 traps
	3 men with myself
40 good traps	2 doz knives
1 doz files	1 Lodge
4 doz knives	Cooking apparatus
20 lbs tobacco	vermillion.
200 lbs grease, if possible	fish Hooks a few sundrys.
3 bales Indian meat	10 lbs powder and lead.
a few small tools	14 pr. Horse shoes.
3 axes	4 pack saddles and Harness.
12 pair Horse shoes (if you have them.)	
4 pack saddles and Harness.	
6 pair of lashes[?]	
25$ for cost of sundrys	
25 lbs. powder and lead with it.	

—said man to do duty the same as the other men and to have no other control than to secure your interest in the division of the skins. In case you are ready to make this arrangement you need make no doubt of my being ready to enter at once on it except that in the mean time I loose my animals.

You to have the liberty of sending a load of goods to pay off the men you furnish. All property at the risk of its owner, neither to be responsible for the debts of the othor.

Yrs &c.

[No signature.]

LXXV.

[The words "Not Sent" are written across the face of the following letter.]

Head of Lewis River   July 4th 1833
Mess Joseph Baker & Son, Boston Masstts.

Gent. Your politeness to me in the little intercourse I had with you in regard to my expedition hither must be my apology for troubling you with this. I hope you will not deem me impertinent interested in the information I send you. I tell you plainly that all my prospects of doing any thing on the coast with no more means than I have still left of my own are at an end. I have traversed the country in many directions and found all those places which [are] accessible to shipping occupied or about to be so by the H. B. Co. who are efficient opponents. The salmon alone without the fur I deem doubtfull. Not that enough could not be traded of the natives by a vessell in the Columbia but when you trade fish of the Indians it is fresh to be sure but not fresh enough to salt for a long voyage. Fish to keep well must be salted immediately from the sceine. If the plan is to catch them yourselves, I think it is at least as doubtfull possibil[i]ty. It appears to me that the impression of the vast quantity of salmon in the Columbia arrises from not considering the vast number of Indians employed in catching what is seen. If each Indian catches three a day it would feed his family and still permit him to bring one along side, and this would give more salmon than would be requisite for a cargo but salmon would in this case be from 6 to 30 hours out of the water which is far too long in this warm climate.

I shall return next year about the time that you receive this and probably endeavor to form some connection to carry on some buisness in this country. One years more experience here will enable me to speak with more confidence of the foregoing matters. The mean time will be employed in a trapping expedition with 11 men south of the Columbia River. I intend to reach the vicinity of St. Francisco. I shall beg the honor of communicating with you on my return. I subjoin a list of the posts occupied or about to be so by the H. B. Co on this coast viz. an oc-

casional post on the Umquoi River which is in latt. about 44 deg.
Fort George or Astoria renewed in 1830 and to be kept up.   One
at Fraizers River which emtys into Pugetts Sound about 30 miles
up. It is in contemplation to move this post to the coast and a little south of the mouth of the River.   One to be established this
year south of Nass.   One already established at Nass.   Also 4
Bgs. and Schs. employed on the coast continuously. One to be
established north of Nass this year.
     The loss of Capt. Lamberts Bg. I suppose you have already
heard.   The Active I have heard has gone to the Islands.   I
have found no means of sending any of the business letters with
which you entrusted me.   The family letters I gave to Capt
McNeil now in the Cos. service to deliver if he fell in with your
vessells.   I am yr. obt. servt. Nathl J Wyeth.
                         LXXVI.
          Heads of Lewis River   July 4th   1832[3]
Wm H. Boardman Esq. (Boston Masstts)
                         Sir Having received from
Capt. Mc.Neil the accompanying letters I take the liberty of addressing you.   I shall return to the States about a year from the
time you receive this and shall then beg the favour to wait on
you with a letter of introduction from Capt. McNeil. It is not in
my power to communicate any information which can be interesting to you other than what I presume is contained in the letter of
Capt. McNeil, except a list of the posts established or about to be
so and the vessells in the employ of the H. B. Co. on the N. W.
coast.   I beg you to believe that I have no interested views in
communication I make.   When I return I shall be able from a
two years experience in the country to form a judgement whether
any thing can be done in it and shall then endeavour to form
some connection to enable me to do it.   Your acquaintance Mr.
F. Tudor will give you any information respecting myself which
you may desire.   I was some years in his service and he knows
me well.   I am yr. obt. Servt. Nathl J Wyeth.

Vz An occasional post at the Umquou River in Latt about 44 deg.
  "   Fort George or Astoria renewed some time since
  "   One 30 miles up Fraizers River which emptys into Pugetts
        Sound.
This post will probably be removed to the Coast a little south of
        the river.
One south of Nass to be established this year
One at Nass, now established.
One north of Nass to be established this year
Kept continually on the coast,
Your Bg Lima Capt McNeil
Diyad [Dryad] Bg. Capt. Kipling
Cadboro Bg. Capt. Sinclair
Vancouver sch. to be launched about May Cap. Duncan

LXXVII.

[The words "Not Sent" are written across the face of the following letter.]

                              Heads of Lewis River   July 4th   1833
F. Tudor Esq. (Boston)
                    Dear Sir   Since my last from Vadcouver of
Jany 16th I have by devious routes and with two men made my
way to this place which is near the back bone of America and in
Latt 46 deg. some minutes.   Excepting 6 weeks which were
spent at Vancouver I have been continually on the march since I
left you.   I can now speak more freely of my circumstances than
in my last.   I have obtained enough furs to pay my expenses
since I left home but they are hidden in the country and I have
not been able to make my way to them as yet.   I remain here
for this and other purposes one year more.   I have recruited 9
more men which makes me 12 in all and 34 Horses and mules.
With these I shall make a hunt and p[e]rhaps obtain what furs
I collected last year.   In the progress of this years hunt I mean
to go southward to near the vicinity of the Spanish settlements in
Calafornia.   If I am unsuccessful this is my last effort and however disagreeable it may be I shall then return home, and solicit
again the place which your generosity once honored me with.
Strict necessity will only bring me to this.   I beg you will excuse,
you know my troubles and altho my course has been different
from what you advised I trust that you will have lenity enough
to excuse what you doubtless deem a weakness and perhaps truly
(a man is no judge of his own maladies.)
     In a letter to Mr. Wm H. Boardman Esq. I hinted that in case
a farther experience should justify hopes of success in this country, I should return with a view to form some connection to enable me to pursue it.   I refered him to you for a farther knowledge of myself.   Allow me to suggest the same to yourself.   In
some of your last communications to me you hinted your intention of quitting the Ice buisness.   I hope you have not done so.
It is a good permanent income to stand upon in case of dis[as]-
trous speculations to which all are liable.   I anticipate that you
have realized much money from your coffee operations.   I cannot see how you can fail of making some.   Be assured if
my wishes would avail anything you would make plenty.   I am
now writing in the open air.   I am shivering with cold, badly
clothed in skins.   Here there is no wood to warm one [and] all
nature seems clothed in gloom.   Be assured I look back upon
what and where I should have been, if but for one thing in great
bitterness of spirit.   Distance as you conjectured has brought no
balm to the wounded mind and physical suffering has not allevi-

ated the mental, nevertheless my perseverence (or obstinacy as you please to term it) is not worn out, and if things go bad the determination to make them go better is not the less. My health is nearly the same as when with you. The bad food and starvation of this country does not agree well with me. I am starting in a dangerous route in case the worst should happen my best wishes are that your prosperity and happiness may be in proportion to your talent and perseverence in buisness and your kindness and favor to myself in better days more I cannot wish you. Be pleased to give my respects to Mr. Gordon.

I am yr. obliged and obt servt.   Nathl J Wyeth

LXXVIII.

["Not Sent" written across the face.]

Heads of Lewis River   July 4th   1833
Mess. Tucker & Williams and Henry Hall Esq. (Boston Masstts)

Gent.   Since mine of 16th Jany last I have made my way to this place but without being able to obtain my deposites of furs or goods.   I have however been able to raise 9 more men making a party now of 12 with 34 horses and mules.   With these I shall make a hunt, and probably reach to near the Spanish settlement of St. Francisco, and on my return obtain my last years deposites of furs &c.   All this if I do not loose my scalp.   If no such accident happens you will see me about one year from the time that you receive this.   In the mean time no orders will come to you from me.   The requisite amt. of furs I have collected, but they are not at accessible places, neither do I deem the buisness of the coast of such certain issue as to induce me to risk bringing out a vessell.   The whole coast as far as furs are concerned is taken up by the H.B.Co.   As to Salmon those of the Columbia only are superior.   A sufficient quan[ti]ty of these could be traded but when you trade a salmon it is from 6 to 30 hours old which is to[o] old in this warm climate to salt well.   It is true it will keep, but salmon badly cured is a common article, and will bring but a small price.   I am quite sure that traded salmon could not be cured so as to be first rate and others would hardly pay sending home. To catch them is a matter that requires much knowledge.   The Indian mode is too slow.   Several good fisherys would be requisite for the sufficient and speedy supply of a vesseel.   I should not venture on the latter mode without myself coming home and putting up the requisite materials and implements for the buisness beside I think as all my men have left me and in future I should have the responsibility of wages to men, it would be more prudent to form a connection if possible and avoid a liability to which my own means are not adequate.

I remain Gent. your obt. Servt   Nathl J. Wyeth

LXXIX.

["Not Sent" written across the face.]

Heads of Lewis River   July 4th   1833
Brother Leonard (New York)
               While I am shivering with the cold
without wood and nothing but a few skins to cover my naked-
ness you are probably enjoying the festivities of the day with
your wife and litttle ones at your side. To think of those things
gives me the blue Devils. Time has not rid me of these and
physical suffering has not lessened the mental but rather points my
mind to the cause. If I can still as of old sing "Heave care oer side
&c" it is rather in obstinacy than in truth or perhaps is more like a
good dinner & wine thrown back from a gorged stomach. I drew
on you from Colville for about $100. In the letter in which I
advised you of it I could not well apologize for the liberty that I
took as I knew it would be examined. If you knew my necessitys I believe you would not ask the reason of my drawing on
you without funds. If you will reccollect I left the land which I
bought of Harvd Colledge under mortgage. This will be due
two years from last March. On this land I have paid $500. My
pride is much concerned in keeping it and my necessitys from the
world. Should I not return in time to make arrangements myself, I beg you to enable Mr.Brown to defer payment by remortg-
aging it. A farther payment of $500 would certainly enable him
to do this and perhaps he can without any further payt. I shall
write Charles to the same effect. That you will do it between
you is my only dependence, and consider that there are enough
things to mortify me without such an experience as the failure of
this would subject me to, still do not for me go farther than
your duty to your-self and family will admit of. I am alone in
the world and if my misfortunes are heavy, there is but one to
bear them, I wish not to drag others into them. As it regards
my buisness in this country what I have done I have done mostly
without help. The furs I have got would in all if in the states pay
my expenses but they are deposited in the earth in remote places
where I was obliged to leave them for want of animals and it is
a chance if I am able ever to get them. I shall give no orders
under the contract for which you are security and I hope you
will consider this in the matter of the land mentioned above. I
have with much exertion recruited my party to 12 men myself included and 34 animals and shall make a years hunt and
endeavour to obtain some of·my furs of last year in the progress
of this hunt. I shall go southward as far as the vicinity of St.
Francisco in New Calafornia and if no accident happens to me and
there is a possibility of so doing I shall be with you about a year
from the time that you receive this. The enterprise I am upon
is a dangerous one but I trust to my usual good luck to bear me

through. Should I give a letter of introduction to you to any
one connected with the Fur trade I wish you would not inform
them whether I am worth any thing or not as it is not for my interest that they should suppose that they have an inefficient op-
ponent. Let them infer what they please but at the same time
extend to them as much hospitality as you possibly can. Reccollect that I have already drawn largely on theirs and am continually exposed to do the same again and do not be startled at
any difference of manners and appearance reccollect that they have
been educated with the Bears of the wilderness. Remember me
affectionately to your wife and the little ones and believe that I
reccollect you as often as I have occasion for your kindness, as
you may well infer from my drafts on your cash, and I hope that
you will do me the credit of doing so at other times. My health
[is] much the same as when I was at home. I send you a Boy.
Please send him to my wife and pay what expenses are incurred
on him to your place.   I am your affte Bro.
Náth. J Wyeth
                   LXXX.

["Not Sent" written across the face.]

                   Heads of Lewis River   July 4th   1833
Bro. Charles (Baltimore)
                   I hope that today you are better off than
myself.   I hope you are in peace of mind and content enjoying
with your friends and family the festivities of the day and I hope
you have a thought too of me. Imagine to yourself a fellow seated on the open and extensive prairie beside a little brook without
a fire in freezing weather and poorly clad in skins with plenty of
poor raw dried buffaloe meat and you see Nat. A meeting with
Mr. Bonneville gives me the power to make up jointly with him
a party for a hunt for this season. I shall not come home this year.
My party is 12 in number with myself and 34 animals. With
these I shall go southward to the vicinity of St. Francisco in
New Calafornia. Since I have been in the country I have collected Furs enough to pay my expenses but they are deposited in
such places as render it at least doubtful if ever I see them again.
They were left for want of horses to carry them. This and other
matters relating to my being worth property or not please not to
communicate to any one connected with the Fur trade even if he
come with a letter from me. If they find out my true circumstances let it be by their own wits. It is not my interest that
they sup[p]ose me worth nothing, at the same time should I give
a letter of introduction to any of them have the goodness to extend as much hospitality to them as you can. Keep in mind that
in this country I am continually liable to receive it from them
and that I have already received much. Your bond for the fulfil-

ment of a contract with Mess Tucker and Williams you may now consider a dead letter.   I shall make no use of the contract with them at least until I see you.   I have a request to ask of you and Leonard jointly.   It is that you would enable Mr Brown to defer the payment to Harvd Colledge for the land I bought of them. It becomes due two years from last March.   I have paid 500$ on this land a farther payt. of 500$ would undoubtedly enable him to remortgage it.   My pride has but little to cling to now save it I beg of you in this respect.   If I return as I expect in about one year from the time you receive this I can arrange the matter myself.   But there is so much [doubt] of my being able to do so that I deem it requisite to make the above request at this time. Please give my affectionate respects to your lady and little ones.

Yr afte Bro.   N. J. W.

LXXXI.

["Not Sent" written across the face.]

Heads of Lewis River   July 4th   1833
Leond. Jarvis Esq. (Baltimore)

Dear Uncle,   Since my last of 16th Jany from Fort Vancouver I have made my way so far across the land with two men but have not been able to go to the places where my furs of last year are deposited.   Circumstances now enable me to raise a small party of men with which to try again if any thing can be made in this country.   My scituation is here far from being comfortable.   Since my last I have seen some suffering and this year I shall probably see much more and with so small a party there is some danger.   Since I have been in the country I have caught furs enough to pay all of my expenses if they were in the States but I do not much expect to be able to get them without as much trouble and expense as would be required to catch as many more and for this purpose I am about starting for a hunt to the southward of the Columbia River.   In the course of this hunt I shall probably go to near the Spanish settlement of St. Francisco in New Calafornia.   About a year from the time you receive this you may expect to see me in your city.   I think there is a good chance to make money in this country.   A good hunter can take an average of 120 skins in a year these are worth in Boston about $1000.   Such hunters can be hired for about 400$ payable in goods at an average of 600 per ct profit.   The animals to do the buisness of a camp cost here about 4$ in goods prime cost in Boston or N. York.   A band of 20 hunters require about 10 men for the various buisness of the camp.   These with transportation horses $3300 for these men do not take all their pay in goods.   The Hunters do not actually cost more than 2000$.   This as you will perceive will leave a large profit.   I am certain that had I the means now here I could

do as well as this.   All the means that I have with me and available only enable me to fit out a party of 12 men and 34 horses
and mules.   This party is one half mine and one half Mr Bone-
villes and myself am to lead it and take one half of the skins.   The
result of this party will show whether my calculation above giv-
en is correct and if so will enable me to follow the buisness.   If it
proves otherwise I shall give it all up and come home and perhaps remain there.   I have made a proposal to the Hon. H. B.
Co. and requested them to direct their answer to your care.   Will
you have the goodness to open their letter and write them that
for reasons above stated I am not with you to do so myself.   Say
to them that I am on a hunting excursion and will stop at some
of their posts where by means of their general letter to the win-
tering partners I shall find if it is accepted and in such case I will
hand over the proceeds of my hunt to meet the requisitions of the
contract, but in fault of finding such information shall proceed to
the American rendezvous in the Mts. where by your means I will
get their answer and act accordingly.   Will you also have the
goodness to send me a copy of their answer and contract if one is
sent not the original as the appearance of it would procure its
being stoped by some interested trader.   This you can do by sending the letters to Mess. Von Pool and McGil or Mr. E. E. March
of St. Louis with a request that they will place the letters in
such hands as they will reach the rendezvous of the Americans in
the mountains.   If all this is to[o] much trouble as I much fear
please make this request over to Charles.   Please give my respects to my good aunt.   I am yr aft Nephew   N. J. Wyeth
                              LXXXII.

              Heads of Lewis River   July 4th   1833
Mr. Thomas Nuttall (Cambridge)
                        Dear Sir   I have sent through
my brother Leond of N. York a package of plants collected in the
interior and on the western coast of America somewhere about
Latt. 46 deg. I am afraid they will be of little value to you.   The
rain has been so constant where I have been gathering them that
they have lost their colors in some cases, and they will be liable
to further accident on their route home.
    I shall remain here one more year.   You if in Camb. may ex-
pect to see me in about one year from the time you receive this.
I shall then ask you if you will follow another expedition to this
country in pursuit of your science.   The cost would be less than
living at home.
    I have several times attempted to preserve birds to send you
but have failed from the moisture and warmth.   Excuse the
shortness of this as I have many letters to write and little time
to do it in.
          Resply Yr. obt. servt.   Nathl. J Wyeth

P. S. By the notes on the paper my journal will show the place from which the plant comes if kept in its proper sheet until I come home.

LXXXIII.

["This letter sent by Mr Ermatinger" written across the face.]

Plain of the Three Butes   July 5th   1833

Dear Sir

Having arr[i]ved at the camp of Mr. Bonneville I take the liberty [of] writing you by this last opportunity to express how much I am under obligation to Mr. Ermatinger for the polite and agreeable manner in which he has dispensed your hospitality to me during the whole route.

I am here in a direct train for the States, and cannot without some extraordinary accident fail of reaching home in Oct. next. Should you visit the states I would feel myself highly honored by a visit or any intercourse which might be agreeable to you for which purpose I have enclosed my direction. Should any of your friends visit the States a letter would procure them any attention which may be in my power.   It will be a pleasure to execute any buisness commands with which you may entrust me. Models of Agricultural implements, seeds and other matters counected with your tastes or buisness.

Resply. yr. obt. Servt. Nathl. J. Wyeth

To Doct. McLaughland   Fort Vancouver.

LXXXIV.

Heads of Green River   July 18th   1833

Mess. Von Phul & McGill

Gent The enclosed draft by Mess. Bonneville & Co. $366.66 I desire you will collect of the Bearer Mr. C. Cerri. If not paid by him at sight, please forward it for collection to Mr Leond. I. Wyeth of the firm of Cripps & Wyeth lace goods dealers New York and oblige

Yr. Obt. Servt. Nathl. J. Wyeth.

LXXXV.

Green River   July 18th   1833

Mr John Ball

Dear Sir I write to inform you that my agents at Boston have sent to the care of Mess Bringsmade Ladd and Hooper of the Sandwich Islands two trunk and some letters for you from thence they will be forwarded to the Columbia River by the first opportunity. I return home by the Yellowstone and Missouri in boats.   I am Yr Obt Servt Nath J. Wyeth.

LXXXVI.

Green River July 18th 1833
Mr F. Ermatinger
          Dear Sir I arrived here on the 16th 9 days
from your camp Saw no Indians but saw the bones of Mr More
killed by the Blkfeet last year and buried them.   He was one of
my men who left me in Pier[r]es Hole last year.   A Mr Nudd
was also killed by them.   All the rest arrived well in the
States. I found here about 250 whites.   A list of the Cos.
and their Beaver which I have seen I subjoin.   I should
have been proud of my countrymen if you could have
seen the American Fur Co. or the party of Mr. S. Campbell.
For efficiency of goods, men, animals and arms, I do not
believe the fur business has afforded a better example or
discipline.   I have sold my animals and shall make a boat and
float down the Yellowstone and Missouri and see what the world
is made of there.   Mr. Wm Sublette and Mr Campbell have come
up the Missouri and established a trading fort at each location of
the posts of the Am. Fur Co. with a view to a strong opposition.   Good luck to their quarrels.   I have got letters from the
States.   The chief news are that the cholera Morbus has swept
through them killing 5000 people in N York and in proportion
elsewhere.   Genl. Jackson president an insurrection in the Southern States on acc. of the Tariff but quelled by Bloc[k]ading their
ports and the repeal of the most obnoxious parts of the same.
About 25 Americans have been killed during the last year.   A
Snake village is here with us.   I find Bonnevilles connections are
responsible [A statement that he has a draft from B. for horses
follows but is crossed out.] he being very short of them.   He
lost one entire party among the Crows that is the Horses
and of course all the Beavers.   A party under Bridger and
Frapp also lost their horses by the Aricarees, also Harris
party lost theirs by the same Inds. who have taken a permanent residence on the Platte and left the Missouri which is
the reason I go by the last named river.   Harris party
did not interfere with any of my plans south of Snake River.
     In my opinion you would have been Robbed of your goods and
Beaver if you had come here altho it is the west side of the
Mts. for Green River emtys into the head of the Gulph of Calafornia.   I give you this as an honest opinion which you can
communicate to the Co. There is here a great majority of Scoundrels.   I should much doubt the personal safety of any one from
your side of the house.
     My Respects to Mr. Payette and believe me yr. sincere friend
                              Nathl J. Wyeth.

     Drips and Fontenelle arrd July 8th 160 men a good supply
of animals.   Obtained 51 packs of 100 lbs ea. Beaver.

Rocky Mtn. Fur Co. 55 packs 55 men well supplied one party not in Beaver sent home by Mr. Campbell.

Mess. Bonneville & Co. 22½ packs. Few goods few horses and poor Capt. Cerry goes home B. remains.

Harris party now in hand 7 packs Beaver and are on foot.

LXXXVII.

Liberty 29th Sept. 1833

Mr Wiggin Abbot (Expected from the upper Missouri soon)

I leave in charge of Mr Samuel some cloths for you. He will also supply you with money sufficient to come to the eastward and for other necessary expenses. I hope to see you soon and remain   Yrs &c

[No signature.]

P. S. When you arrive at Baltimore call on Wyeth and Norris for me.

LXXXVIII.

Liberty Sept 29th 1833

Dear Sir (E. M. Samuel)

(Present) As it is my present intention to return across the mountains to the Columbia the next Spring I deem it requisite to open some arrangement for the purchase of the necessary outfits so far as horses harness and men. I wish to know what is requisite in order that you commence the prosecution of the above. Do you require a remittance or will you draw drafts as fast as disbursements are required? The amt. of responsibility will be from 3 to 4000$. An answer to the above I shall receive in Baltimore to the care of Mess. Wyeth & Norris.

I further request that Wiggin Abbot may be supplyed with money to pay his expenses to Boston. He will come down the river with Mr Sublette and is directed to call on you. I also request that the suit in regard to the notes which Capt. Hill alledges I gave him may be defended. For all expenses which you may incur please draw on Chas Wyeth directed as above.

Yrs. &c N. J. W.

LXXXIX.

Steam Boat Oct. 4th 1833

Dear Sir.

When at the Station above I paid the small draft which I had before given Doct. Fellows on you.

I leave with this at Mr Allens a small bundle of clothes for Abbot.

Yrs &c N. J. W.

To E. M. Samuel Esq Liberty Mo.

P. S. Mr Aull says he is willing to swear that Johnson when he brought him the note in question expressed himself uncertain when he got it also that he saw the freight paid. Could not the testimony be used?

XC.

Steam Boat Mo. River   Nov. 4th[Oct. 4th]   1833
Fred. Tudor Esq. (Boston)
        Dear Sir Since my last from Colm. River of Jany 16th, I have made my way to this place on boat below Fort Leavenworth and make haste to inform you of the same.   I shall probably stop a few days in Balto. Philad. and N York and will not probably arrive at home sooner than the 10th Nov. Expecting so soon to see you there is little to write further than to say that I have arrived in good health and spirits, and that nothing would give me more pleasure than to receive a letter from you at Baltimore.   Should you have any buisness to transact on my route to Boston I should be glad to serve you in any way you may direct.

[No signature.]

XCI.

Steam Boat Mo. River   Oct 4th   1833
Mess. Tucker & Williams and Henry Hall Esq. (Boston)
  Gent.   I write merely to apprise you of my arrival so far as this.   I shall be in Boston about the 10th next month when I shall be able to confer [on] matters of buisness [better] than by letter.   I received your letter of 19th Dec. 1833[2] through Mr Sublette on the heads of the Colorado of the West, and can hardly express the pleasure that it gave me.

Yrs &c   N. J. W.

XCII.

St. Louis   Oct. 9th   1833
Mr. E. M. Samuel, (Liberty Missouri Enclosing his order on Ed. Tracy of St. Louis for 200$)
        Dear Sir   I arrived here to day. Above you have your order for 200$ not used.   I shall put the buisness of the counterfeit note into the hands of one of the gentlemen named in your memo.
  My respects to your good lady and Mr. More and my thanks to yourself for the many attentions you have shown me

I am yr obt. Servt. N. J. W.

XCIII.

St. Louis Oct. 9th 1833
Mr. M. G. Sublette (at St. Louis) Dear Sir
        According to promise I write but can say nothing farther than when with you. You may depend on the contract or the bond, and you will hear from me within 9 weeks stating possitively which.   I leave this place

for Louisville to morrow and shall write you directed to the Post office here.   If you write to me direct to Cambridge Masstts care of Mr. Jas. Brown.

Yr Obt Servt.   N. J. W.
XCIV.

St Louis   Oct 9th   1833

Mr M. G. Sublette (Left at Towns[?] Hotel   St Louis)
   You will find a letter in the Post Office for you.

Yrs &c   N. J. W.
XCV.

Cincinati   Oct 17th   1833

(To Genl. Harrison)
                    (present)   Sir   The enclosed I received from your son on the Big Horn.   I met him on Green River on the Colorado of the West and was with him some 20 days.   He is in good health and told me that he should remain in the Indian country through the winter.   He has taken an outfit from Fitzpatric & Co of some few horses and men for the trapping buisness.

It would have afforded me much pleasure to have delivered the note in person but haste prevents.

&c   N. J. W.
XCVI.

Baltimore   Oct 21th   1833

Sir (London)
            In answer to a letter which I wrote to you from Fort Colvill dated March 12th 1833 I received information that the said letter had been transmitted to you.   I request that an answer may be sent to Mess Cripps & Wyeth Merchts N. York which will be in season as I arrived too late to proceed to the Columbia by vessell this year.

I have made a contract for the delivery of a quantity of goods to Mr. Sublette and Mr. Fitzpatric partners under the stile of the Rocky Mountains Fur Co.   Shou[l]d your Co. make the agreement which I propose I would fulfil the contract with the R. M. F. Co. goods from the States and hand over the furs received at Walla walla or Vancouver and the furs so delivered to be in lieu of the security which is proposed in my letter to you as above.

(To Geo Simson Esq. or the Gov. or Agent of the Hon. Hudsons Bay Co. London)

I am yr. obt. Servt.   Nath J Wyeth
XCVII.

Baltimore   Oct 26th   1833

Bro. Leond. (New York)
            Will you have the goodness to call[on] Mr. Alfred Seaton and ask him if in case two small drafts made

by Bonneville & Co. amt. about $416 and which on my arrival at St.Louis I left for presentment to Mr.Cerry who brings down the returns of said Co. are not paid by said Cerry if he will pay the same. These drafts we[re] drawn on Mr Seaton and others at 60 days sight provided Mr Cerry did not elect to pay them at St.Louis at sight.

I shall await here the arrival of Charles, if I do not get notice from him that he will remain long enough to see him in N.York. The enclosed letter I wish sent to England by the first conveyance and if you think proper you can direct to the care of Mr Cripps or any one who will see it delivered as I am not quite certain of the direction. Please seal it

Yrs &c N. J. W.

XCVIII.

Baltimore Oct. 27th 1833

Mr.Wm. H. Boardman (Boston)

Sir Having to wait here a few days I enclose two letters which I received from Capt. McNeil on the Columbia. On my arrival I will do my self the pleasure to call on you with a letter of introduction from Capt. McNeil

I am &c N. J. W.

XCIX.

Baltimore Oct 28th 1833

Old Jonas

On board the Bg. Calo[?] Capt. Percival you will find 2 Indians one Trunk one rifle pair Elk Horns pacage of papers small bundle of cloths which please deliver at my house. The freight and passage is paid. She will sail about the 1st Nov. Shall be with you soon and am

Yrs &c Nathl J Wyeth

C.

Cambridge Nov. 8th 1833

Mr Henry Hall and Mess Tucker and Williams

Gent. In order to understand the nature of that branch of the Fur trade in which I propose to operate I deem it requisite to enter into a short account of its size and progress. The statements which I shall make are such as I have heard and am confident are in the main true, but I do not pledge my self that every circumstance is so but only that I have heard them and believe them to be so and that the inferences are such as my best attention to the subject warrant.

About 12 years since Mr Wm H. Ashley engaged in the Indian trade essaying by various means to obtain furs. At the time he engaged in this undertaking he was bankrupt, but was a person of credit, which enabled him to get the requisite means. His first attempts were predicated upon the possibility of trading furs from the Indians in the interior for goods. In this he was not successful, and in the event became much reduced in means, and credit, but in the course of this buisness perceived that there was plenty of Beaver in the country to which he had resorted for trade, but great difficulty to induce the Indians to catch it. After many tryals of trading voyages he converted his trading parties into trapping parties. In the first establishment of this buisness he met with all the usual difficulties incident to new plans but still made something. About this time a Mr. Gardner one of his agents met a Mr. Ogden clerk of the H. B. Co. in the Snake Country at the head of a trapping party. Gardner induced the men of Ogdens party to desert by promises of supplyes, and good prices for furs. The furs thus obtained amounted to about 130 packs or 13000 lbs. worth at that time about $75000. The following year Ashley sold out to Smith Sublette & Jackson for about $30000 and left the buisness, after paying up his old debts, worth about 50000$. Smith Sublette & Jackson continued the buisness until 1829 and sold out to Milton Sublette Frapp Jervais Bridger and Thomas Fitzpatric, and in the stile of the Rocky Mountain Fur Co. for 30000$, dividing among them about 60000$ for I think three years buisness. This last firm has continued the buisness since have paid the purchase money and have cleared their stock of goods and animals requisite for the buisness in the country but not being buisness men and unknown where the goods are to be bought have been dependent upon others for their sup[p]lies for which they have paid enormously to Mr. Wm. L. Sublette brother to a member of their firm. They have been together three years and have made two returns amounting to 210 packs of furs, value nett about 80000$ and received two outfits of goods, first cost about 6000$ for which they have paid about 30000$ and for returning their furs about 8000$ leaving them after paying the first purchase about 12000$ some of which must be due to men who have not received their pay in goods leaving them with little property except their Horses Mules and Traps and a few goods, and unavailable property.

Since the commencement of this species of buisness severall persons have attempted it, but all are now out of the way except Mess Dripps & Fontenelle fitted out by the Am. Fur Co. and Mess. Bonneville & Co. fitted out by men in New York. Neither of these last named Companies as far as I can ascertain have made money to any great extent, owing to enormous prices paid for goods. The country to which these parties resort is extensive and there is plenty of room for them and many more, and if *they* made a little money, I do think if proper means are used that much could be made. After this short account of the present state of the buisness I proceed to sum up the expense of conducting it, as it is now done, in order to shew where a saving may be made. I shall omit saying any thing about duties on coarse woolens and other goods, used in this trade, which have to be paid when goods are sent by way of St. Louis and which may be saved when sent around the Horn.

The dry goods for an overland trip are best found in New York and the other articles in St. Louis. A small charge must be added for transport to St. Louis for those bought in N.York, say on 4000 lbs. including

Ins. & Sundrys ....$	160.00
Baling of the above and Sundrys bought at St. Louis..	100.00
50 pack saddles and 50 Riding Do	250.00
Hobbles and Halters for 100 animals........................	150.00
Shoeing for 100 animals...	50.00
Corn and sundry for Horses....................................	50.09
Saddle Blankets..	100.00
50 men for 5 months at 15 per month......................	3750.00
Provisions to Buffaloe...	100.00
Pack covers...	50.00
Am[m]unition	100.00
100 animals...	3000.00
Guns..	300.00
First cost of goods...	3000.00
Six months interest on all charges except wages........	222.00
	11382.00

being the Cost of transporting goods (including the first cost) of the value of $3000 from St. Louis to the Trois Titons Long 110 deg. west Latt. about 43, Air line distance 900 miles.

In making an estimate of the cost of transporting the same amt. of goods from the head of navigation on the Columbia I shall make the difference in time and force required which from some knowledge I think just and also cost of Harness and Horses.

50 pack Saddles and 15 riding do to be bought of the Inds for about 25 cts. ea in goods........................	17.00
Halters and Hobbles for 65 animals........................	17.00
Buffaloes for blkts..	30.00
15 men for 4 months at 15 per month......................	900.00
Provisions...	100.00
Pack covers...	50.00
Amunition	25.00
Guns..	90.00
65 animals at $5 ea..	325.00
First cost of goods...	3000.00
	$4554.00

Interest for 10 months on all charges except wages of men 182.00

$4736.00

being a difference of $6646.00 in fav of transporting goods from the first rapids on the Columbia to the Trois Titons Long 110 deg. west, Latt. 43 deg N. (and 400 miles air line) over and above St. Louis.

I have assumed a calculation of $3000.00 because I have contracted to supply that amt. of goods as per the enclosed copy of contract and not because it is all that is required for the interior. The amt. now consumed in the section of country with which I am conversant is about 12000.00$ first cost in N York. Whether in the end I could supply all goods wanted may be a question and of which you can judge as well as myself, but that men can be employed to trap beaver and paid as far as their wants require in goods the same as is now done I feel not the least doubt and to almost any extent, and that it can be done to a profit is proved by the fact that the buisness is one of great profit even as it is now conducted from St. Louis.

I shall now detail what I think may be done in order to get the goods wanted to the Columbia and the Furs home in such manner as that no part of the expense of the vessell may be charged to them. Salmon have been brought from the Columbia to Boston and I think sold for about $16 per bbl. but I believe in not the best order which I suppose arose from their having been caught too long before they were salted. This I was told by persons who saw them put up. And if salmon are traded from the Indians there will always be some difficulty in this respect, but if salmon will bring $12 per bbl. they will pay all the expenses of the vessell and leave a large allowance for the expenses of the post, at which they are caught. I make no doubt that enough could be taken when once the proper mode is adopted, but I have not been on the Columbia below the first rapids in the Salmon season, and should feel doubtfull as to the expediency of ordering out a vessell before I have made a thorough examination at the proper time of year. While there last winter I sounded the bottom to ascertain [the] depth on the fishing grounds and if the bottom was clear of snaggs and rocks and found it favorable. I have every confidence when the proper mode is known and adopted that this branch of the buisness will pay all the expenses of the vessell and leave the fur trade free from all charges in the shape of freight. The prominent advantages of supplying my own or the trapping parties of other concerns from the Pacific instead of St. Louis are saf[e]ty of the country traversed, and consequent saving of men, shortness of distance, and low price and abundance of Horses on the Columbia. The latter circumstance alone would enable any company doing their buisness by that route to make a proffit equal to all expenses of transporting. The Horses in the mountains are brought from St. Louis chiefly, and cost about $30, and when you consider that a trapping party uses 3 at least to a man this alone is a large and continual saving in the buisness.

I will now proceed to state what I propose to do if I can find the means, and for the security of such persons as shall furnish me, I can give such names as I believe would be satisfactory. These names I will bring forward at the proper time. The enclosed contract was made with Mr. Fitzpatric and Mr. Sublette of the Rocky Mountain Fur Co. when I was in doubt whether I would be able to perform it but knew I would be able to pay the default. The contract as you will perceive will amt. to little more than carrying me into the Indian country free of expense and procuring the buisness of a very efficient concern, in this light I hold it to be valuable.

I propose to fulfill this contract. This done if the Rocky Mountain Fur Co will sell me their remaining furs at such rate as I can make money or will pay me for transporting them to St. Louis I will fit out a party sufficient to send them down with all other furs then on hand. That they will do so I believe because if I supply them with goods no other party will be there to do it, and they will not have the means of doing it themselves in the country. If they should not do so, then I will proceed to a safe country on the Columbia River where some furs may be traded and there leave them with a few men leaving some men and a trusty person to keep them and trade as many more as he can. The residue of my party (their apparatus having been brought out at the same time with Sublettes goods) will be employed in the trapping buisness. During the last of the salmon season of 1834 I will be on the Columbia in order to see in what mode the Salmon may be taken in such quantity as will do for a vessell and also endeavor to make returns by some vessell that may happen to be there. If no such opportunity should occur then the furs must either remain in the country until a vessell can come out to receive them such vessell bringing apparatus salt bbls. &c for taking home a cargo of salmon and bringing also goods to supply the parties or when the first outfit is exhausted the whole return, and afterwards commence the undertaking by sea. In the mean time a proposal has been made to the H. B. Co. to supply goods in the country and receive the furs as per the enclosed copy of proposition.* Should I have no partners in this buisness I might in case of their [H.B.Co's] acceding to it deem it for my interest to close with them, if I had partners I should probably not. Should you agree to give me the requisite supplys and I should afterwards close with them then you shall be entitled to your commissions the same as though the af-

---

*See copy of proposition in connection with No. LXXIII, p. 58.

fairs passed through your hands. Should you join me as partners you will of course exercise your judgement in regard to
it, but I have no expectations that the Co. will accede to it and
made it with a view to get their ideas on the subject as much as
with any expectation that they would close with me.

In case you agree to supply me for commissions and Interest
the amt. wanted will not be far from 8 to 10,000$ and wanted
some by the first of January and from that to 1st March and in
any case the cash would be required at the same period but the
amt might be varied if you took partnership according to your
views but I deem the smallest investment the best until more experience is obtained.

I will in conclusion observe that I consider all the coast and
country North of the Columbia completely occupied by the English, and all east of the mountains by the Americans. From these
countrys I expect nothing, but all that country lying south of
the Lewis Fork of the Columbia and west of the mountains as far
south as the settled parts of the Mexican territory is yet unex-
plored or nearly so. Into this section of country I have been,
and have myself taken more than a pack of beaver in less than a
month, and the furs of this region are excellent from their color,
and goodness, and without doubt are reasonably abundant.
One reason why this country has been so much neglected is that
in it there are no Buffaloe, and hunters cannot live in the luxury
that they like. Still with good economy food enough may be found
from the beaver, Elk, deer, and goat, of which there are some. Otter are plenty and good. Furs in this country would be good except about three months in the summer and by approaching the
sea coast where the climate is warmer the hunt might continue
all winter and thus add a great amt. to the years hunt without
adding any thing to the expense.

& &c N. J. W.

Enclosing copy of contract with Fitzpatric and Sublette and
proposal to the Hon. H. B. Co.

CI.

Cambridge Nov 10th 1833

Bro Leond. (N York)

Enclosed you have a note against Wyeth &
Norris [for] Three Hundred and Sixty Five dollars which please
place to my acc. and forward me the same in order that I may
give you my note for the balance which is all I can do for the
present.

Am now in treaty with Mess. Tucker & Williams and as soon
as the result is known I will write you fully. All well here and
the wills destroyed at my request.

Yr Afte Bro. N. J. W.

CII.

Cambridge   Nov. 11th   1833

Mess. Editors

Having while on a recent visit to the Columbia Received much attention and kindness from the English Traders there I deem it a duty to express my gratitude for the same, more especially as I am frequently asked the question if I was never molested by them.   By all their acts toward myself I am fully convinced that all persons who from any cause may come into contact with them will receive honorable and gentlemanly treatment.   Among the many to whom I am under obligation I wish to name Chief Factors John McLaughlin and Finlinson, Chief Trader Francis Horon, Mr. Francis Ermatinger and Mr. Pambrun.   Among the American Traders I have received much attention from Mr. Mckenzie and Mr. Laidlow of the Am. Fur Co and Mr. Wm. L. Sublette.   To all the above gentlemen I tender my thanks

Yr. Obt. Servt.   Nathl J Wyeth.

CIII.

Cambridge   Nov. 10th   1833

Bro. Jacob (Galena Mo)

Having arrived here I take the first opportunity to forward your account in order that it may be settled while I am at home which is the more easy as there appears to be little difference between us.   The horse which you took in the mountains was charged to me by the Co. at 75$ but in your acc. I charge just enough to make balance between us.   Int. is so nearly even that I say nothing about it. $150 is credited by me to you because that amt. which I took of Mess. Norris & Wyeth in Baltimore is charged to you in your acc. with them which should have been charged to me.   The $94.50 in your acc. is cash paid for medicines and money lent at various times.   The $40 is the amt. which I paid the Pacific Trading Co. as per your agreement with them.   Will you have the goodness to forward me as soon as possible your acc. against me, that is just reverse the Dr. and Cr. sides of the annexed receipt and forward it by mail, also please let me know how you are doing.   All well here.   Nudd was killed last winter in the mountains, and Trumbull died at Vancouver on the Columbia.   All else well as far as I know.

Yr Afte Bro.   N. J. Wyeth

CIV.

Cambridge   Nov 10th   1833

Mess. Joseph Baker & Son (Boston)   (This letter sent also to W. H. Boardman)

Gent   The following has been collected from the clerks of the H. B. Co. during my stay west of the mts. and altho not very definite may serve to show what opposition you may expect from them. It has been gathered from so many persons that I am inclined to think that its truth may be relied on.

Yr Obt. Servt. N. J. W.

An occasional post on the Umquou River in about Latt. 42 deg. Fort George, or Astoria renewed about 1830 and to be kept up. A Fort at Fraizers River which emtys into Pugets Sound about 30 miles up the river. It is contemplated to move this post to the coast and a little south of the river. A Fort south of Nass to be established this year. A Fort now established at Nass. A Fort north of Nass to be established this year

To be kept on the Coast

Bg. Lima   Capt. McNeil
" Dryad   "   Kipling
" Kadboro   "   Sinclair
Sch. Vancouver "   Duncan to be launched in June.

CV.

Cambridge Nov. 12th 1833

Bro. Perry (Newburg Vt.

I arrived home on 6th inst. in good health and spirits and am very buisy in making arrangements for another trip. I hope to get men the next time who will stick to me. On arrival I found all well and much the same as when I left. It would afford me much pleasure to see you this winter but I do not think it possible for me to spare the time required for a visit to your place. I regret to find that a deserter of mine has been publishing lies in some paper near you. Much that he says can be contradicted but would operate as an exposure to young Livermore which I would wish to avoid on acc. of his parents. It appears to me that the letters of Bell go at least to shew that he was guilty of Horse stealing and if his character is much known to your vicinity his statements will meet with little credit, and will not require from me any notice in fact I have neither time nor inclination to go into such a subject with such a fellow. Please give me your Ideas on this matter.

You gave me a letter to a gentleman at the Sandwich Islands. This I sent by a vessell bound there.

My journey to the Pacific was attended by very few of those romantic adventures or terrible sufferings or privations supposed to be incident to such journeys. I do not think I have been without food for two whole days together and from cold we suffered nothing. I have not read Mr. Balls letters but suppose they will give a pretty fair idea of the country and journey for I believe him to be a man of veracity and not inclined to exagerate. John Wyeths book is one of *little lies* told for gain. I hear with regret that you have lost your second child and with

pleasure that you have a new daughter.   Be assured that I sim-
pathise in your pains and pleasures.
    If you wish I will send you the letters of Mr. John Ball from
the Columbia and a review published in a periodical edited by Mr.
Welland in this town of John Wyeths Book these two would if published in some of your papers probably convince those who have
read Bells letters that there is room for doubt at least. I shall write
to S. K. Livermore but consider him entitled to no explanation from
me on acc. of his having consented to have public letters from a
deserter and thief to be addressed to him when I could not answer
and calculated to make an injurious impression against me, which
when the subject had once passed from the public mind it was
impossible to alter.
    Please give my respects to your good wife and family and be-
lieve me   Yr Aft Bro.   N. J. W.

CVI.

["Not Sent" written across the face.]

Cambridge Nov. 13th   1833
S. K. Livermore Esq.
                    Sir I have returned to Cambridge and find
that during my absence publick letters have been addressed to
you in answer to a call from you to the writer for information
concerning the desertion of your son from my party.   Now I do
not object to your right to enquire into a matter which so nearly
concerns your family, but I do object to your right to publish,
or of aiding or abetting the publishment. This I conceive you
have done.   Had I been in the country at the time the case
would have been different.   The injury is now done and thousands have read the slander who can never see the answer, even if
I should make one which I am not disposed to do. Had you
made only private enquiries I should have considered myself
bound to give you information on the subject at the first opportunity, and then you would if you thought fit have had a right
to publish what you pleased, but as it is I do not think myself
bound to go into the subject with you. My case has by you been
tried and the result at your instigation published. No opportunity was given me to explain in the case.   I consider myself
treated with injustice and until these things are differently explained to me or I should see them in a different aspect, the
friendly relations in which we have heretofore been are broken.
                    I am Your obt. Servt Nath. J. Wyeth

CVII.

Cambridge Nov 12th 1833
Le[o]nd Jarvis Esq. (Baltimore)
                    Dear Sir   I have called as you requested
to see about a shawl to be sent to Vermont. It has been forward-

ed but so lately that there had not been time for you to hear of it.

I am much engaged at this moment in endeavoring to make arrangements to return to the Indian Country and think I shall succeed. In the mean time I have offers in the ice buisness from Mr. Tudor more than equal to anything I left and shall close [with him] in case I am unable to succeed in the other project.

If you will advise me in regard to answering or not answering the calumnies and lies which have appeared since I left, I will take your advice but if they do not do me much hurt except with strangers I am strongly inclined to say nothing. Two reasons induce to this that my time is too much occupied is one. Another is that some exposures of character of near relatives might be the consequence and generally in such matters the character of the individuals at last govern the public belief. I ask your advice.

I found all well here and now I have been here a few days I am tired. There is little to interest. I have nothing to do except making preparations to go and I begin to wish them done that I may be off.

Please give my respects to my good aunt. Wife likes her dress much and I am getting my pants. made up. As soon as I can conclude what I shall do I shall write you in full.

Yr Afte Nephew   N. J. W.

CVIII.

[No address or date.]

To Mr. Henry Hall and Mess. Tucker & Williams (Boston)

Gent. Agreeable to arrangement I make the following proposal. viz

You to furnish what capital is wanted to fulfil my contract with Sublette & Co. and the sum wanted in order to send a vessell to the Columbia river with goods for the Fur trade and materials for the salmon fishery Interest to be charged and credited before any dividend of profits you being entitled to commissions on buisness done here 2½ per ct on disbursements 2½ per ct Sales and guarantee and being at the risk of the ultimate loss of the buisness if any should occur. I will then engage in the buisness for such time as may be agreed on you being bound as well as myself to continue the buisness during such time and make the requisite disbursements, myself having the entire control of the buisness in the Indian country and on the Pacific. Under the above terms I will engage in the undertaking for twenty five per ct. of the profits that may accrue. The risk I run is of any remuneration except there should be profits.

Yrs &c   N. J. W.

CIX.

Cambridge   Nov 19th   1833

Mess Von Phull & McGill (St. Louis)

Gent   The enclosed dupli-
cate is of much importance.   I have sent it to you in order to be
certain that Mr. Milton G. Sublette will receive it, and you will
much oblige me by putting it into his hands if possible, otherwise
send it by as certain a conveyance as you can find.   I request
that you will be careful to avoid passing it through the hands of
his brother Wm. L. Sublette.

If the small demands which I gave you against Mr. Cerry are
paid please inform me of the same if they are not, on the receipt
of this, please forward them to Mess Cripps & Wyeth New York.
In this last case I will in the spring call on you and pay the
charges that have been incurred, or you can ask them of Mr. E.
M. Samuel of Liberty Mo.

(Inclosing the following letter to M. G. Sublette,)

(Duplicate) Original sent to Sublette.

Mr. M. G. Sublette

Sir   This is to inform you that I am now ready
to fulfil the contract made with Mr. Fitzpatric and yourself on
the 14th Augt 1833 at Big Horn River and to request that you
will as soon as possible come to N. York where I will meet you.
If by letter you inform me when you will be there please use
this letter as an introduction to my Brother of the firm of Cripps
and Wyeth Pearl St. N York importers of Lace goods, and
leave with him directions where you may be found.   I particularly wish to see you soon as I am about dispatching a vessell
round Cape Horn to the mout[h] of the Columbia and would if
possible wish to make contract to supply your Co. the following
year.   I am &c.   Nath. J. Wyeth

CX.

Cambridge   Nov 20th   1833

[The "20th" is written over a "17th".]

Bro. Leond. (N. York)

As requested I enclose note to St. Felix [for]
$768.50 but not payable to his order.   If this is wrong I will
alter.   I shall endeavor to have the matter settled as you propose
in regard to what may be still due me from the estate.

The proposal in your letter of 11th inst. I deem impracticable
and shall not attempt.   I am offered much better than when I
left off by Mr. Tudor who importunes me much to stay.   He has
made $40000— since I left which includes two years buisness.
This is in the ice, not including coffee on which I do not think
he will realize much.   In a few days I shall know certainly what
I shall do and will then write you fully.

Tell the little ones that I shall send by the first opportunity some small books for them. Perhaps I shall be in N. York soon. Keep me as well informed as possible of any variation that may take place in furs this in order to appear at home on the subject.

Yr. Afte. Bro. N. J. W.

CXI.

[No address.] Nov 17th 1833

Mess. J. Baker & Son

Gent Below you have an estimate of the furs brot. in by the way of St. Louis for 1832 and 3. I have marked those which I have seen. The rest are from information which is as nearly correct as is requisite for your purpose. These furs are Beaver and otter, Land, about 1-20 of the latter.

I am Yr. obt. Servt. Nathl J Wyeth

90 packs from St. Fee
Seen— 30 Am. Fur Cos. party in the Mts. under Dripps and Fontenelle
Seen—140 Rocky Mt. Fur Co. brot home by Wm. L. Sublette
120 Traded by the Am. Fur Co. at their posts on the Mis-
—— souri (Astors Co.)
380 packs of 100 lbs. ea. 1832.

Seen— 62 Am. Fur Cos. party under Dripps and Fontenelle in Mts.
Seen— 61 Rocky Mtn. Fur Co brot home by Wm. L. Sublette
Seen— 30 Bonneville & Co brot home by Cerry to Alfred Seaton N. York.
90 Am. Fur Co Traded at their posts on the Missouri
60 probably from St. Fee returns not made when I left St.
—— Louis.
303

The above are nearly all that came into the western States From the Arkansas and the Mississippi few Beaver are brot and whatever the quantity may be it must decrease yearly.

CXII.

Boston Nov. 20th 1833

To Geo. Simson Esq

Sir Since my last from Baltimore dated Oct. 26th 1833 I have ascertained that there was still time to forward a vessell to the Columbia to reach there by first of the salmon season and a vessell is now in a state of forwardness for this purpose, consequently all further negotiations for the present are at an end in regard to this subject. Had I been sure that you would have accepted I would have entered into no other arrangement but uncertain of this I could not let the opportunity pass. I regret that I have troubled you so much in this matter.

I am Yr. Obt. Servt. Nathl. J. Wyeth

Supplement to letter of 20th inst. to Leond I Wyeth N.York [No. CX] enclosed in same sheet at same time viz To day the thing is closed, the vessell to be sent round the Horn at once. In the concern I have no risk further than I take stock. Have the full management out there and one fourth of all profits. I take one eighth of the stock ⅛ still open. Stock 20000$ they to provide for the remaining ⅛ if no one offers on my part. 'Tis a bad bargain but the best that I could do. I shall be in N. York soon. Please forward the accompanying letter by the first Packett.

Yr afte bro. N. J. W.

CXIII.

Cambridge Nov 20th 1833

Bro. Charles (Baltimore)

It is now a matter settled that I go again to the Pacific. A concern is made up here to invest $20000. I have for my services one quarter of all profits and no risk. So far I have the liberty of taking one quarter of the stock. I have taken one eighth there is still one eighth open which the partners here provide for in case I do not meet it. I am to have the entire control of the buisness in the Indian Country and on the Pacific. I shall give up all your liabilities. No new ones will be asked of you but you must give $1000 before the 1st March. If you can do this my ⅛ is provide[d] for. Please give me your answer soon, and let it be yes. Shall be in N.York soon and will write you at what time in order to meet you there if you can come.

Yr. Aft. Bro. N. J. W.

CXIV.

Cambridge Nov 31th 1833

Leond Jarvis Esq (Ba[l]to.)

Dear Uncle On my return from a journey eastward I found your very acceptable fav. of 17th inst. In regard to the matter on which I asked advice I am happy to find that we agree. I did not ask your advice because I had any doubts as to the best course to pursue but because it was a matter in which the feelings of my friends were more concerned than my own. Had you advised different your advice would have been followed because I think one who has done so much for the respectability of his family has a right to be consulted in such matters. You say to all whose opinions you value on proper occasions vindicate your self. I value your good opinion much and will therefore explain a few circumstances of which Bells letters treat. John Wyeth tells many *little* lies but they are of not much consequence. In Bells first letter to S. K. Livermore he says "One landing was at Point Comfort. Here our Captain was determined to make up lost time, and accordingly treated himself and some of the company very liberally to champaigne and the usual effects of intemperate drinking succeeded.'' I deny none of these facts, but I deny the intended inference. Some of the men were worse of what they drank and Bell much more drunk than any other. If Bell had told that he threw a handkerchief full of eggs from the pier into the boat, or that I ste[e]red the boat to the vessell through a thick fogg about three miles with nothing to guide me but the stars he would have told the truth and the inference would have been somewhat plainer who ''exhibited the effects of intemperate drinking''. Beside this it is nonsense to suppose I had any lost time to make up. If I had had such a strong disposition to loose no time in drinking I might have carried a plenty of liquor with me. The fact that I carried some shews that there was no very *strong* desire for it. The facts out of which this very *popular* story was made are these. After a long and squally voyage during which most of the men had been sea sick and had lived very *poor on salt beef and pork*, we anchored off old Point Comfort and I went ashore with some five or six of the men to procure some oysters eggs &c. I ordered a supper for those with me and after supper I think two Bttles of Champagne and one of Made[i]ra were drank and I believe some ardent spirit. Afterward the landlord treated to some more I presume on acc. of the novelty of the Enterprise or some slight acquaintance with myself. Having got what stores I could for those on board and seeing that the frolic had gone far enough I returned on board with no more wine in my head than I have carried from your table. The answer to what Bell says of promises about purchase of Horses is all a lie. I never verbally or otherwise engaged to make other provision than what I might deem suitable and proper. All discression in this matter was reserved to myself by agreement, and the fact that they started is proof, that I did not. Can one man compel 24 men to go with him against their will, and would the men have started if I had broken my promises in the manner stated, or would they have gone at all if the equipment was evidently insufficient. The fact is that no other idea was ever held up to them except that of marching. If this was not the case why did they march across the Aleganys. S. K. Livermore well knows this, for with him I corresponded on the subject of Thomas learning music for marching and in my letters to him dated Jany 23d & Feb 6th 1832 of which I have copy he will have the same expressed, the same in regard to hunting dresses &c. Tis all a lie that I made any promises on these subjects. The agreement states that the party shall be provided in the usual way and manner of trading parties, and this I can prove. Bell states that Weeks expressing a determination not to go I compelled him by put[t]ing him under arrest and afterward let him off on paying over to me all the money he had, and adds ''leaving him *almost* destitute of means to accomplish his return" he might have said *quite*, if the first part of the statement was true.

The facts were these. The day before I left the last of the settlements I sent John Wyeth with a yoke of oxen and some sheep out to horse guard. He returned near night stating that the sheep strayed, and that he tied the oxen, and went after them, but when he returned they had broke loose and he could nowhere find them. I suspected all was not right, and sent a man to the place with John. This man returned and told me that John could shew no place where cattle had been tied, such place he would have known by the tracks (before morning they [were] found tied in a different direction) About this time Thomas Livermore told me that Johns gun was not in camp. I had the men called to arms. When it was discovered that Weeks and John Wyeth had no equipments they we[re] called upon to produce them, and refused. I put them under guard, and a short time afterward Weeks offered to go and get them, and while out attempted to escape from the man sent with him, but finally produced the equipments. In the morning the Company was called together. I stated to them that I had no power to release any of the parties to our compact, that in regard to John he being a minor having been put under my charge by his father and having no means of satisfying the concern for the expenses incurred on his acc. I should carry him on, but this I would propose that Weeks should be released provided that he would indemnify for expenses incurred by the concern over and above what he had paid in. This passed by a vote according to form, and by vote also it was provided that he might be released by paying $40 and keep his cloths and equipments, which were Co. property. This Weeks at first refused to do. I then told him that he should go if I tied him to the tail of a horse. Soon after he paid the $40 and was released. The whole buisness was done by vote of the Co. and at the time recorded by the clerk of the same. Now if the Co. as Bell says had been deceived and abused could one man have exercised such control over them. The fact is that the Co. generally felt much insenced at this attemp[t] at desertion and secconded me fully and strongly in punishing it. The companion of Bells desertion, was the person who informed against those fellows viz. Livermore. In regard to the arbitrary conduct during the twelve days which Bell remained with me after this, I have only to say that I expected implicit obedience to my orders and was determined to enforce it at all hazards. Notice was given that those who lagged behind would be put on guard. They lagged to get rid of some work which is always to be done immediately on reaching camp, and those who avoided this labor I thought ought of right to make compensation by doing some other. Jacob was once put on guard for this

offence. Livermore might have been but I do not reccollect it.
It was the buisness of any one sick or disabled to report himself
to the Doct. and after examination he was entitled [to] and received any indulgence that the circumstances of the party would
allow. Livermore complained of his feet once. I required to examine them, he refused and said his word was enough. I did
not think so, and required him to do the same duty as the others.
I had before experienced much impudence from Livermore. He
at one time told me, I lied. I told him to prepare himself to return home from the next landing for that he should go no further with me. Before we got to the next landing he came and
expressed a willingness to go before the whole Co. and make an
apology. After this the matter was overlooked. His conduct
was always bad. The night before we left Boston he and Bell
were out all night and said they slept at a friends in Boston.
When we arrived at Baltimore Bell had a clapp and this was the
reason that he rode over the mountains at my expense. He takes
care to tell none of these things and this was the tyranny to
which he was subjected. Livermore spent on this trip beside the
$50 which his father gave him for his outfit near $50 which he
borrowed on various pretences of me, and something which you
gave.

[''Insert here the Postscript'' is written across the beginning
of the following paragraph.]

The suggestions in your letter concerning family quarrels prevented me sending to Mr Livermore a letter which I had
written not in anger but in a spirit of just rebuke for what I consider great meanness. I allude to his suffering a letter written to
Bell to be published and Bells letters to be addressed to him. If
these things were done without his consent he should have dis-
claim[ed] them, but he has aided in the dissemination of them and
thereby made it a positive consent instead of an implyed one. I
cannot overlook that as far as he is able he has assisted to get up
an impression against me, when I had no chance to rebut it. If
on the one hand I withhold an expression of my feelings for the
course he has pursued on the other I shall withhold all explanations of things concerning which he might otherwise have enquired. I have enquired for Kendal at the Stables and Taverns,
he appears not to be known at either place. My impression is favorable to him I hope he will turn out well,
as much that you may get the suitable reward of your
exertions for him as for his own good. In regard to my own
plans I say that I would now entirely change my plan of life and
as old as I am not deem success unatanable, could I once convince
myself that my talents are as good as you seem to believe they are
but in this matter every man must judge of himself and make up
his own mind as to what he is most fitted for. I have never allowed myself to abandon any serious project that I had formed.

Pursuant to this plan of life I have urged on from the beginning this western enterprise and I shall give it up only when I am convinced I am destitute [of] the means to pursue it. I have obtained the means of pursuing it and by relinquishing too much of the profit I have avoided responsibility beyond such extent as I am able to meet.

Please give my respects to my good aunt and accept for yourself the best wishes of—

[Subscription written but crossed out.]

Postscript inserted in the body of the letter.

In regard to the fitness of the arrangements for the voyage There were purchased 34 animals. There were 19 loads of goods leaving 15 spare animals, beside two that were individual property and 24 persons started. I call all animals loaded with provisions spare ones becaus[e] in less than 20 days they would all be released from their loads. If the men had took good care of the animals they could have rode half of the way but instead of this they lost or stole two horses before they lef[t] the settlements. Livermore stole three and I killed one more in trying to overtake him. Beside this some who were fearful to go on and disliked to back out endeavored to ruin the expedition by ruining the horses. Tin pots and picketts have been found under the pack saddles and the backs of many of the animals were soon ruined and in consequence we were all on foot except the sick or disabled or those who were hunting. It is not true that I rode the day before Livermore and others deserted. That day myself and Mr. Buck[?] went out to hunt on foot. This fact I distinctly recollect from having found a horse that day. The day that they deserted I rode the newly found horse to hunt and being out of camp and able to go ahead of the party they were enabled to effect their intention, a thing they would not have dared attemp[t] had I been in camp. The provisions carried with the party wer[e] one chest Tea pepper and salt, Corn meal 450 lbs. Bacon one yoke oxen sixteen sheep this to last until we should reach the Buffaloe country which we did in 22 days.

N J W

CXV.

Cambridge Dec 2d 1832

Bro Perry

Your very acceptable fav. of 25th ulto is at hand. In regard to what I propose now I answer the same as at first viz. to make money out of the fur trade. So far I have lost some money and have gained some experience and hope yet to make out. Am now fitting out a Bg. to go round the Horn to Bring out some goods and bring home a cargo of Salmon. 1st March next I shall go to St. Louis and start overland again with some goods which I have contracted to deliver to a concern in the mts.

with the furs received for these go [on] to the mouth of the Columbia and send them home by my Brig take the goods which she has brought out, and up again to the mountains exchange goods for furs employ residue of year in trapping Beaver until salmon season (having left men making barrels through the winter) This done another vessell comes by arrangement takes the salmon and collections of the year. I take of her more goods and so the same round again. I take across the land about 40 men hired at the west men here will not do. I am of your opinion about Bells letters and shall not notice them. I have not written to S. K. Livermore but consider his conduct as dishonorable. The letters were addressed to him by his consent, because he circulated them and has not said publicly that they had not his consent. I shall not give him any explanation in the buisness and consider he has forfeited all claim to it. If horse stealing is a crime anywhere it was under the circumstances that Bell and others did it. I would prosecute if it were not for Livermore. I had never any connection with H. J. Kelley farther than that I might have gone in company with him if he had gone in season but I had no view farther than trade at any time. I will not meet you half way. I wish to see the wife and young ones. I shall if I can possibly find time come all the way and bring wife but this is uncertain. I have been East and go to N. York soon. After my Brig is off may have a little leisure time. The Review I can not send as I know of. If I do please send it back again as soon as you can as it will be a part of a sett. I mail this with all of Balls letters which I have and they contain the whole I believe.

Y &c N. J. W.

CXVI.

Cambridge Dec 4th 1833

Mess Samuel & More

Gent Enclosed you have an order on Mess. Von Phul and McGill St. Louis for whatever ballance may be due me with them.

In pursuance of the plan about which I spoke to you you will oblige me by commencing to purchase mules and horses. The first I am most anxious to get. 60 of each at least will be wanted. As fast as you get the animals have them put under the charge of some suitable person and kept together. You will of course exercise your judgement whether in regard to the question the cost of buying now and feeding until spring will be more than purchasing at once when we want them, and whether we could collect so many animals at a moments warning.

The amt. due me if draft has been paid from Mess. Von Phul and McGill is about $400 on which please commence to purchase animals as you can meet with them cheap, and in the mean time please designate where we can place funds for further purchase of these animals. N. York or N. Orleans will be convenient to us. On this subject please address yourself to Mess. Tucker and Williams Boston.

I am Yr Obt Servt   N. J. Wyeth

CXVII.

Mess Von Phul & McGill
            Gent Any funds of mine which may be in your hands on the receipt of this please hand over to Mess Samuel and More of Liberty Missouri and oblige

Yr Obt Servt   Nathl J. Wyeth.

Boston   Dec 4th   1833

CXVIII.

Cambridge   Dec 9th   1833

Mr Jas Worthington (Flonsante Co Missouri)

Dear Sir I shall be going to the Mts. as early next spring as the grass will permit and shall be glad of your company with as many persons as you may have with you and such goods as you may choose to carry.   I shall have a vessell sail for the mouth of the Columbia in about ten days with goods and if you should follow the buisness of Beaver catching I do not doubt that I could hereafter supply you with goods in the Mts. much cheaper than you could pack them up yourself.

You will know my movements from Mr. E. M. Samuel of Liberty.   In the mean time I remain

Yr. Obt. Servt.   N. J. Wyeth.

If you write direct to Cambridge Massachusetts.

CXIX.

Cambridge   Dec. 9th   1833

Bro. Charles (Baltimore)

            Your very acceptable fav. of the 26th ulto. is at hand and would have been answered sooner but I have been down East and could not.   You say that you will let me have the $1000 dont fail me on any acc. as serious inconvenience would be the consequence.   Your understanding of the foundation of the present expedition is correct.   I can take no further risk than the one eighth.   I may risk my life but will not risk loosing so much as that with health and industry I can retrieve myself.   I will go the whole Hogg no further than this.

I shall be in N. York soon but shall be there again in February, and as you think it will not be convenient to you to see me there I will not expect to see you until Feb.

I differ with you as to the notice in the Courier it is not sharp enough to cut.   I have taken the advice of Mr. Jarvis and to all that has been said I shall answer nothing and shall let character determine mens minds.

I have not the least reason to find fault with Leonard and perhaps in the end he will be the better able to render assistance than now, and I am more in want of it. I have now many offers to take part in this enterprise over and above what I can use and all that makes it requisite for me to take any of the stock is to shew confidence in it. We have bought a fine new Brig and she is nearly ready for sea.

In regard to the arrangement of the matters between Jonas and father I do not believe that I can better them. They are now on good terms and Father does not wish any thing to be done. Quarrel they will more or less under any circumstances. I do not think Jonas has done as well by the place as he could but he or any one else would have a hard task to prevent all mischief to the trees during times of hurry. Contrary to what you fear I found things as well here as such matters can well be after what has passed. I turn from home and friends only because I have not yet done what I have undertaken.

I have been very buisy and cannot write you as much at length as I could wish but perhaps I shall be more at leisure after the vessell is off and do not be affronted if I serve my best friends worst. "Whom the Lord loveth he chasteneth." I have written a long letter to Mr. Jarvis on the subject of the statements that have been made by the deserters and if Mr. Jarvis pleases he can shew it you. Brother Perry advised me not to notice Bell at all, as his character would not entitle him to credit at home. Give my respects to your good wife. I am sorry for her complaint but can suggest no remedy. Remind me to the little ones.

I am Yr. Afte. Bro.   N. J. Wyeth

CXX.

Cambridge   Dec 9th   1833

Hon Lewis Cass. (Washtn)

Dear Sir   Accompanying you have an introductory note from Genl. Ashley. The object of addressing you is this. There are west of the Mts. many gentlemen and servants of the Hudsons Bay Co who have Indian wives and families and who are desirous of retiring from active life but they can not well mingle in society as it is constituted in G. Britain or the U. States. They wish to locate themselves on the Wallammet or Multnomah River, a river coming from the south into the Columbia. They express themselves indifferent as to which Govt. they may come under. There are now on this river nine families of Trappers who have good farms. An answer to the following queries or an expression of opinion from so high a source in regard to them would be very acceptable to a class of men who are at a loss to know where they may best spend the remnant of lives of toil and danger. Viz

1st To what extent may they take up land.

2d What price will be demanded pr acre if the Am. Govt. should take possession of the country.

3d Can they be sure that they will be allowed to keep possession at any price.

4th If they are not allowed to keep the land will any allowance be made for improvements.

I shall go early in the spring to the country west of the Mts. and would be pleased to communicate any assurance or opinion which you may do me the honor to give on this subject.

I should be happy to impart any information of which I may be possessed to the Govt. if it is deemed desirable.

With Great Respect I have the honor to be

Yr Obt Servt.   Nathl J Wyeth

Hon Lewis Cass
   Secty. of War
     Washington

CXXI.

Boston   Dec 10th   1833

Mess. Thomas C. Rockhill & Co (Philad)

Gent   Above you have draft for Seventy Nine dollars and Seventy Five cents which please place to the Cr of Mess Samuel and More of Liberty Mo. of which please inform them and receipt for the same in my fav. to them and oblige   Yr. Obt. Servt.   N. J. Wyeth.

CXXII.

Cambridge   Dec 12th   1833

Bro Leond. (N York)

Yours of 9th inst is received. In regard to calculations about vessell &c will run over them with you soon and personally.

Good did quite right in regard to the draft which you say has been shewn you Drawn by Abbot fav. of Sublette & Campbell on M. G. Sublette to be charged to me. Abbot is much my debtor, has never had any authority to draw on me, but had authority to take up money of Mess. Samuel & More and Wyeth & Norris and them only and of both he took up money and some more of me. When he arrived here two days since, he never mentioned to me any thing of this transaction. He is now gone. There must be something irregular in this buisness. A. has been gaming. I shall not pay unless some shadow of an obligation can be shewn why I should. I can conceive none which can be made to appear in this case.

I regret to say I have not seen Mr. Osgood and do not know where to find him otherwise should not fail to call and see him.

I am waiting for Capt. Lambert who has gone to see his family expect him every minute. When he comes shall leave directly for your city in order to purchase goods, and as you say

All well.   N. J. Wyeth.

CXXIII.

N York   Dec 18th   1833

Mess. Tucker & Williams Boston
                              Gent   Arrived here on the 16th
I can find no callico shirts here. 200 are wanted which you had best set making as soon as possible. Figures are wanted but stripes will do if the other cannot be had. Let the colors be bright and the stile gay.

Yr Obt Servt.   N J Wyeth

CXXIV.

N. York   Dec. 18th   1833

Mess. Tucker & Williams Boston
                              Gent   I have completed pur-
chases all except scarlett cloths or stronds of which there are none in this place. You will have to pick up what you can to cost not more than 1.80 per yd. From 5 to 10 pieces must do. W cannot buy many at this rate. If nothing better can be found scarlett Duffle must be used. One Bale Blue Am. sheetings one unbleached, still wanted. I do not find them here, so you can buy them if you can find them.

I am yr. obt. Servt   Nathl J Wyeth

CXXV.

N York   Dec 19th   1833

Mess. Tucker & Williams Boston
                              Gent. I write to apprise you
that no vessell can sail before Saturday for Boston which will give you a little more time. Still no scarlett stronds except about 2 pieces at 1.75 pr yd. Shall find amt. of bill in order to insure as soon as possible.

Yrs &c   N. J. Wyeth

[An illegible P. S. of four words.]

CXXVI.

N. York   Dec. 20th   1833

Mess. Samuel & More
                              Gent. I am here purchasing goods to send
round the Horn by a vessell, and have not yet had the time to make the arrangements proposed in your letter of Nov. 6th with Mess T. C. Rockhill & Co nevertheless you will oblige by proceeding to purchase Horses and mules to any extent you deem prudent not exceeding the directions contained in my letter of 4th inst. Also to engage 30 men to leave your country in

last of April and first of May next and for 2½ years. Engage none but those you think good men. At my first opportunity on returning to Boston I will forwd. to you a form of agreement with the men and also complete an arrangement with Mess. Rockhill & Co. by which funds will be placed to your Cr. as fast as you expend it in the purchase of animals.

You can engage at the lowest possible rates 35 riding saddles (Spanish) These are for the men and should be of the cheap kind without any finery about them, then 6 of a superior sort for *us gentlemen* but still not expensive but good and plain. The residue of the harness I will have made here and bring it on with me.

I have to request that, if you can find Sublette, you will urge that he come here sooner than Feb. he ought to come at once and not leave the purchasing of his goods to the last minute. Write to him to this effect if you know where he is and represent to him that these goods should leave N. York or Boston by the 20th Feb. in order to be at the upper settlements in time for an early start.   I am &c   N. J. Wyeth.

CXXVII.

N. York   Dec 20th   1833

Mr. M. G. Sublette St Louis

Dear Sir   Not having heard from you since your arrival and heard nothing of your intentions except from E. M. Samuel of Liberty I write to urge you to come here immediately. It is important that you should select your goods in good season as you will be able to do it much cheaper and get better kinds when you have time to look about you than when you are hurried, beside I am desirous of a spree with an old *Mountaineer* these folks here wont do. My Brig will sail in a few days for the Columbia with goods enough for an outfit for you another year. Abbot passed this place a few days since. When you come to N. York call on Mess Cripps and Wyeth Pearl St. Please write me as soon as you can and inform me when you will start for this place.   Yr &c N. J. W.

CXXVIII.

New York   21st Dec. 1833

Mess Tucker & Williams Boston

Gent   I leave this to day in the steam Boat and will probably be with you Monday morning but for fear of accident write to inform [you] that I have purchased one small bale of scarlett cloths of 10 pieces. This will obviate any necessity of your buying at disadvantage as we can do without more of this article.

Mr. Thomas informs me that he has purchase[d] 5 Purcheons Rum being all he can find in this place entitled to Debenture.

[Subscription written but crossed out.]

CXXIX.

Cambridge Jany. 2d 1834

Bro Leond.

I have this minute received a letter from Mr Milton Sublette informing me that he leaves Pitsburgh on 26th Dec. for N. York. What I desire is that you induce him if possible to come at once to Boston, but if you cannot do this, you will have the good[ness] first to drop me a line to the care of Mess Tucker & Williams, and in the mean time if he is in great haste, let him commence selecting goods, in which please render him what assistance you are able, making all your purchases at 6 mos. and oblige

Yr. Obt. Servt. Nathl J Wyeth

Enlcosing copy of contract with Fitzpatric & Sublette.

CXXX.

Cambridge Jany 2d 1833[4]

Mr. M. G. Sublette

Dear Sir Yr. esteemed fav of the 26 ulto. is at hand. I am at this moment much engaged in fitting out a vessell for the mouth of the Columbia. I have written to my brother to urge you to come at once to Boston as the gentlemen who are concerned with me are desirous of seeing you, but if haste renders this out of the question, I will come to N. York as soon as I know that you are there, of which I have requested my brother to inform me immediately on your arrival. If you cannot come to Boston and are in much haste you can select the goods that you want when you please, and I have requested my brother to assist you in this matter, I would prefer however that you would not begin until I come but in this do as you please.

I am Yr. Obt. Servt. Nathl J Wyeth

CXXXI.

Cambridge Jany 6th 1834

Bro. Charles, Baltimore,

I write to say that I shall draw on you for one Thousand dollars payable 1st March.

The stock of our Co. will amt. to 40,000$ which makes even an ⅛ a full back load in these times and therefore if you have any more loose cash, and wish to give *it a good circulation* you had better lend it to me, however I have not a face to ask you a direct question of this sort in these times, but only make the *slight* suggestion. But I have provided to meet in some shape my obligations by becoming indebted to the concern in case I cannot raise my share, but I have great repugnance to resort to this measure.

Our vessell sails to morrow and in the course of the week I shall go to N. York to meet Mr. Sublette in order to purchase goods for our overland trip. I think I shall be in N. York from the 12 to the 20th inst.

In going out I shall pass through Baltimore but shall make little stay.   I am too buisy at present to write about family affairs
and have not even made up my journal of last trip in such form
as is suitable to leave.   I do not know when I shall have time to
do any of these things, for in addition to my other concerns I
have those of Mr. Tudor to attend to for the winter.

I am yr. afte. Bro.   N. J. W.

CXXXII.

Boston   Jany 4th   1834

Mr M Sublette (N York)

Dear Sir   I have received a note from
my brother informing me of your having arrived in N. York.   I
should come immediately to see you were it not that I have already written to urge your coming here and am afraid of passing
you on the road.   When I have got your answer whether you will
come here or not I shall move to see you.   In the meantime permit me to suggest that there are great advantages to be derived
from an interview between yourself and the gentlemen who are
concerned with me in this undertaking, among the most important of which is the establishing in your mind of a perfect confidence that any contract that may be entered into with you or
your partners will be fulfilled.   When you have arrived here you
will be able to satisfy yourself in this matter.   Also it is
important that you make some arrangement for sending home
your furs over and above those which you pay us for the goods
which we are to deliver to you.   If you should wish to avail yourself of the opportunity afforded by our vessell an agreement for
the same can be made here and also for transporting them to
the vessell.   If it is possible to come to any agreement on these
subjects an insurance might be effected to cover the risk of
the sea on such amt. as might be shipped.   Beside the above
reasons, there are many goods which can be purchased as well
and *some* better here than in N. York.   The great difficulty
which your concern has encountered and· the enormous expence
in getting your supplies has induced me to suppose that you
would avail yourself of any opportunity which on reasonable
terms would obviate all the difficulties and much of the expense.
Such opportunity is now within your reach.   By means of our
vessells employed in the salmon trade we can take out goods and
bring home furs to any extent to the Columbia.   These goods
we can purchase cheaper than goods can be purchased to send
over the mountains because on some of them we get the draw-
back of the duties.   The packing up from the Columbia is neither
difficult nor expensive, horses there are comparatively cheap and
in that country there is little danger consequently few men are required.   These advantages we are willing to divide with you, in
order that by getting your goods on reasonable terms you may be

able to monopolise in a great measure the trade of the mountains, and thus, much enlarge the amt. of goods which you will take from us. One other convenience of this route is that all your men which are wanted for camp keepers could be had from the islands these men would be better than those you get from the States for such purposes and much cheaper. One other advantage to be derived from pursuing the buisness through this route is that if you succeed in breaking up the other companies as you certainly can do, when you get your goods so much cheaper you will prevent the influx to [of?] small traders and others who by their competition continually injure your buisness and spoil your men. Should the above considerations strike your mind as they do mine you will I have no doubt you will see of how much importance it is that parties who in the course of events may have such large engagements with each other should meet and establish a mutual confidence which will afterward facilitate all buisness and in such case I shall expect to see you in Boston in the course of the week. I was in hopes that you would be able to spend the winter with me and go to St. Louis together in the Spring, but in your buisness prevents we will let you go after you have spent a week with us.

I am Yr &c N. J. W.

To M. Sublette Esq

CXXXIII.

Boston Jany 7th 1834

Mess. Samuel & More (Liberty)

Gent. Mr. Abbot will hand you this. I send him for the purpose of taking care of the animals which you may purchase, and for assisting you in the same under your direction. I request that you will be extremely careful in the purchase of animals and be sure to get none but what are hardy and as many mules as possible. As to price I am in hopes that having so much time to purchase in you will be able to buy horses for $25 that are first rate working animals and mules at 40$ but if you should not you must give a little more. 75 mules are wanted and 25 horses and to this extent you are authorized to make purchases. Some competent judge must select these animals. Before this you will have received the requisite assurance from Mess Rockhill & Co.

In regard to Abbot I wish you to supply his absolute wants until I come which will be about 20th April and nothing farther. He is a little inclined to be extravagant and I do not wish to pay for it.

If you have not yet made an absolute bargain in regard to the saddles for which I wrote in my letter of 20th Dec. you can leave off the stirrups as they can be had cheaper here than with you, but if already you have made [a] contract do not alter it.

I am Yr. Obt. Servt.   N. J. Wyeth

CXXXIV.

Boston   Jany. 7th   1834

Mr. Wiggin Abbot

Sir   You will proceed with all possible despatch to Philadelphia, you will there call on Mess Grant & Stone and request them to procure a duplicate of the letter which they requested Mess. Thomas C. Rockhill & Co. to send to Mess Samuel & More of Liberty in behalf of Mess. Tucker & Williams of Boston. With this Duplicate and the letter I have given you to Mess Samuel & More, you will proceed immediately to Liberty. When arrived you will deliver duplicate and letter, and act under Mess S. and M. in procuring animals, and keeping those that are purchased, taking good care that they are kept fat. Without interposing in any direct manner with Mess S & M. I wish you to ascertain the real cash value of horses and mules, and it would be well to let them see that you take note of these things, this, not that I doubt their good faith, but they having much buisness on their hands may be deceived as to the value of animals.   Also if you think the animals they purchase are unsuitable you will give them your opinion.   I have requested Mess S & M. to supply you with what cash you may want for necessary expenses only but I am in hopes the money with which you are supplied here will prevent any considerable expenses on your acc.   Your time will commence on your arrival at Liberty, and what you spend on the road will be charged to you, therefore keep an accurate acc. of the same. You will be allowed $300 for the first years services, you finding you[r] own clothing.   We do not agree to furnish any clothing or other supplies between the settlements and the Columbia river. At that place and during the year you will be charged 50 pr ct. advance on what shall be sufficient for your own use.   After the first year an agreement for farther services must be made.

Nathl. J. Wyeth.

(Added by Mr Abbot)

Having carefully examined the foregoing instructions from Mr Nathl J Wyeth and having agreed with him to render my services in conformity thereto I hereby acknowledge myself to be entirely under his directions and do promise and obligate myself to perform to the best of my ability all that may be required of me by him and that I am entirely satisfied with the compensation stipulated for as herein expressed, and the manner in which I am to receive the same.

Signd by   Wuggin Abbot.

[The discrepancy in the spellings of Abbot's name occurs in the copy.]

CXXXV.

Boston   Nov. 23d   1833

Mr. Alfred Seaton,
                    Sir   We will take your furs within one hun-
dred miles of Horse Creek of Green River and convey the same
to the Columbia and thence to Boston for thirty seven dollars and
fifty cents per pack of 100 lbs.   We obligate ourselves to take the
usual care of these furs on both parts of the route, furs to be delivered to us during the month of July 1834.   The risks that you
are to run includes that of our vessells going out to the Columbia.
                    I am Yr Obt. Servt   Nathl J Wyeth

CXXXVI.

Boston   Jany. 4th   1834

Bro. Chas. (Balto.)
                    I have mailed to you a package of printed paper
which please keep two days when if Mr. Abbot does not come to
take them of you please forward them to Mess Samuel & More of
Liberty Missouri in Clay county.   Please give Abbot no money
should he apply to you for it as I have given him as much as I
wish to trust him with.
                    I am &c   Nathl. J. Wyeth.

P. S.   Papers will not come as above

CXXXVII.

Boston   Jany 8th   1834

Mess Samuel & More   Liberty Missouri
                    Gent.   Having written
you under date of Dec. 20th from N York and on 7th inst per Mr.
Abbot I now write to recapitulate, and to make sure that you receive the requisite instructions in case Abbot should be delayed from
any cause, viz purchase 75 mules and 24 horses with [as] much
dispatch as you can consistently with economy, place same under some suitable man if Mr. Abbot does not come that they
may become w[o]nted to the band.   Be careful to get serviceable
animals.   If so many mules cannot be had you must make up in
horses. Also 35 common Spanish riding saddles without stir[r]ups
bridles or girths these I can get cheaper here.   6 of a little superior kind but still not expensive for my own use and some
other gentlemen, also you can be looking up 2 bulls and 8
cows for driving overland to stock a fort also one yoke of cattle
for provisions, fat for eating, and about 30 sheep.   If these cattle
can be purchased at any time it had better be delayed until the
last of the purchases.   Probably I may want a few more animals
than above ordered but this will do for the present.
                    I am Yr. Obt. Servt.   Nathl. J. Wyeth.

To find Longitude

To get Polar distance. . . Take declination of Sun from Nautical almanac for the date which we suppose to be 11th Jany. 1834 which is 21 deg. 50 min. 17sec. which correct for Long. from Tab. 5 Bowditch deriving you[r] knowledge of Long. from the last observation and dead reconing added.

Say, Sub.	1 min. 45 sec.
	21 deg. 49[8?] min. 32 sec.

Correct for time Say 3 Hours A. M. as
per Table 5 Bowditch which is = add   1 min. 07 sec.

	21 deg. 50 min. 39 sec.
Add to 90 deg. to obtain polar distance	90 deg. 00 min. 00 sec.
Polar distance	111 deg. 50 min. 39 sec.

In making the above reconing with Capt. Lambert we added instead of 90 deg. 90 deg. 50 min. 39 sec. which will make an error through[ou]t the whole calculation for we made polar distance 112 deg. 58 min. 18 sec. and this sum therefore I use hereafter instead 111 deg. 50 min. 39 sec. which is the true distance. After rejecting seconds which we always do if under 30 and add if over

1st The Cronometer to be made to agree with Greenwich time by adding or subtracting its rate as the case may be

2d Take the Suns altitude, and it is best to do it when the Sun is rising of[or?] falling the fastest, which read directly from the quadrant and we will suppose it to be   68 deg. 10 min.

Which always divide by two	34 deg. 5 min.
To which if the Lower limb is taken always add	16 min.
	34 deg. 21 min.
On Land for refraction always subtract	1 min.
Which will be the true altitude	34 deg. 20 min.

Corrected altitude as above	34 deg. 20 min.
Corrected Latt. which is got from Last obs. and dead rec.	45 deg. 20 min.
Polar distance from above	112 deg. 58 min.
Add together	192 deg. 38 min.
Which always divide by 2 which is	96 deg. 19 min.
Subtract Suns altitude	34 deg. 20 min.
Which is remainder	61 deg. 59 min.

In Taking out Log[a]rithms reject the index when it is 10.

Cor[r]ected altitude as
above   34 deg. 20 min.   (from Tab. 27)
Corrected Lat. as above 45 deg. 20 min. Secant of Lat.   08314
    "   Polar distance
    as above   112 deg. 58 min. Co. Sec. poi. dis 03587·
Add together & Halve 192 deg. 38 min.
Half   96 deg. 19 min. Co Sine Half
Subtract Suns alti   Sum   9.04149
    as above   34 deg. 20 min.

Remainder   61 deg. 59 min. Sine of remain-
                                         der   9.94587
    Half of this sum   19.10637
    is   9.55318

Log. 9.55318 = in time to   9 H 12 min. 32 sec.
Add equation of time from almanac as date   8 min. 13 sec.

    Mean time   9 H 20 min. 45 sec.
Greenwich time, which ad[d] to 12 to make it
    greater than Mean time if not so before
Which we will suppose to be 4 H 5
    min. 3 sec.   16 H 5 min. 3 sec.

from this subtract mean time   9 H 20 min. 45 sec.
    Which is the Longitude in time   6 H 44 min. 18 sec.
Which by table 21 Bowditch is Longitude 101 deg. 4 min. 30 sec.

To find Lattitude

28th Jany 1833 observed   48 deg. 25 min.
Index error   oo   oo

                                           48 deg. 25 min.
Half altitude   24 deg. 12 min. 30 sec.
Suns Semi diameter   16 min. 16 sec.

                                           24 deg. 28 min. 46 sec.
Refraction on Land   1 min. oo sec.

                                           24 deg. 27 min. 46 sec.
Subtract from 90 deg.   90 deg. oo min. oo sec.

                                           65 deg. 32 min. 14 sec.
Suns declination for date   18 deg. 10 min. 30 sec.

    Latt.   47 deg. 21 min. 44 sec.

CXXXVIII.

                        Boston Jany 12th 1834

Mess Samuel & More
            Gent On the other side you have copy of
agreement, with a note on the back. Should you engage the 30

men named in my letter of the 20 ulto. 15 of them must agree to this note, as it may be desirable to let Sublette have some of the men when I reach the mountains.   Mr. Sublette is now with me. At his suggestion I request you to consider if men and animals could not better be got in some of the lower counties than in Jackson and Clay and if so you can make any suitable arrangement for doing it.   Endeavor principally to get French and mules and make no advances until I come. Make no agreement with any one that you think likely to back out or that you do not think a good man.   The french are generally much preferable.

I desire that as soon as you receive this you would send weekly to the care of Mess. Von Phul and McGill a statement of what you have done, in order that when I arrive at St. Louis I may know what you have done, and be able to make what purchases or engagements [as] are wanted while I am coming up the country.

I shall probably be with you by the middle of April.

I am Yr. Obt. Servt. Nathl. J. Wyeth

CXXXIX.

Boston   Jany 14th 1834

Bro Leond.   N. York.

Mr Sublette requests me to ask you to inquire at the office for letters for him, and in case you find any you can forward them to the care of Tucker & Williams. This until the first day of Feb. after which time you can keep them and he will get them when he comes.

I also wish you would inform me as soon as you can if there are any red stronds or scarlet cloths to be had in N. York and on what terms.   If Mr Wm. L Sublette calls on you he can direct his letters to his brother to Mess. T & W as above

I shall be with you about the 12th Feb. next

And I rem Yr Obt Servt   N. J. W.

CXL.

Boston   Jany 15th   1834

Mr Thomas Nutall

Dear Sir   I write to say that I shall pass through Philadelphia sooner than I at first contemplated say 18 to 21st Feby. and possibly shall leave St. Louis by the 20th March and the upper settlements by the 20th of April. Should you not be in Philadelphia when I pass you can join me on the route or at St. Louis in which place you will hear of me at Mess. Von Phull & McGills.   If when you arrive at St. Louis I have gone you will then find me at Mess. Samuel and Mores in Liberty Clay County where I shall remain until the 20 certainly, perhaps longer.

Hoping I may have the pleasure of your company from Philad.
west, I remain   Yr. Obt. Servt.   Nathl. J. Wyeth.

CXLI.

Cambridge   Jany 25th   1834
Saml. L. Dana Esq. (Waltham)
         Dear Sir   Altho a stranger I have de-
sired to call on you to thank you for a piece of service you
did me in your review of the Book of Jno. Wyeth, by Benj Water-
house.   It enhances the obligation that it was done for a stranger, in his absence, and that it was so well done that the liar and
his pander were annihilated.   Much buisness prevents my ac-
knowledging to you in person, but be assured that I shall take
with me to the prairies and forests a sense of the favor you have
conferred on me and those who feel an interest in me.
                              I am &c   N. J. Wyeth.

CXLII.

Cambridge   Jany. 26th   1834
Brother Perry   Newbury (Vermont)
                    Finding that it will be impos-
sible to visit you as contemplated before leaving these parts, I
write to say good bye, to you and yours.   If you wish to write to
the Sandwich Islands, I will carry letters which I can send by our
vessell to their destination.   I leave this place on the 7th Feb.
and should your letters reach here a little later they could be forwarded to St. Louis.   There is little to say at this moment more
than if good success attends me this time it will be long before I
shall return but if on the contrary I meet with disasters, I shall
soon be back and probably be obliged to remain for want of
means to make a third trial.   Mr Sublette is now with me which
is the reason of my leaving so much sooner than I expected.   All
connections are well.   Wife sends her love.
                    I am Yr Afte. Bro. Nathl J Wyeth

CXLIII.

Cambridge   Jany 29th   1834
Mr Hallett (Editor of the Boston Dayly Advocate)
     Dear Sir   I have not been able to find the author of the piece
in your paper of 23rd Jany. 1833.   I leave this for the westward
on the 7th Feb. and therefore can have no farther time to attend
to this matter.   I have not the least doubt that could the author
of the communication be found he would give Jno. Wyeth as his
authority.   Now as the Book of Jno Wyeth is at variance with
this communication it only remains to shew that Jno. Wyeth is
the author of both to shew that no credit is due to anything that
he stated.   It will be some trouble to you perhaps to find the person who sent the communication but I have confidence enough
in your disposition to see justice done, to ask you to do so, and ask

him for his authority. If he gives Jno. Wyeth, I will then ask
you to compare the book with the communication and state in
your paper the difference which you may find.

As I conceive, you have inadverently done me an injury. It is
in your power to do me a favor that will more than compensate.
I ask no more than truth and justice and I have no doubt that
you will incur a little trouble to render it.

I am Yr. Obt. Servt　Nathl. J. Wyeth.

CXLIV.

Cambridge　Jany. 31th　1834

Cousin Noah (Hingham)

Yours of 28 inst. is received. I leave
this on 7th Feb. but cannot take books across the continent 4000
miles the risk and transportation would be five times their value.
Our vessell for this year has gone but one will go yearly by which
any thing may be sent that his friends wish. Articles to be sent
to Mr Ball should be left with Mess Tucker & Williams Central
Wharf Boston. If his friends [wish] to send letters I will take
charge of them with great pleasure and he will get them in
Sept. next.

I should have notified Mr Balls friends of this opportunity but
I did not know where to find them. If the person you mention
will inform them I will be obliged to him. Letters for him may be
sent to the care of Mess T. & R or Chas. Wyeth Baltimore who
will forward them to me at St. Louis until the 10th day of March
next after which time they cannot overtake me as I shall leave
the western settlements about the middle of April next.

Respy Yrs.　N. J. Wyeth

CXLV.

Boston　Feb. 3d　1834

Bro Charles

My Indian boys are on board the Hem.[?] Bg. Nitor
bound for your place. I wish you would watch and on their
arrival place them at some suitable place to board see that their
washing is done &c until I come. Buy for them what clothing
they stand in immediate need of and pay $20 for their passage.

I leave this on the 7th inst and shall tarry for a few days in N.
York to buy goods and be in Balto. about the 15th inst.

In the mean time I am Yrs.　N. J. W.

CXLVI.

Boston　Feb. 23d[?]　1834

Mr Wm L. Sublette　N. York,

Dear Sir　Your fav. of 30th ulto. is
at hand. Your brother is here and we leave in company for New
York on the 7th inst where we shall remain about 5 days then to
Philad. there remain 2 or 3 more then to Baltimore there re-

main 2 more.   If I do not see you before please leave word with
my brother in Baltimore where you can be found, as I am anxious to be in company on the route westward.   I place little re-
liance on any information or on any reports through the Am. F
Co. especially by Doct. Harrisons hands.   There may have some
small disaster happened and a small one it must be to amt.
to no more than $7000 when it reached St. Louis through such hands.
You well know the great pains taken by rival companies in the
mountains to discredit their opponents.   My brother of N. York
informed me some time since that a draft drawn by Abbot on M.
G. Sublette chargeable to me was shewn him, which having no
instructions he refused to pay.   This is all the information I have
received of this draft.   I presume it is [for] supplies for Abbot on
his passage down.   If so for any reasonable amt. I shall pay it
when I see you.   I regret that you did not forward it to me with
the account or whatever else it is founded on.   Abbot never notified me that he had drawn such a draft.   Had the buisness been
properly done I should have avoided having it said that a draft
on me had been returned unpaid.   I shall call on Mess Gill Cam-
bel & Co. if I do not see you in N. York, but if you could possibly wait my arrival in N. York it would af[f]ord me much pleasure.
I should urge your coming to Boston were it not so late.   If you
think of going to Washington I would like to keep company.
I am Yr Obt. Servt   Nathl. J. Wyeth

P. S.   Miltons foot is I think a little better.

CXLVII.

Boston   Feb 4th   1834
Thomas Nuttall Esq.   Philad.
Dear Sir   Your esteemed Fav. of 30th ulto is at hand.
I leave this on the 7th inst. and may be in Philad by the 16th,
but probably not until 18th or 20th and by the time we can reach
the Ohio, I think it will be open.   I am pleased that there will
be one more added to our society.   As he will probably have no
servant I would not recommend to him to take many goods.   His
stock of clothing would I should think be all that he will require.
I should advise him to take three mules but three horses or two
mules would do.   What little clothing he may want in the country he shall have on such terms that he will have no reason to
complain.   I do not see that he need provide anything before
reaching St. Louis more than he has unless he carrys *implements
of science.*
I will deliver the message to Mr. Brown.   I have engaged Capt.
Thwing* who is well versed in taking observations to accompany
the expedition and have provided suitable implements.   Can you
get some cherry, peach, apple, pear, apricot, plumb, and nectar-

*The author spells the name of his Captain with a "w" this first time.

ine stones to take with us? Mr. Sublette is now with me and will
come on in company.

Resply Yr. Obt. Servt. N. J. Wyeth.

CXLVIII.

Boston   Feb 5th   1834

Mr Joseph Thing
          Sir   The following buisness requires to be at-
tended to before you leave Boston. viz
     Ship to Baltimore to Mess. Wyeth & Norris
     7 tents and 45 oil covers, which find at Bell & Cowleys
     Indian Rubber Boat   "   "   " Tucker & Williams
     Two Traveling Cases   "   "   " B. C. Weld Camb.
     100 Beaver Traps   "   "   " Brainerds.
Also bring on with you a memorandum of all the bills Charged
by Tucker & Williams to the overland expedition in order that I
may have with me the means of knowing at any time the amt.
invested in this part of the buisness.   At N. York and Baltimore
of the gentlemen to whom I give you letters you will obtain farther advices from me provided you do not find me with them.

&   N. J. W.

CXLIX.

Boston   Feb. 5th   1834

Bro Chas.
          The bearer is Capt. Jos. Thing who goes out with me
as the second in command.   Whatever buisness I leave with you
relating to this expedition or any letters to me you will please
hand over to him, and shew him such attention as may be in
your power and oblige

yr. Afte. Bro. N. J. Wyeth

CL.

Thursday   evening   Feb 4th   1834   Boston.

Mess. Tucker & Williams   Boston

Gent

                              I do not think the traps
will be according to sample therefore it will be requisite to examine them carefully and compare them with the pat[t]ern, which
is in Brainerds possession.   They should be equally well finished
with the pat[t]ern and by contract are to be set for one week and
then rejected if the springs do not come up fair or are broken.   I
have agreed, if he would have all of them finished by the 7th Feb.
to give him $15 over and above the contract.   If Brainerd will
not agree to have them set on board the Packett and take back
all that do not prove good on their arrival in Baltimore, it will be
requisite to retain them in Boston one week in order to try them
by setting at the end of which time, if the springs are unbroken
and come up fair and they are as well finished as the sample he

will be entitled to $165 for one Hundred traps, this provided they are delivered to you on the 7 inst. but if delivered after that time he is only entitled to 150$.

I am Yr. Obt. Servt. Nathl. J. Wyeth.

CLI.

Providence   Feb 4th   1834

Jno Pickering Esq.

Dear Sir

Your favor of Feb 4th reached me only last evening consequently I could not call on you as requested. It is not in my power to answer the queries contained in your letter from memory but I will preserve the vocabulary which you sent and endeavour to give the information desired at some future time. Probably I will write to you again before leaving the States and after rejoining the Indians, but if I should not do this I will on the first occasion write you from beyond the mountains.

If you wish to write me on these subjects your letters will reach me by being left at Mess. Tucker & Williams on Central Wharf, both before I leave the States and afterward, and be assured that it would afford me much pleasure to give any information in my power.

I am &c N. J. W.

To Jno. Pickering Esq.

[A letter to F. Tudor Esq., Boston, written Feb. 7th, from Providence is omitted. It is devoted exclusively to explanations of suggested improvements in the process of harvesting ice.]

CLII.

New York   Feb 10th   1834

Mess. Tucker & Williams (Boston)

Gent Your letter of the 9th inst. was received today containing letter and copy of letter from Mess. Samuel & More. The copy is in answer to one of mine of Dec. 4th 1833 and the letter was written about the same time and contains nothing important. An answer to all that is contained in these two letters is in letters which I wrote to these two gentlemen on the 20th Dec. and Jany 7th 8th and 12th last which they appear not to have received at the date of their writing. A copy of these letters I would forward to you but have not time to write them off.

I hope you will see that the traps are good. His engagement was to have them done by the 7th. I do not know if he is bound to notify you of their being done. It is important to get them as soon as possible.

I shall write you as often as anything transpires of interest and in the meantime hope that you are not affected by the late failures.

Will you have the goodnees to send me amt. of the balance to my Cr. on your books in your next as I wish to enter it against you in my new books and have mislaid the acc. which you rendered.

I am &c N. J. W.

CLIII.

N. York Feb. 10th 1834

Wm. L. Sublette Esq. Philad

Dear Sir I arrived here in co with Milton yesterday Mng. and was disappointed in not finding you here, and write to say that we shall probably be in Philad. by the 16th and there hope to see you.

I am &c N. J. W

CLIV.

N. York Feb 11th 1834

Mess Thomas C. Rockhill & Co. (Philad)

Gent I have notice[d] that Mr Samuel of the firm of Samuel & More of Liberty Missouri left for your city on the 6th of Jany. I am very desirous of seeing him. Will you have the goodness to inform him that I shall remain here until the 16th inst. and then come to Philadelphia, provided you know where he is at this time.

And oblige Yr. Obt. Servt. N. J. Wyeth

CLV.

N York Feb 11th 1834

Bro Charles (Balto)

I have your fav. of the 10th of Jany last. I leave this on the 16th and remain but one day in Philadelphia and then to your city and hope to see you once more.

Yr. Afte. Bro. N. J. W.

CLVI.

New York Feb 11th 1834

Mess Tucker & Williams Boston

Gent Finding that there would be some cash bills to be paid here I have this day drawn on you at sight for 600$ No 1, which will probably be all this side the Aleganies at less time than six months.

I am &c N. J. Wyeth

CLVII.

N. York   Feb 12th   1833 [4]

Mess Tucker & Williams Boston

Gent Herewith you have duplicate of my letter of yesterday and copy of letter to Samuel & More which last will give you a view of the present state of affairs with them.

I am &c N. J. Wyeth.

CLVIII.

New York   Feb 12th   1834

Wm. L. Sublette Esq. (Philad)

Dear Sir Yours of the 6th inst was received by way of Boston today An answer to its contents has already been sent you and I presume you have received it before this. I only write to say that Milton leaves this in the morning for your city and I shall be there by the 16 and will expect to find you at Gill Campbell & Co.

I am &c N. J. Wyeth.

CLIX.

New York   Feb 12th   1834

Mess Tucker & Williams (Boston)

Gent Your fav. of 10th inst is at hand. If the Black smith will not consent to the traps being sent to Baltimore and abide the result on their examination there they must be tried by setting one week in Boston and as soon thereafter as possible have them forwarded to Mess Wyeth & Norris. If sent by the 24th inst I shou[l]d get them in season but I would take none after the 20th including time of tryal. I note what you say as to residue of goods and of Capt Thing.

In regard to drafts from the mountains they cannot be made on Samuel & More but must be made on some first rate house in St. Louis or on the bank as arranged.

In regard to the $6000 which I am to draw on you for from St. Louis I *may* make an arrangement with Samuel & More for a part, but I have not yet seen him and do not know where to find him, but have written to Philadelphia, but at the same time I would not like to make an arrangement with him for the whole. I request that you will *immediately* furnish me with a credit in in St. Louis of at least 3000$. If Thomas C. Rockhill & Co would accept my drafts there would be no trouble at least I think so, or if you would make yourselves known to Mess Von Phull & McGill of St Louis I think that would answer; but I can not pick up horses cheap without cash in hand nor can I wait until I get to Liberty to get it, for I must make some purchases before. As I leave this 2 days hence and then make haste westward you must be aware that there is not a moment to loose in this matter.

I am yr obt Servt   N. J. Wyeth.

P. S.   Your next please address to the care of Mess Grant & Stone Philad.

[The following is written across the above letter: Do not omit to have all the chains sent whether the traps are or not.]

[A letter to Frederic Tudor, Esq., Boston, dated "N. York Feb 12 1834" is omitted. Like that of the 7th inst. to Mr. Tudor it contains only suggestions pertaining to the management of the "ice business."   Mr. Wyeth closes the letter by saying, "Excuse the liberty I take in these matters I cannot forget the habit of thinking that I have still something to do with ice"]

CLX.

New York   Feb 15th   1834

Bro Jacob. (Galena)

I leave this place on my way west on the 15th inst. and shall be in St. Louis from the 5th to the 10th [of] April and would be much pleased to see you there.   The ur-gency of my buisness prevents my coming to see you, otherwise I would do so.   I have in charge for you some books which I shall send from St. Louis to you if I do not see you there.

I am Yr. Afte. Bro.   N J Wyeth

CLXI.

N York   Feb 14th   1834

Rev Jason Lee. (Baltimore)

Dear Sir.   I have received your fav. of 11th inst in answer to which say that I leave this city to mor-row morning and proceed directly west and remain but five or six days at St. Louis.   You will hear of me in St. Louis by calling on Mess Von Phull & McGill.

I think I received and answered a line from some one in west-ern Mass. but am not certain.

&c &c   N. J. W.

CLXII.

New York   Feb. 14th   1834

Mess. Tucker & Williams (Boston)

Gent   On the other side you have a list of drafts drawn on you up to this date also a list of bills paid.   I am obliged to keep the originals as vouchers in making up the invoices for Sublette.   I shall forward them from the up-per settlements by private hand and in the mean time shall con-tinue to forward only lists of bills.

The good[s] from this place I shall ship to Baltimore by sea, be-ing cheaper and will be in time.   Enclosed you have all the ma-terials for invoicing if you deem expedient.   If you write me as early as the 16th you can direct to the care of Mess Wyeth & Norris Baltimore but if later and until the 18th to the care of Josiah Lawrence & Co. Cincinati, after which time to the care of Mess Von Phull & McGill St. Louis and they will forward the letters to me wherever I may be at the time.

I am yr. obt. Servt. N. J. W.

(Enclosing bill of lading,and drafts drawn to date and bills paid.) viz.

No.	1	Feb	11th	fav.	of	Cripps & Wyeth	sight	600.
"	2	"	14	"	"	F. Gebard	6 months	149.85
"	3	"	14	"	"	R. H. Osgood & Co	8 months	253.
"	4	"	"	"	"	F. B. Rhodes	6 months	388.08
"	5	"	"	"	"	Robbins & Painter	6 months	484.92
"	6	"	"	"	"	Sindam & Jackson	6 months	571.75
"	7	"	"	"	"	Wolf & Clark	6 months	484.65

Bills paid

Feb.	13	Jno H. Albee	No.	1	8.87
"	"	Smith & ———	"	2	5.85
"	"	N. H. Weeld & Co	"	3	13.50
"	"	Girding & Siemon	"	4	17.37
"	"	———	"	5	17.58
"	"	Platt Stout & Ingoldsby	"	6	3.38
"	"	Hide Hitchcock & Greenman	"	7	3.00
"	"	Baily Ward & Co.	"	8	11.50
"	"	W. &. E Clark	"	9	61.09
"	"	Stryker & Smith	"	10	18.86
"	"	R H. Osgood & Co.	"	11	253.00
"	"	E. D. Sprague & Co.	"	12	11.94
"	"	E. J. & E. White	"	13	39,00

N. J. W.

[The following is written across the face of the above letter]
P. S. Out of the 2543.59 deduct, not shipped by the Othello

20 rifles   200.00

2 spades   1.75

30 doz.Scalping knives[?] 41.25

———

243.00 or

$2300.59 to be invoiced

Bill	to	F. B. Rhodes	No	14	$388.08
"	"	F. Gebard	"	15	149.85
"	"	Robbins & Painter	"	16	484.92
"	"	Sindam & Jackson	"	17	571.75
"	"	Wolf & Clark	"	18	484.65

CLXIII.

N. York   Feb 14th   1834

Capt Jos Thing (present)

Sir   You will please call on Mess. Wolf & Clark Pearl St. and ascertain if they have shipped to Mess Wyeth & Norris Baltimore some Rifles and Indian Knives for me and if so you will bring on with you the bills lading but if they have not you will bring these goods with you by the boats and railroads provided this route is open but if it is not you will have to ship them which do by the first vessell.

This is all that occurs to my mind now. You will attend to any suggestion which Mess. Cripps & Wyeth may give in relation to this buisness, and oblige   yrs &c   N. J. W.

P. S.   There are at Wolf & Clarks 20 rifles, 2 spades, and 30 doz scalping knives.

CLXIV.

Philadelphia   Feb 18th   1834

Capt Thing

Dear Sir   Having found the cloths which I wanted in this place, it becomes expedient to have the goods still in N. York forwarded as soon as possible, therefore please bring them on by the Boats and Rail Road as soon as you can get them.

Yrs &c   N J Wyeth

CLXV.

Philadelphia   Feb 18th   1834

Bro. L[e]ond

I have found in this place the Scarlett Cloths which I wanted, will you have the goodness to inform Mr. Stewart that he need not buy any on our acc.

Please forward any letters that may come to you for me on or be-fore the 19th inst. to care of Charles Balto.

And believe me yr. afte. Bro.

Nathl. J. Wyeth

CLXVI.

Philadelphia   Feb. 18th   1834

Bro. L[e]ond. (N. York)

Herewith I introduce to your acquaintance Mr. E. M. Samuel of Liberty Missouri. I have received from him the utmost kind-ness and attention when it was particularly acceptable. Any atten-tention that you shew him will much oblige me.

I hope you are by this much better than when I left you and am anxious to get a letter from you informing me of the state of your health.

Yr Afte. Bro. N. J. Wyeth

CLXVII.

Philadelphia   Feb. 18th   1834

Mess Tucker & Williams (Boston)

Gent I have seen Mr. Samuel. He assures me that the buisness of purchasing mules and horses is going on as fast as economy will permit and thinks we will have no difficulty as to men or animals.

I do not feel like trusting to any particular house at the westward for funds, inasmuch as by possibility they might not be able to give me the amt. of cash that I might want. The amt. disbursed by you in Boston with what I have already drawn for is about $3900 and possibly here or at Cincinati I may draw for 600$ more and $2000 which you arranged for through Rockhill & Co. This will leave of the original sum of $16000 $9500 of which amt. 5500$ [are reserved] to meet my drafts from the mountains [payment] must be made through the bank as arranged.

I have procured from Mess Grant & Stone letters of credit backed by one from Mess T. C. Rockhill & Co. and you will please forward to Mess Grant & Stone authority to draw on you for 4000$ at sight whenever they have paid my drafts to that or a less amount. Also please forward the letters of credit from the Cashier of the Branch in Boston to the Cashier of the Branch in St. Louis to the care of Mess Von Phull & McGill.

Herewith you have notice of bill drawn on you from this place and also bills paid here also duplicate list of bills drawn on you from N. York as per my letter of 14th inst.

I leave for Baltimore at 7 in the morning and Remain,

Yr. Obt. Servt. N. J. Wyeth.

CLXVIII.

Philadelphia   Feb 18th   1834

Mess Grant & Stone

Gent Since seeing you it has occured to my mind to request you to forward letters if any should come for me to the care of Mess. Wyeth & Norris of Baltimore. Also to say that my first draft on you will be No. 10, and follow in regular series till the amt. is completed.

I am Yr Obt. Servt N. J. W.

CLXIX.

Philad.   Feb 18th   1834

Capt Thing,

Dear Sir I write merely to say that there is nothing for you to attend to in this place except to call on Geo. W. Carpenter Druggist Markett St. and see Mr. Nuttall and let him know that you are going on, he wishes to keep company with you.

Yr &c N. J. Wyeth.

CLXX.

Balto.   Feb· 20th   1834

Col. E. W. Metcalf   Boston

Dear Sir   Your esteemed fav. of 8th inst. reached me on my arrival here last night.   In regard to the subject of it I think you have a right to suspect almost any thing (from that quarter) but I assure you that I have no knowledge in regard to it.   I am well aware that what you state in regard to the contract was common report at the time but I have not the slightest idea of what prevented its going into effect.

I desire you would believe that there is no desire on my part to withold information on this or any other subject and should be at all times pleased to correspond with you.

Respy. Yr Obt Servt. N. J. Wyeth.

CLXXI.

Balto.   Feb. 20th   1834

Mrs Deborah Powers (Lansingburg New Troy N Y.)

Madam   Your fav. I have received, and most gladly communicate the information you desire.   Please direct your letter to the care of Mess von Phull and McGill of St Louis to reach there by the 15th April.   I have frequently endeavored to find the directions of Mr Balls friends but had not succeeded.

You may be assured that your brother shall want nothing that I can supply on my arrival out.   I will make some enquiries about the Box which you speak of.

And Remain Yr Obt. N. J. Wyeth

CLXXII.

Baltimore   Feb. 21st   1834

Capt Thing   Balto.

Dear Sir   I leave here bills lading for Two Cases goods for Wm. G. Sublette, also Bills lading for goods from Philadelphia also Bills lading of goods from N. York and the Bills lading sent by you from N. York.   In addition to these goods you will have those from Boston of which I presume you have the bills lading, as they have not been sent me.   On the receipt of all these goods you will have the Cases &c overhauled and made strong and put them on board the wagons for Wheeling or Pitsburgh taking receipt for the same in the usual manner.   Have its weight marked on each box, in order that there may be no need of weighing more than once.   If by the time you have done this the traps have not come, you will leave them behind, in which case I have left directions with Mess Wyeth and Norris to take care of them.   All charges incurred of the Two Cases of Wm. G. Sublette you will keep separate.   Pay all bills here and take and preserve all the bills and bring them on.

I leave here $150 for you which I have charged to you. You will call on Mess. Josiah Lawrence & Co. of Cincinati where I will leave a line for you

[No signature.]

P. S.   You will manage the reshipping the goods when it is requisite.   You will find here 2 cases marked S. 16 and 17 and a barrel [marked] S No 18.

CLXXIII.

[No date.]

Mr Bradenburgh [?]
          Dear Sir   You will oblige me by seeing that 2 cases goods for Sublette and Campbell and one for me per the Union line from Phila. are brought to the store also if goods from Boston or N. York should arrive before Capt Thing comes have them brought to the store.   All these goods are to be sent to Wheeling or Pitsburgh and you will oblige me by putting Capt. Thing in the way of doing this in the best manner and advise him as to the suitableness of the cases.   Expenses to be paid by Capt Thing.

Should any goods come after Capt Thing leaves this you will oblige me by forwarding them to Von Phull & McGill St. Louis in the best manner.   Some traps are the only [things] which I now expect will be too late for Capt Thing and the expenses on these Mess Wyeth & Norris will pay and and collect the same of Mess. Tucker & Williams of Boston.   Please address me to the care of Mess Von Phull & Mc Gill of St. Louis.

There is here a package of letters for Wm. G. Sublette also the two cases goods which please deliver [to] him.   You will find him at Bells House[?] on Saturday or Monday.   If he wishes the goods can come on with Capt. Thing.

All letters for me you will please forward to the care of Mess. Von Phull & McGill St. Louis and if Bills of lading are wanted for the goods from Boston you open letters for me to find them.

N. J. W

CLXXIV.

Baltimore   Feb. 21st   1834
Mess. Tucker & Williams Boston
          Gent.   Herewith you have duplicate notice of draft drawn on you from Philad. and notice of draf[t] from this place, and list of Bills paid here.   I have lef[t] with Wyeth & Norris $150 to the Cr. of Capt Thing for the payt. of freight of goods out.

List of Bills paid here

No. 21,   Wyeth & Norris   35.18
 "   22,   Thomas Tyson   35.93
 "   23,   Densmore & Kyle   69.78

Duplicate notice draf[t] as per letter of Feb. 18th from Philad.

viz Liter Price & Co 6 months, 230.18. Draft Drawn from this place Feb. 20th fav. of Mess. Wyeth & Norris $300.00 at sight.

I am to leave this to morrow morning therefore in [the] future please address all your letters to the care of Mess Von Phull & McGill of St Louis.

I am yr obt. Servt. N. J. Wyeth

CLXXV.

Baltimore   Feb 22nd   1834

Capt Thing (Baltimore)

Dear Sir   Since mine of yesterday it has occurred to me that it would be well to try an observation with our instrument during the time that you will be waiting for the goods, this in order to see that you have all the requisites and such as are suitable. If you find any thing deficient you will purchase it here if possible. The sextant had better cross the mountains in your trunk if you can find the room. You will examine the two cases carefully and see that all is tight. The bbl. of Rum at Wyeth & Norris will require to be carefully examined to see if it is tight and the Boxes should be hooped.

If you find that there is not enough money left for you you will obtain more by shewing that more is requisite of Wyeth & Norris.

I am Yr. Obt. Servt.   N. J. Wyeth

CLXXVI.

Pitsburg   March [Feb.] 26th   1834

Capt Thing

Dear Sir   Since writing you at Baltimore it has occurred to me that some medicines for the clap and pox may be wanted the men often contract these disorders before they leave the settlements and unless there are some remedys the consequences are bad often inducing the men to desert in order to obtain relief. They should be of small bulk and little cost, and please get them at the first place that you can find them. Of these medicines we have plenty on the Brig and probably very few cases will occurs before we reach her.

I am Yr. Obt. Servt. Nath. J. Wyeth

CLXXVII.

Pitsburgh   Feb 26th   1834

Dear Wife (Camb.)

Since leaving home have had good luck enough to get so far and being detained here one day have time to write you. About the time this reaches you it will be time to get the things about the house in order. Please send my compliments to Mr. Weld and request him to see to it the small trees must be dug round except those set out last fall. Have them all trimmed but tak[e] off only dead branches. Have the the fences righted up and all things made decent, in order that when I send any friend to you you may be able to receive him.

Give my love to all friends and excuse this short letter. I have many to write and am unused to writing to ladys any way.

Yr afte Husband   N. J. W.

CLXXVIII.

Pittsburgh   Feb. 26th   1834

F Tudor Esq. (Boston)

          Sir   Your fav. of 17 inst. came to hand at Baltimore. The very flattering and liberal expressions used in it demand an acknowledgement. I am quite well aware of the value of testimonials from such a source and persuaded that I owe to similar ones the power to proceed in an enterprise which you are pleased to say has disappointed some of your expectations.

It affords me much pleasure to hear that the ice buisness is like to assume an importance worthy of the perseverance and talent bestowed on it for so many years. If true satisfaction is to be found it must be I think in the success of ones plans against the current of the worlds opinions and the ridicule of fools. I do not doubt that the extended ideas which you take of the buisness are sound and the belief affords me gratification unalloyed except by a fear that I shall have no part in the excitement of the strife or the glory of victory.

While you are successfull in N. Orleans these oppositions in Charleston are not of so much account, and up to the time that I left circumstances to me indicated an unexampled success in these but other p[l]aces aside I am persuaded that experience enables you to manage an opposition to perfection.

In regard to my returning to the ice buisness I can only say that "I am pledged" to the buisness I am in, as long as those concerned in it carry it on in the right spirit but I will not suffer small and parsimonious views, in others, to ruin me past redemption, or consume my time and prevent me from availing of a great opportunity. I consider the buisness I am now in as of sure result but will not yield adequate returns until the third year. In the mean time if those concerned fail in confidence or preseverance all is ruin and I shall not again essay to trouble the waters of these seas. *Having* engaged good fait[h] impels me to leave nothing undone to make this thing successfull and if so to pursue it for the benefit of all, but if they put this out of my power and you are inclined I shall then return on the best terms I can to the ice buisness.

I shall write you at all opportunities and next from the rendezvous in the Rocky mountains when I will give you any indication that may then appear as regards the probable result of this buisness.

I note the kind wishes at the end of your letter if mine in return are an equivalent you have plenty of them and be assured sincere. I am yr. obt. Servt.

Nathl J Wyeth.

CLXXIX.

Pitsburgh Feb 26th 1834

Mess Tucker & Williams (Boston)

Gent Some conversation while on my route hither and a previous acquaintance has induced me to give letters of introduction to Mr. Ira Smith of St. Louis directed to you. He thinks of visiting Boston on his return from Santa Fee and if so he will present them at that time and also to communicate to you the following ideas. The present letter on this subject is only intended to call your attention [to the matter] in order that you may collect what information you can in regard to it, and if such examination is favorable to the project and after those now in hand have been made to pay and leisure afforded to establish new sources of profit then to take hold of it. The following statement is my view of the Santa Fee buisness, derived however from superficial observation. viz

First cost of goods carried to St Fee and duties paid
the Mexican Government $100,000
Outfits and expenses on same 50,000
Profits and interest in the States between the importer
and the St Fee Trade 25,000

$175000

Returns made from St. Fee in Specie and Beaver $200000
Profits remaining to the St. Fee Traders $ 25000

This is I presume about the result of the trade. The goods are carried to St Fee by about 30 distinct traders in about 75 wagons. The largest trader has rarely more than 12 wagons. More than one half of these people are farmers and buy their goods on 12 months, and often mortgage their farms and consequently are obliged to make returns the same year, and will not follow the trade more than one year with bad success under any circumstances and certainly not when you consider that unless there is a sufficient company it is not possible to go through on the Sta Fee route. The idea that I have is this (when we are ready to make such large investments) take $50000 first cost of goods to the mouth of the Columbia with say $5000 in silver to pay the duties transport them up country and encamp there near Sta Fee and enter only to the amt. of 5000$ duties from the sale of these goods get the means to enter the residue. The mildness of the climate west of the mountains will enable to bring these goods to Santa Fee two months earlier than the St. Louis traders will come during which time considerable sales will be made when they come put the goods down so that they must loose at the same time buy them out so that they will loose a little. They must return in about 2 months, after which time and during the rest of the year goods will resume their accustomed prices. The sales of the first year will probably be one half consumed in purchases made. I do not believe that a company could be got to go from St Louis the next year if so a very small one and must be treated the same as the first after which time I think it is a matter of absolute certainty that we should get the whole trade. I have not made the requisite enquiries but do not calculate on any saving of distances by taking the goods from the Columbia but only of duties merch[an]ts profits in States and animals and in transporting to which there will be an offsett of interest. I think that after the 3d year one third of all the returns of the trade might be profit. The route from the Columbia to Santa Fee is the same in part as to the mountains and the returns such as would not interfere materially with the cargo of Salmon being entirely Beaver and specie.

Mr. Smith is Brother of the Smith killed on the Sta Fee route in 1829. He bears an excellent reputation here and thinks he would put $10000 into such a buisness. He has been two years in this trade and is the largest Dealer in it. If anything should be done it would require another partner in the Indian country, and I presume no better person could be found. I object however to any further proceeding in this matter other than collecting information until what we have now in hand has proved itself which will be about three years then if successfull and it be found expedient, I am for it. In the mean time let us blow the coals, that the fire in Smiths mind may not go out. It is a buisness that he opened to me and I think that he may be kept in tow until we are ready to say yes or no.

I am desirous to get the Hudsons Bay Cos. public sales in London and all other information touching furs that can be obtained which please forward by next vessell

I am yr. obt. Servt. N. J. W.

CLXXX.

Wheeling   Feb 27th   1834

Mr. Jno. Bradenburgh [?]   Baltimore

Dear Sir   There is a package of letters for Mr. Wm. L. Sublette at the store which please have forwarded to the care of Mess A. and G. W. Can & Co St Louis. The Goods which belong to Mr. Wm. G.* Sublette you will please have forwarded with mine

&c N. J. W.

---

*The second initial of Wm. Sublette's name was uniformly written as "G" in the letter book. A reviser has however written an "L" over the "G" in almost every instance. The "L" has alone been given wherever it thus occurs.

CLXXXI.

Cincinati   Feb 28th   1833[4]

Capt Thing   Present,

Dear Sir   I leave here no buisness   for you to attend to but wish you would call at the Post Office in Louisville where if I purchase any thing I shall leave a letter for you. Should you be in want of money here you will obtain it of Mess. Josiah Lawrence & Co.

I am Yr obt Servt.   N J Wyeth

CLXXXII.

Cincinati   March 1st   1834.

Mess Tucker & Williams   Boston

Gent   Yours of 18th ulto. received here.   What you say of the traps is good.   I presume that you have rec[e]ived notice before this that Capt. Thing joined me in N.York, and of the arrangement I made in regard to drafts from St Louis.   From this place I drew on you for $300 in fav. of Lawrence & Co sight.   I purchase no goods here Sublette preferring to buy his Powder in St. Louis which is better for us. $165 of this money goes to pay a draft which Abbot drew on me in fav. of Mr. Sublette of which I had no notice until lately and did not justly owe but choose to pay to save discredit.   After I have finished spending I shall endeavour to forward means by which you will be in funds to the extent of my deficiency so far as I shall then know it but am afraid that if money continues as present in Boston I shall not be able to come quite up to the mark.

Duplicate notice

Draft fav. of Mess. Wyeth & Norris [at] sight for $300.00 Feb. 20th 1834

N. J. W.

CLXXXIII.

Cincinnati   March 1st   1834

Mess Grant & Stone   Philad.

Gent   I write only to inform you that my first draft will be from St Louis No 11 having since I wrote you had occasion to draw one draft more on Boston than I expected.

And remain   yr obt Servt   N J W

CLXXXIV.

Louisville   March 3d   1834

Mess Allison and Anderson   Louisville

·Gent.   For fear that in the hurry of buisness you might forget my directions   I recapitulate viz Mark from 20 upwards.   W. and ship to Mess Von Phull & McGill of

St. Louis by first direct opportunity.   Capt. Thing calls on you
before you have done this deliver them to him,
and oblige Yr Obt. Servt. N. J. W.

CLXXXV.

Louisville   March 3d   1834

Capt. Thing   (Louisville)
Dear Sir   You will find at Mess Alli-
sons & Andersons 3 bbls Alcohol and 11 packages Tobacco,
provided they do not ship the same before you arrive in this place
in which case you will proceed direct to St. Louis.
I am &c   N J Wyeth

CLXXXVI.

Louisville   March 4th   1834

Mess Von Phull & McGill   St. Louis
Gent   Above you have Bill Lading   of
some goods which if they arrive before me please receive and take
care of until I come
And oblige Yr Obt Servt. N. J. W

(Enclosing Bill Ladings 11 packages Tobacco, 3 bbls alcohol
and 3 coils of manilla rope.)
CLXXXVII.

Louisville   March 5th   1834

Mess. Tucker & Williams (Boston)
Gent   Permit me introduce to your acquain-
tance Mr Ira G. Smith from him you can obtain much useful information in regard to the Santa Fee buisness in which he has
been engaged some years. Any assistance which you can
render him in Boston will much oblige your
Obt. Servt   Nathl. J. Wyeth

CLXXXVIII.

Louisville   March 4th   1834

Mr. Jas. Brown   Boston
Dear Sir   Herewith I introduce to your acquaintance Mr. Ira G Smith. Any politeness or attention which
you can shew him will much oblige
your old friend   Nathl. J. Wyeth

CLXXXIX.

Louisville   March 5th   1834

Bro. Charles (Baltimore)
Allow me to introduce Mr. Ira G. Smith
an acquaintance of mine to you.   He is just from Santa Fee and
will amuse you with long storys of Indians &c.   Shew him what
attention you can and oblige
Yr afte Bro   Nathl. J. Wyeth

One of the above to Leond. I. Wyeth.

CXC.

St. Louis   March 10th   1834

Mess Samuel & More

Gent.   Since   mine of 12th ulto. I have
not heard from you and do not know   what   you have done in regard to Horses, mules and men and desire that as soon as possible you would inform me.   I shall engage here if possible 20 men
but shall not purchase animals,   The riding saddles please get as
heretofore ordered.

While in Philadelphia I   saw   Mr. Samuel with   whom I arranged in regard to money   matters   and he informed me that he
had written you on the   subject.   In addition to the money that
you have   received from Mess Von Phull & McGill and the letter
of Cr. from T. C. Rockhill & Co. I shall want about $3000
which in all will be about   5400$.   Please inform me if this will
[be] convenient at your earliest opportunity.

And oblige Yr Obt Servt   Nathl. J. Wyeth.

CXCI.

St. Louis   March 11th   1834

Mr Jas. Brown

Dear Sir   Expecting, as usual, to be a little
short of fulfilling my engagements to the company with which I
am concerned I have to request of you the favor of getting a dis-
count for me provided they call for it.

I have left with Tucker & Williams a note   against   F. Tudor
for $300 also one against Jonas Wyeth 2nd $1000. These you know
are perfectly good and if not formal can be used collaterally
and are due about the 1st Sept and Dec. next.   If you are not at
liberty to endorse owing to stipulations with   your partners you
might probably get the Colonel by *way of importance* to do it
or some one else.   If you will exert your self in this matter you
will essentially serve me.   I shall write to T & W. to call on
you for this purpose if they find it requisite.

Yours of the 17 ulto. was received am sorry your neighbors are
cracking and glad that you are not.   Shall write you again just
as I leave the world.

Yr Afte Friend,   N. J. W.

CXCII.

St. Louis   March 11th   1834

Mess Grant & Stone

Gent.   This is to inform you that I have this
day drawn on you for $1000 at 10 days sight fav. Mess. of A. and

G. W. Ken* No 11 for the amt. of which please draw on Mess.
Tucker & Williams Boston as arrange[d] and oblige

                              yr. ob Servt.   N. J. W
    CXCIII.

                         St. Louis   March 13th   1834
Mess Tucke[r] & Williams   Boston
              Gent.   Your favours of the 18th and 22nd
ulto. are at hand.   I presume you have before this received my
letter of 21st Feb from Baltimore and 26th ulto from Pitsburgh.
Your letters of Cr. on the Branch Bank here for $4000 I shall not
be able to use and I have already drawn from this place on Mess.
Grant & Stone for $1000 10 days sight.   For remaining $3000
of this credit I shall endeavour to get the time provided by your
letters with the bank, from Samuel and More.   But Mr. Samuel
having gone to Liberty the day before your letters were received
and having made an arrangement with him it might be a serious
disappointment to him not to obtain my bills to make his pay-
ments at the East but still it will amt. to about the same thing as
the bills will be drawn much later.   Had your letter arrived one
day earlier I should have avoided drawing say No. 11 at so
short a sight.   The Cr. of $5500 to be used from the Mountains is
entirely satisfactory.
    The Traps will be in Season under ordinary circumstance and I
have taken out an open policy for $3300 from Pitsburg to this
place on such goods as may be shipped at 1 pr ct.
    I note that you have written to Mess Samuel & More.   Mr.
Coxe charges on drafts one per ct. and Interest 6 pr ct.   I
have hired here for 3 years one man $300 pr An. one for $250
per An. 18 at $250 for 18 mos. time to expire in the Indian
country.   Advances and Horses will exceed the estimate I think
but can not yet say how much.   I arrived here the 10th inst
having had as I believe the Cholera on the route but am now well.
    Fitzpatric was robbed by the Crow Indians of his horses and
goods but has made 2300 lbs. Beaver and 2 of his parties not
heard from when he wrote.   Should his other parties do as well
it will be a good hunt after all.
    Seaton sends out a party of about 40 men and we propose to
join company through the dangerous country.   This with super-
numeraries will make us about 120 strong enough to flog all the
Indians in the country.   Of my own funds here I shall not be
able to collect more than 600$.   In the mean time I have written
to Mr. James Brown firm of Hilliard, Gray & Co who is my at-
torney to get discounted some of the notes which I left with you
which under any ordinary circumstances he will and can very
readily do if you will call on him and this is all the arrangement

_____
    *Written "Can" when previously mentioned.

which I can make to meet any deficiency that may appear against me. The Cash paid by me from my own funds in this place will not exceed $600., which is in addition to what stands to my Credit with you.

I this day received a letter from the Gov. of the Hudsons Bay Co. in London in regard to the proposition which I made them and of which you have a copy in my letter of Nov. 8 18,33 deferring a definite answer to the same until the express from the Columbia was received it appears that their ships were last year frozen up at Hudsons Bay in consequence of which they had no news from the Columbia of the year in which I was there.

                    & &c   N. J. W.

CXCIV.

St. Louis   March 18th   1834

Bro. Jacob

       I had hoped to find you here or at least a letter from you but do not, and therefore write to say a sort of farewell before I again encounter the uncertainies of the wilderness. After leaving you at the rendesvous we moved on with tolerable comfort and success in the way of Hunting and trading until we arrived at the Coast where we found the vessel that I had expected had been lost. This was a signal for the rest to desert and truly I was glad to be rid of them altho thereby all the proceeds of the expedition were sacrificed or buried in the Mountains. I then commenced my return with two hired men and during the time from the 1st March last until the 10th Oct. made my way to St. Louis and in due time home. The old concern being dis[s]olved, I formed a new one and am now on my way to the Columbia having sent a vessell round the Horn and am taking a company of 50 men overland to go over again the toils and suffering and perhaps the losses of which you saw a part, and this will either make or break me. Thus much for myself.

I hear that you are doing well and have far the best practice in your place. Industry will keep this and economy will make it ample for your wants. Yrs. of the 8th Dec. last I received and mark that you say that your "prospects are great and getting better, as you always knew they would be, if once disengaged from your friends as they *ludicro[u]sly* stile themselves who have always weighted you down &c stifling all your energies &c." Whether friendly to you or not or whether I ever stated myself to be, imports nothing and whether you intended me or others imports as little. All the comment I can make on the passage, is to ask you, who supported your early life of idleness and dissipation, until it was beyond the power of any friends to do it longer? and who on your return from the Mts. enabled you to avail yourself of your present prospects? I have never yet read a passage which so strongly indicated the truth of one of Rochefocaulds maxims viz.

"If you would wish to make a man your irreconsilable enemy do him a kindness he cannot repay["]. I have done you the favor not to shew this letter to your friends believing that you did not appreciate the words when you wrote them and that it might be only an exebition of that inconsiderateness which forms a part of your character.

I hear that you are to be married and to one who is said to be worthy of you or any one else. Altho you do dot seem to allow that I should call myself your friend yet perhaps you will admit me to sug[g]est that economy will be the best mode to maintain that independency which you have now so fully declared more especially as in regard to it I have been wanting as well as yourself. Be assured that much of the comfort of your married life will depend upon your being able to maintain a respectable appearance among your acquaintance. Want and pleasure do not associate, and beside if your income can be made sufficient nothing would be more to your credit than to pay off some of your small debts to the Eastward. This would make your father much more comfortable than he now is and would in the end I have no doubt afford you more pleasure than you could purchase with the same money in any other way.

It affords myself and your other *friends* no little pleasure to hear that your exertions are praiseworthy and that at last you are likely to make a man of yourself that you have quit all sorts of dissipation and have formed industrious habits. That you may continue in this c[o]urse is the sincere wish of

Yr afte Bro   N. J. W.

CXCV.

St. Louis   March 19th   1834

Mr Nuttall

Dear Sir   Capt Thing informs me that you wait information from me before you leave Philad. I can not tell exactly what time I shall leave St. Louis, but of this I am certain that you will have no time to spare after you receive this and when you arrive at St. Louis call on Mess Von Phull & McGill who will inform you if I have gone up the river in which case follow as fast as you can. At Liberty or Independence you will hear if I have started and how long. If I have not been gone more than three or four days with a good horse you will easily overtake me before you come to any dangerous country following the trail of my horses.

I shall probably not leave Independence before the 25th April and perhaps not quite so soon. Much depends upon the grass whether it is fit to feed the horses or not. At present appearences indicate an early spring.

I am Yr Obt. Servt.   Nathl. J. Wyeth

CXCVI.

St. Louis   March 21st   1834

Mess Samuel & More

Gent   Enclosed you have list of men which I send up.   The passage is $5.50 a piece which please pay for all that are delivered, and when they arrive please find some house where they can stop and cook their food.   Supply them with provisions until I come and let them cook for themselves.   I shall be up in the next Boat.

I have paid the Capt $25 which please deduct from his bill unless he shows that he has supplied these men with provisions which he is authorized to do in case those on board run short.

Yr &c   N. J. W.

P. S. Having blkts on the route I have given these men none. If you could hire their lodging cheap I would pay for it or get them some bedding until I come by paying for the use of it.

Also authorizeing Mess. Samuel & More to pay one dollar extra for any of the men who did not wood on the way and in proportion to the distance if they should desert.

N. J. W.

CXCVII.

St. Louis   March 28th   1834

Mess Samuel & More   Liberty.

Gent   Your fav. of 20 inst came to hand to day.   I am sorry that you have made a contract for saddles at 10$ each.   You have either mistaken the kind I wanted or have paid far too much.   Such as I wanted without stir[r]ups or girths as I ordered them can be had here at $4 each.   Please get off from taking as many as you can of these saddles, and if you have not already engaged 6 better ones that I ordered you may leave it until I come.   You do not tell me what you are giving for animals or how many you have bought.   I shall probably come up on the next Boat say in about eight days from the time you receive this.

In the mean time I remain

Yrs &c.   Nathl. J. Wyeth

CXCVIII.

St. Louis   March 28th   1734

Bro Leond

Allow me to introduce to your acquaintance an uncle of Bro Jacobs intended, Col. Geo. W. Jones of Galena.   He gives so good an account of the Doct. that I know you will take great pleasure in conversing with him

Yr. afte Bro.   Nathl. J. Wyeth

CXCIX.

St. Louis   March 31st   1834

Dear wife   (Cambridge)

Your fav. of 13th came to hand this morning and was very acceptable. I am glad to find you will take some care of the trees. Perhaps they will not grow for our use but some one will get the benefit and it will be pleasant to leave even such a memorial of our having once existed. It is true that Mr. Fitzpatric was robbed by the Crow Indians but I was in hopes that you would not hear of it. I knew it before I left Cambridge but did not wish to alarm you. I do not think there is much danger with so large party as I shall have.

Mr. Nuttall and Mr. Townsend another naturalist passed through this place to the rendezvous last week and their goods went by the vessell so there is no doubt of his going. The Missionarys came here this morning. Mr. Abbot is at the rendezvous taking care of the horses. Batiste and the Indian I have also sent up to the rendezvous. Batiste continues a pretty good boy. I shall think of your request for seeds and pretty stones while I am on my way out, and certainly shall not forget my promise to send for you if there is any chance of doing so with propriety but you must not be too sanguine a thousand circumstances may prevent it altho I desire it much. I feel as much as you can do the lonesomeness of my way of life but you know the success of what I have undertaken is life itself to me and if I do fail in it they shall never say that it was for want of perseverance. But this is my last attempt and if I am not successfull I must come home and endeavour the best way I can to get a living and to pay my debts which will then be heavy. Still I am yet sanguine that I shall succeed. I will take good care of myself and perhaps the life which began in turmoil may yet end in quiet and peace and our sun go down from a clear sky. I should be desolate indeed if I thought that the residue of life was to be as unsettled as the past, and I cannot but reproach myself that I have made you in some measure a widow while you ought to be enjoying yourself. I am afraid that you will brood over hopes that have been blasted by me who should have been with you to fulfil them and at hand in time of need to cherish and support. These things make me melancholy and I half believe I have got the Blues.

Jacob writes me that he is about getting married. The people from Galena all say that he is doing well. I hope so but cant. help doubting whether it is permanent.

Good bye My Dear wife and may God bless you.

N. J. Wyeth

CC.

St Louis   April 3rd   1834

Mess Samuel & More   Liberty
                    Gent. Your fav. of the 28th ultó.
came to hand this evening. I note that you are getting horses.
120 horses if good would do me. To this number you can purchase. If you can get mules allow that 3 are as good as 4
Horses. As to price you are the best judges, but I am in hopes
that 30$ a piece will buy good horses and $40 mules. I wrote you
on the 28 ulto. about saddles &c. I do not wish you to do anything more until I come in regard to any thing except Horses
and mules. Please get the animals shod as fast as you buy them.
    I am on the Ioway with all my goods and leave this in the morn-
ing and have hired men enough with the 20 I have before sent
you except 6 which please engage if you can find cheap and
good but not otherwise.
                    I am yr obt. Servt. N. J. Wyeth

CCI.

St. Louis   April 3d   1834

Mess Grant & Stone   Philad.
                    Gent. I have drawn on you this day fav.
of Mess Von Phull & McGill 90 days sight No 12 for $700 for
which amt you will draw on Mess. Tucker & Williams as arranged and oblige
                    yr. obt. Servt. N. J. W.

CCII.

St. Louis   Ap 3d   1834

Mess Tucker & Williams   (Boston)
                    Gent I have this day drawn on you No 13.
$600 90 days sight fav. H. S. Coxe cashier of the U. S. Bank in
this city, also this day No 12 on Mess. Grant & Stone Philad.
$700 90 dys sight of which I have advised them.
    All the goods have arrive here and are reshipped and insured to
Liberty. I shall leave this in the boat in a few minutes and shall
write you in full from the upper settlements forwarding acts[.] of
disbursements and the certain arrangements of the expedition.
                    I am yr. Obt. Servt. N. J. W

CCIII.

Independence   Ap. 17th   1834

Mess Tucker & Williams
                    Gent. Your fav. of the 21st ulto. came to
hand to day. The last of mine which you acknowledge is of the
1st March since which I have written you advising of the following draft viz A and G. W. Ken 10 days sight on Grant & Stone
No. 11 $1000 March 11th—Von Phull & McGill 9[0] days on

Grant and Stone No. 12 $700 April 3d—H. S. Coxe 90 days on Tucker & Williams No 13 $600 dollars Ap. 3d making about $6062.45. The amt you speak of as paid for Abbot was not paid on Company acc. but on my own. He gambles but is usefull to us and owes us too much to have him stopped. To day I have drawn on you No. 14 fav. H. S. Coxe 90 days $343.37 also same on same date and time $3000 making in all to this date about 9500$ and there will be yet some more. Several items not included in the first estimate conduce to this such as insurance of these vions, [?] passage for myself, Abbot, Thing and two Indians. The opposition of the 4 companies have made me pay heavy advances on men and high prices for horses, in addition to which I have been obliged to advance about $500 to Milton Sublette which arose from this circumstance viz last year Sublette & Campbell took out to the mountains Capt Stewart & Doct. Harrison and authorized Milton Sublettes Company to credit them and draw for the amt. These drafts Sublette & Campbell refused to honor and pay as soon as they ascertained that we were to supply Milton Sublettes Company with goods unless Milton Sublette would remain at home in which case Sublette & Campbell offered to settle the acts. and pay the Drafts. Sublette & Campbell are going out with a party of men & goods to the rendesvous to the mountains. Under these circumstances I felt myself obliged to make the advance above stated to M. G. Sublette and also to purchase a more expensive kind of animals then I had at first intended in order to be first at the rendesvous which I consider very important. So far I am ahead and shall leave the settlements on the 26th or thereabouts at which time I shall forward you acts. in full, Invoices muster roll &c.

I am now packing up. All the goods have arrived here safely. I have 20 more horses to purchase. The season is early and everything favorable except that the expense will be greater than has been calculated, but as you do not complain much of hard times I am in hopes that you will meet it willingly and request you to believe that every exertion has been made to keep it within bounds. There are none of the Dignitaries with me as yet and if they "preach" much longer in the States they will loose their passage for I will not wait a minute for them.

I am &c   N. J. Wyeth

CCIV.

Indpendence   April 25th   1834

Mess Tucker & Williams

Gent. To day I drew my last draft on Mess Grant & Stone 30 days sight No 16 2515.66 fav. of Samuel & More. You will be surprised at the amt. I have drawn but without abandoning the enterprise I could not avoid it and there being no chance to refer to you, I have taken the responsibility and must abide the consequences if you choose not to ratify my act. I should have drawn on my own means but I have not got them. There have been by the government and the trading companies purchased here above 1000 Horses which accounts for the great increase in the price. I have been obliged to advance to men or not get them and once in for it I have been obliged to pay their other debts, or loose them. Many of them having been taken by the officers. I shall make out Invoices, musters, and accounts due from men and my own account with the concern. These I shall send from the Kansas Agency. I should do it here but officers are continually taking the men and making more expense beside time is of the greatest importance. I go in the morning and can make out these papers at nights. It is like keeping a bag of fleas together to keep the men in this whisky country

In haste. You will please pass to m[y] Cr.

yr obt. Servt. Nathl. J. Wyeth

CCV.

Independence   April 26th   1834

Mess Tucker & Williams

Gent. Notwithstanding what I wrote you yesterday I have drawn to day yet another draft fav. of Mess. Samuel & More No 17 $120 sight which I hope and believe will be the last. I have lost 4 cattle and 2 horses and in case I do not find them to day I shall leave them behind. Excuse my brevity at this moment as I have many things to do and shall write you again as advised in mine of yesterday.

Enclosed you have a note of W. Abbot to me which please hold for collection. This is the debt which I paid for him to Sublette & Campbell as advised in mine of 1st March from Cincinati and credit the same to my acc. and oblige

yr obt. Servt. Nathl J Wyeth

CCVI.

Kanzas River   May 2d   1834

Mess Tucker & Williams

Gent This is my last this side of the mountains and with it you have my acc. with bills and copies of bills that are required as vouchers in the mountains also a list of people terms of engagements and charges against men. I am not sure that these papers are accurate as they were made up in camp and in very wet weather and much to attend to. I have lost 2 Horses 4 cows. 2 men deserted and I expect some more will. I am the first as yet in the Indian country. Excuse me from writing more as I am fatigued to[o] much.

yr obt. Servt. Nathl. J. Wyeth.

P. S. I have not sent you the invoice of my own goods because they will probably be all charged to disbursements in case I send out a trapping party. I have therefore supposed it best to charge all except Sublettes Invoice to Disbursements and credit that account when any part of it was sold.

CCVII.

Little Vermillon   May 8th   1834

Mess Tucker & Williams

Gent I am sorry to say that Mr. M. G. Sublettes leg has grown so troublesome that he is to day obliged to turn back and by him I write this. He has given me an order on his partner for the amt. of advances made him payable in furs. I regret this circumstance much but it was unavoidable as he was perfectly unable to go on. 4 more men have deserted since mine of 2nd inst. 2 men I have hired. No more horses have been lost. The bills and acts. were forwarded by the same conveyance as the letter of the 2nd inst. We have now crossed the Kanzas and are about 60 miles above the Agency or 120 from the western limit of the state of Missouri.

In the acts. which I forwarded to you you will observe a mistake of 343.37 which you will please credit to my acc. Wishing you all manner of good success and the same myself somewhat on your account I remain

Yr obt Servt.   Nathl. J. Wyeth

CCVIII.

One day this side the Blue   May 12th 1834

Dear Sir Wm Sublette having passed me here, I am induced to write to you by this opportunity and hope you will get it. You may expect me by the 1st July at the rendesvous named in your letter to Milton which which you sent by Dr. Harrison who opened it and I presume told Wm Sublette of the place. I am not heavily loaded and shall travell as fast as possible and have a sufficient equipment of goods for you according to contract. Cerre will be much later than me and also the Am. Fur Co. Milton left me a few days since on account of his leg which is very bad.

I am yr obt. Servt.   N. J. W.

To Thos Fitzpatric or Co.

In the Rocky Mountains.

P. S. I have sent a vessell around the Horn with such goods as you want and would like to give you a supply for winter rendesvous or next year on such terms as I know would suit you.

CCIX.

Sweet Water   June 9th   1834

Mess Thomas Fitzpatric & Co.

Gent. I send this to inform you of my approach with your goods. I am now two days behind Wm Sublette, who I presume is with you by this. Milton informed

me that you would rendesvous near the mouth of the Sandy. In
case you do not I wish you would immediately inform me by express. I am now one days march above rock Independence and
shall continue to come on at a good rate and for the present follow the same route which I came by two years since. I wish
that you would defer making any contract for carrying home any
surplus furs that you have or for a further supply of goods untill
I come as I have sent a vessell to the mouth of the Columbia
with such goods as you want and am ready to give you a supply
for winter rendesvous if you wish, or for next year, and also to
send home by her, at a low rate, such furs as you may have and
can make you advances in St. Louis on them to pay men &c.

I am yr. obt. Servt.   Nathl. J. Wyeth.

CCX.

Hams fork of the Colorado of the West   June 20th   1834
Jas. W. Fenno Esq.   Atty. at law   Boston

Dear Sir   According to
arrangement I write you. I have as yet no certain knowledge of
how the buisness I am now in will prove, or for how long a
time it may detain me. Our getting no furs as yet, renders it
quite probable that it may be given up soon. My partners may
get discouraged, if no returns are made the first year, and if they
do I shall be compelled to give the thing up. You may feel
yourself quite certain on the return of the first vessell if another
is not sent out immediately that I am coming home soon. Having been the instigator of this enterprise I cannot be the first to
abandon it and have no disposition to do so, but if those engaged
with me do not support me in a proper manner so as to enable
me to prosecute it successfully I must turn my attention to some
other buisness. It is perhaps impertinent in me to advise and
quite likely you will think me interested, nevertheless, if you will
keep yourself aloof from the ice buisness for a time I think there
may be an opportunity to commence it more favorably. For
some years the buisness has been too successfull to induce proper
ideas of its value and if you should enter the buisness as an agent
you will run the chance of change of opinion which might be
fatal to any project on the subject. Little as the above amounts
to it is all that I can say. Affairs have not yet given any decided indication to enable me to be more definate. This much to
shew you that I have not forgotten the subject.

I hope you have got the patent arranged in such a manner
that you can clap the screws when occasion calls.

Our route hither has been attended with success so far as travelling but not otherwise. We have had no fighting and [have] seen
few Indians and what horses we have lost have been worn out
and not stolen. The companies here have all failed of making
hunts, some from quar[r]eling among themselves some from having

been defeated by the Indians and some from want of horses, and what few furs have been taken have been paid to the men for their services leaving none for me. I shall build a fort on Lewis River about a hundred and fifty miles west of this which is in Latt. 45 deg. 15 min. Long 112 deg. 15 min. and there deposite my goods for sale when there is Beaver to pay for them.

While I am here turning Indian probably you are turning civilized that is getting married and settling down to all the comfort that can be imagined, preparing yourself an easy chair for after life. That you may find not thorns when you expect Down is the wish of

your friend and Servt. Nathl J. Wyeth.

CCXI.

Hams Fork of the Colorado of the West   June 20th   1834

F. Tudor Esq.

Dear Sir   With no adventure worth relating in the way of Battle or hardship I arrived here on the 19th inst. having left the settlements on the 1st May. And feel it a duty to write to you altho I have not much to say. The contracts which I made with the companys here have not been complied with and in consequence I am obliged to establish a fort, which I shall do on Lewis River about a hundred miles west of this for the purpose of trading my goods and then leave part of my men at it and then proceed to the Columbia for the further prosecution of the buisness. The failure of adequate returns by the first vessell may possibly discourage those who are concerned in this thing at home and in case you find that a vessell is not sent out as soon after the first returns as possible you may expect to see me soon and in such case with a determination to take any reasonable chance in the ice buisness and stick to it the remainder of my buisness life. I cannot in conscience ask you to defer any thing for me nor can I be the first to abandon this undertaking having been first in it, but will not prosecute it further than there is a reasonable chance of success.

We have here none of what you call the comforts of life but have heart and health, and are yet young and after all not discouraged which is one half. If I cannot succeed I will fail after a fair tryal but not before.

That you may in the evening of your days enjoy that comfort and satisfaction for which you have striven so hard and long is the wish of one who feels under heavy obligation to you.

I am yr obt Servt. Nathl. J. Wyeth

CCXII.

Hams fork of the Colorado of the West   June 21st   1834
Leond Jarvis Esq
                    Dear Sir   I have not time to write much or
much to say, but I cannot omit saying a little.   So far this buisness looks black. The companys here have not complied with their
contracts with me and in consequence I am obliged to make a
fort on Lewis River to dispose of the goods I have with me.] I
think I can in a little time realize good returns, but in the meantime the concern at home may get discouraged and if they do the
whole is spoiled, and I shall be obliged to give up the buisness.
After leaving a part of my men to take charge of the fort I shall
proceed to the Columbia and probably get there about 1st Sept.
The place I am now at is Latt 41 deg 45' Long 112 deg. 35'.   If
I am obliged to return home again it will be to stay and endeavour
to pay off the debts which I will then owe, and believe that I can
do so in time with health.
    Accept Dear Uncle my wishes for your happiness and also that
of my good Aunt, and believe me
                    Yr Afte. Nephew   N. J. W.

CCXIII.

Hams Fork of the Colorado of the West   June 21st   1834
                    Dear Parents   I arrived here on the 19th
inst without accident after a very quick voyage and no fighting.
All as yet looks as   prosperous as could be expected (you
know however that I do not expect much and am therefore not
so likely to be dissappointed).   I hope you get along in quiet and
peace with Jonas.   The idea that this may not be the case occasions me some uneasiness.   I can not say how soon you may
expect to see me but of this be certain, that there is little or no danger here except of not living quite so well as I could at home.   I
hope you will do all that you can to make my wife comfortable
and happy and yourselves the same.   I have many letters to
write and not much time at present but shall write you by the return vessell.
    Love to all.   With many wishes for your health and hap-
piness
          I am yr affectionate Son   Nathl J Wyeth.

CCXIV

Hams Fork of the Colorado of the West   June 21st   1834
                    Dear Wife   I have but little to say to you
in a letter, but much buisness with you, if I were at home.   I
got here safe and well, but whether I shall do well is yet uncertain but I will try.   Miltons leg got so bad that he did not come
with me.   Mr. Nuttall is well and is cursing the tittle tattle of
Cambridge in high style.   It would do you good to look into

our tent just now and see how fat I am.   Be of good cheer and
make yourself as happy as you can until I come or send.

Give my respects to your mother and Aunt Rebecca and love to
Caroline   Baptiste send[s] compliments.

yr afte. Husband   Nathl. J. Wyeth.

CCXV.

Hams Fork of the Colorado of the West   June 21st   1834

Mr Jas Brown

My old friend I cannot write at length but there is
a feeling when I write to you that I feel to no one else.   In long
array comes up the wits and wine the social converse and the
sunny side hills of old times.   Are they gone forever?   Yes from
me, but as the hearts of kings tremble at the name of Napoleon,
so mine vibrates to the recollections of old joys.   I am not now
able at once to heave care "over side" and the Bon[n]y Boat the
Jovial crew, Chaplain and all would   now be insufficient to fill the
void.   I believe that times of Careless Joy have gone by for me,
and speed to them.   And now we look forward to those quiet
times when the wicked cease from troubling and the weary are
at rest.   Are the heavens Black or is the gloom in my vision?
The latter must be true for still youth and I[n]trepidity look upon
as fresh a world as ever and wlll not believe "hic Transit Gloria
mundi to be true."   If you think me Blue remember that I am
hard to convince and all are unwilling to believe themselves
astray.

In regard to my affairs manage them as well as you can.   My
scituation is not such as to justify your incurring any risque on
my account.   I would like to keep the Colledge lott if possible
because I think that let affairs turn as they may I will be able to
come home and in a little time clear myself of any incumbrance.

I hope your buisness is prosperous and not so burdensome as
to destroy comfort.   Mine here still looks squally but obstinacy
and hope guide the way.

Be so good as to give my respects to all friends and especially
to your good wife and love to little ones.

And believe me as of old your affectionate friend

N. J. Wyeth

CCXVI.

Hams Fork of the Colorado of the West   June 21st   1834

Col. E. W. Metcalf

Dear Sir   As I promised, I write to say that
in gallant stile, I bore your acceptable present of a cap over the
Rocky Mountains and in perfect saf[e]ty arr[i]ved a[s] far as this
on our long route Latt. 41 deg. 45 min. Long.........

Perhaps you may think it strange that I write when I have so
little to say I do so to induce a correspondence with one who is

well able to inform me of the state of affairs at home and who perhaps will be willing to take the trouble to inform me. We have in this country little to interest the mind when once the novelty of white Bears Buffaloes and Indians is worn off which is now pretty well the case with me. Mr. Nuttall is with me and well and has made an immense collection of new plants preserved also there is a Mr. Townsend who has found a good variety of new birds and preserved them. I shall establish a fort on Lewis River which will be about 150 miles west of this for the purpose of trade and then go to the mouth of Columbia River for the further prosecution of it.

Should you consent to correspond you can leave your letters at Mess. Tucker & Williams Central Wharf. In the meantime accept for yourself and family my best wishes

Respectfully yr obt Servt.   Nathl. J. Wyeth

CCXVII.

Hams Fork of the Colorado of the West   June 21st   1834

Bro Charles,

All well, but I am afraid not doing as well as might be expected but will do all I can "and then trust to providence." My affairs are at the present in too unsettled a state to express any opinion of the event. I shall write you again by the vessell. In the mean time I am going about 150 miles west of this to build a Fort and that done shall proceed to the Columbia to build another there for fishing and then the Deil knows where after Beaver.

Give my love to your wife and believe me that old kindness is not diminished on the contrary I look back to the fondness that has so long sweetened our intercourse as the Brightest spot on memorys green and the brighter for the darkness and desolation which encompasses me.

yr. afte Brother   Nathl. J. Wyeth

CCXVIII.

Hams Fork of the Colorado of the West   June 21st   1834

Bro. Leonard

I do not know what mood to write you in. Is money scarce? If I knew so I would indite you the Blackest kind of a letter and dip my pen in gall and wormwood and indulge my own fancy while tallying with yours.

Affairs in this region are going bad   Murder is rife and distrust among themselves makes the whites an easy prey to Indians. There has been little Beaver caught and of that little I get less than I ought. As yet there is no positive indication of the event of this buisness. I shall do all I can and if those at home do not get discouraged it will yet turn out well but of this I am afraid.

I leave this about the 1st July and then go west about a hundred and fifty miles W. on the Lewis River to make a fort for trade thence to the Columbia to build another then out trapping and trading with a party. I shall write you by the vessell and hope to have good news to send but if not shall say nothing. Here are plenty of Buffaloe and other good things to eat and so far no Indians to trouble us, but continual watching is tiresome and at last men get willing to lay down and take their chance. I hope your difficulties have ceased and with less damage to your affairs than you apprehended still I think let what will come you will fare as well as the best and come out bright at last.

Give my respects to Mess. Osgoods and their families and my regular built[but?] hearty good will to you[r] lady and little ones, and believe me

yr. afte. Brother Nathl. J. Wyeth.

CCXIX.

Hams Fork of the Colorado of the West June 30th 1834
Mess. Von Phull & McGill
Gent. I herewith enclose a draft, Fitzpatric Sublette & Bridger on Sublette & Campbell $1002.81 twelve mos. from date dated July 1st 1834 also one same parties 4 months $864.12 same date. These drafts or the proceeds of them you will please collect or hold subject to the directions of Mess. Tucker & Williams of Boston.

I take this opportunity to say that my journey so far has been prosperous and pleasant and attended [with] no accident and to express to you my sincere wishes for your health and prosperity.

I am yr. obt. Servt. Nathl. J. Wyeth.

CCXX.

Hams Fork of the Colorado of the West July 1st 1834
Latt. 41 deg. 45 min. Long. 112 deg. 34 min.
Mess Tucker & Williams
Gent. I arrived here on the 17th inst. and Wm Sublette arrived two days before me. This he was enabled to do by leaving one half of his goods and horses on the route, which of course I could not do. On arrival the Rocky Mountain Fur Co. refused to receive the goods alledging that they were unable to continue buisness longer, and that they had dis[s]olved, but offered to pay the advances made to M. G. Sublette and the Forfeit. These terms I have been obliged to accept altho they would not even pay the interest on cash advances for there is no Law here. I have also sold a few goods at low prices. The proceeds of the Forfeit &c and Sales after deducting a small amt. for payment of wages of men who have gone home, from this place, I have forwarded to Mess. Von Phull & McGill of Saint Lonis subject to your order, in one draft Four months from date July 1st 1834 for

$864.12½ and for $1002.81 same date 12 months both by Fitz-patric Sublette & Bridger, accepted by Sublette & Campbell of St Louis.

In addition to not fullfilling their agreement with me every ex-ertion is made to debauch my men in which they have had some success, but I have hired enough of theirs to make up, and do not fear falling short of troops. These circumstances induce me to quit their neighborhood as soon as possible.

I shall proceed about 150 miles west of this and establish a fort in order to make sale of the goods which remain on my hands. I have sent out messengers to the Pawnacks, Shoshonees, Snakes, Nez Perces and Flatheads to make robes and come and trade them at this Post. I am under the impression that these Indians will make a good quantity of Robes whenever they find they can sell them and I believe the Transportation will not be too expensive for the value of the article beside which I have no doubt that toler-able good returns of Beaver may be made at this post. I propose to establish it on a river called Portneuf on Snake or Lewis River.

I feel much disappointed that the contract was not complied with. Had M. G. Sublette been able to come I think it would have been. I much fear that the gentlemen at home will get dis-couraged if no returns are made the first year. I shall do the best I can but cannot now promise anything immediate. If I find on arrival at the mouth of the River that Lambert has not done much I shall think myself justified in detaining him another year.

I have drawn no drafts from these mountains.

Bonneville & Co. I have not seen, but he is not far from me on my proposed route. I fear that he has done nothing of conse-quence. I shall endeavour to take home his Beaver what there is of it if I can get an adequate price. I think his concern is finished.

I should forward you an Invoice of goods on hand and a memor-andum of transactions here but have not time without delaying my march. Capt. Thing altho a first rate man is even a worse scribe than myself and it is all we can do to make the proper charges and to look after our men and Horses and having to lose some time in making a fort, time is the more precious. I think that I will be with the vessell about the 10th Sept. next and af-ter arranging at the Post on the Columbia shall try my fortune at a winter Hunt for Beaver.

I have now with me 126 horses and mules in good order and 41 persons all told that are in the employ, and can hire as many more as I want. The amount due for wages is trifling. Almost all the men take up as fast as they earn, and would faster if I would let them, in goods at about 500 per ct. on the original cost. Our expenses after this year will be very small, and I have strong hopes as ever of success notwithstanding appearances so far.

I am yrs   Nath. J. Wyeth

CCXXI.

Hams Fork   July 1st   1834

Mr. G. Sublette
         Dear Sir   I arrived at [the] Rendesvous at the mouth
of [the] Sandy on the 17th June. Fitzpatric refused to receive the
goods he paid however, the forfieit and the cash advance I made
to you this however is no satisfaction to me.   I do not accuse you
or him of any intention of injuring me in this manner when you
made the contract but I think he has been bribed to sacrifice my
interests by better offers from your brother. Now Milton, buisness
is closed between us, but you will find that you have only bound
yourself over to receive your supplies at such price as may be in-
flicted and that all that you will ever make in the country will go
to pay for your goods, you will be kept as you have been a mere
slave to catch Beaver for others.
         I sincerly wish you well and believe had you been here these
things would not have been done.   I hope that your leg is better
and that you will yet be able to go whole footed in all respects.
                    I am Yr Obt. Servt.   N. J. Wyeth.

CCXXII.

Hams Fork of the Colorado of the West   July 2d   1834

Mess Von Phull & McGill
                    Gent.   I enclose three small drafts drawn by
me on Fitzpatric & Co whole amt. $98.25, which please collect
and hold to the order of Mess.Tucker & Williams and oblige
                    Your obt Servt   N. J. Wyeth.

CCXXIII.

Bear River   July 5th   1834

Fr[i]end Ermatinger
                    Your esteemed fav. of [the] 12th ulto. reached
me by the politeness of Mr. Newell on Hams fork of Green River.
Mr. N. also informed me of the particulars of the battle with the
Blkfeet.   It must have been a capital mixture of Wine and Gun-
powder.   I am happy to hear that you had some success last year
but am afraid that you will do but little this season.
         I am quite happy to hear that the Doctor remains at Vancouver.
I shall soon have the pleasure of seeing him.   I suppose that Mckay
has "thought of it" by this time and perhaps felt of it too, and
you too seem to have done more than thought of it.
         The latter part of your letter I shall answer when I see you,
which will be, I think in the course of the year.
         .I am now on my way to meet a vessell that I sent from Boston
to the mouth of the Columbia and hope to be there by the 1st
Sept.

You have also enclosed a letter for Mr. Payette whose son is now with me.

I came up with goods and about 50 men 130 horses. The goods I will have to leave for sale somewhere her[e]abouts with part of the men. I have got no Beaver and have sold but little and that for Drafts which I hope are good

I have again to repeat to you the advice which I before gave you not to come with a small party to the Am. Rendesvous. There are here a great collection of Scoundrels.

I have a great desire to see you and repay you in part for all the kindness which I received from you last year. Please give my respects to Mr. Horon and all my accquaintances that you may happen to see and believe me

yr obt Servt and Fr[i]end   Nath. J. Wyeth

CCXXIV.

Bear River   July 5th   1834

Mr Francis Payette

Dear Sir   I received your esteemed fav. of 14th May from Fort Nez Perces.

Your son is now with me and will go to the mouth of the Columbia to arrive there about the 1st Sept. He has learned to speak English to read write and cypher tolerably well. He learns fast considering how broken his time has been. We teach him a little on the route but cannot do as much as I could wish. He is an active lad and appears contented. I should be pleased to hear from you at all times and especially good news. Letters addressed to the care of the Doctor at Vancouver would reach me.

I am yr obt Servt.   N J Wyeth

CCXXV.

Sept 1st   1834 (at Grand Ronde)

Capt. Bonneville

Dear Sir   Yours of this morning I have, and in answer can only say that I shall send a clerk and an outfit of goods up to the Fort as soon as I get down, and shall come myself with it as far as where you now are, and probably be there in about 7 weeks from this time. I will enlarge the outfit a little so as to meet this trade, and will trade with them personally at your present camp, if they will be there, or I will send a clerk to them at any place they shall designate, provided they do so before my passing the Grande Ronde. The time and place must be designated in time in order that I may give the proper directions to the clerk.

I shall bring up goods so that in case you should alter your mind as to purchasing you could still get a supply. But if I could see

you personally at the Grande Ronde when I return it is likely
that we might make a joint buisness of it.

It is very like that I may detain the Brig until next summer,
in which case I would like to freight home your furs, which I will
do at 37½ per lb. Insurance included and receive them at the
Grand Ronde.

[No signature.]

CCXXVI.

[No address given.] Sept 1st 1834

Capt Bonneville

Dear Sir I got your note of to day late this evening, and am obliged to you for the trouble you have taken. I will
meet the Nez Perces at the A-show-to River within 8 weeks. I
Hope to meet yot before this, and would be pleased to make a
joint affair of it much better than to proceed alone.

Your Beaver traded from the Skiuses [Cayuses] is so much
seized from the common enemy in trade, so far so good.

Respectfully yrs. Nathl. J. Wyeth

CCXXVII.

Copy of letters of introduction addressed to Leond Jarvis Esq. J.
Wyeth, L. I. Wyeth Chas. Wyeth and James Brown in fav. of
Capt W. Stewart.

Oct 6th 1834 Columbia River.

Permit me to introduce to your acquaintance Capt William
Stewart an English gentleman who has been traveling in the
Rocky Mountains during the last year. From his intimate acquaintance with the affairs of the Mountains he will be able to
satisfy such enquiries as you may wish to make respecting those
regions. Any attention that you can shew him will much oblige
me.

& &c N. J. W.

CCXXVIII.

Columbia River Oct 6th 1834

Capt William Stewart

Dear Sir Enclosed you have a few letters addressed to some of my frends. They will be happy to see you and
to hear from me and if convienient you will oblige me by de-
livering them. Also enclosed you have your account which you
can pay to Mess. Tucker & Williams, or to either of the gentlemen to whom the letters are addressed and request them to do it.

I am yr. obt. Servt. N. J. W.

CCXXIX.

Columbia River Oct. 6th 1834 (40 miles above the mouth.)
Frederic Tudor Esq. (Boston.)

Dear Sir Since mine of 20th June last I have built

a Fort on Lewis River and raised the Am. Flag in a new region amid the din of powder and the effects of alcohol common on such occasions. I assure you the Fort looks quite as warlike as a pile of of ice but not quite so proffitable. After accomplishing this I made for this place and met the vessell on the 11th Sept. she having then just arrived after a disasterous passage of 8 months caused by being struck by lightening off Valparaiso. Consequently I am obliged to delay the vessell until another year which will delay for that period at least any decision as to the duration of this buisness, it looks black enough at the present time to induce an opinion that it must terminate soon one way or the other.

I find by some English publications that you[r] ice adventure to East Indies attracts much attention. Should this branch of your buisness appear to be of value would it not be possible to raise up some trade from this coast to enable you to send vessells from this to Calcut[t]a. I think the ice might be obta[i]ned a little north of this, I can not think if any cargo that could be brought here from the East Indies.

I am anxious to hear how the speculation ended and if you find sufficient encouragement to continue it, also how your ordinary ice buisness has succeeded the last year and what has been the result of your coffee affair. Permit me to ask the favour of a letter from you by the first opportunity.

I am now buisy in making an establishment on the Multnomah about 50 miles from its mouth and one on the Columbia at this place. This winter I go up Lewis River to make one more Fort on its waters and one on the south side of the Great Salt Lake. In the Spring I shall return and ascertain if I can put up a cargo of Salmon.

With wishes for all manner of prosperity for you,

I am yr. obt. Servt. N. J. W.

CCXXX.

Columbia River   Oct 6th   1834

Jas. W. Fenno Esq. (Boston)

Dear Sir Since mine of 20th June I have built the Fort that I then mentioned on Lewis River, Long 112 deg. 30 min. W. Latt 43 deg. 14 min. N. I arrived on the Columbia and met my vessell on the 11th Sept. she having been struck by lightening on the passage out and detained in consequence to repair at Valparaiso. She entirely missed the salmon season and I am obliged to detain her to another year.

I still think of the old buisness and hope if this fails to find an opening left to resume it. When I shall be at home is uncertain. This buisness looks very bad at this time. We have failed in every thing for the first year. I shall do all I can one year more, which will I think shew whether anything is to be done here or not, and I will not be long in closing the concern when I find that there is nothing to be made.

You will be careful not to make any disclosures as it regards the prospects of our buisness here which might be injurious.

I am anxious to hear from you and obtain information of how the agitated question now stands. In the mean time believe me your obt Servt   N. J. W.

CCXXXI.

Columbia River   Oct 6th   1834

Friend Brown

My last was from Hams Fork of the Colorado of the West since which time I have been building a Fort on the Snake or Lewis Fork of the Columbia which I named Fort Hall which took me until the 6th August on which day the Am. Standard was raised in regions remote from its usual habitation and amid the noise of revelry and gun powder it floated in the gaze of the astonished Savages. After accomplishing this I proceeded to the mouth of the Columbia where on the 11th ulto. I met our ship. She had on her way out been struck by lightening which occasioned a detention of three months by which our season for fishing was entirely lost. I shall detain her until another year and if she is then not able to bring home good returns I shall close this concern as soon as possible and return home with a flea in my ear.

My route from this to the Salmon season of next year will be from this place to Fort Hall Latt. 43 deg. 14 min. N. Long 113 deg 30 min. W. thence to the Great Salt Lake where I propose to build another Fort and thence back to this place to be here by the 15 May next to be ready for the Salmon.

I am extremly buisy and can not say much but wish you and your family all the good wishes you can imagine

Yr fr[i]end and Servt   N. J. W.

CCXXXII.

Columbia River   Oct 5th   1834

Dear Wife

I am here but have had no good luck. The vessell was struck by lightening on her way out and detained so long that the salmon season was past. She will therefore have to remain here until another year. In the mean time I shall cruise about the country and see what I can find.

I have built a Fort on Snake river near the middle of the Continent, one here, and made a farm on the Multnomah. If by another year I find that the buisness is to be successfull I shall send home for you, if not I will come home myself.

I hope you mak[e] your self comfortable and happy. It is the only good policy to enjoy ourselves while we can

Yr afte. Husband   N. J. W.

CCXXXIII.

[No address or date]

Jacob Wyeth Esq.

I am here buisy as can be fitting out parties making farms, Forts, and preparing for next years fishing. The vessell met with an accident which detained her so long on her passage that this years salmon fishing entirely failed. I shall try it one year more and if then there is no better success to be had I shall quit it and come home and attend to whatever buisness I can find wher[e]by to make a living.

I hope that no further difficulty with our tenant has disturbed your comfort and that all things about the place go on well. From what I heard when I was at St. Louis Jacob must be married by this time and if so I suppose you have heard of it. From the representation of very respectable people from Gelena he is quite a reformed man diligent and successful in his profession and respected by those who know him. The lady to whom he was about to be tied is said to be of the first respectability and every way worthy. I have no doubt that she will exercise a very salutary influence over him.

I can not say when you may expect to see me but in the meantime I am well here and with a little more success could be very happy.

I am yr afte Son   N. J. W.

CCXXXIV.

Columbia River   Oct 6th   1834

Brother Leonard

I have no good news to impart. The vessell miscarried owing to having been struck by lightening on her way out so that our fishing is defer[r]ed to another year. After so long an abstinence I feel hungry for a little success. I have built a Fort as I mentioned in my last on Snake or Lewis River in Latt 43 deg. 14 min N. Long 113 deg. 30 min. W. and raised the Am. Standard in a new region amid the noise of guns and the Sound of revelry. I met the vessell to a day, and two months after both expected to arrive here. I have commenced a fine farm on the Multnomah. Were all I wish to see, and they are not many, here I think I should never wish to return. I journey this winter into the interior to the vicinity of the Great Salt Lake and shall probably make 2 more Forts, and return hither about the 15th May next to see what can be made of the Salmon fish[e]rys. If at the close of next year our prospects are not brighter you may expect to see me back again, following with fresh spirits some new or old plans of profit or improvement.

I only write to you to evince that my mind still looks back to the good and worthy that it has left behind, that it compares the

Hideous squaw with polished white woman the faithless savag
with the upright and buisy white man, and sees the difference
Give my respects to the Mess. Osgoods and their family and m
love to your wife and children and let them hear the name of thei
uncle if they do not see him.

Yr. afte Bro.   N. J. W.

CCXXXV.

Columbia River   Oct. 6th   1834

Bro. Charles
   Since my last of June 21st 1834 I have made the establishmen
then spoken of on Snak[e] River in Latt. 43 deg. 14 min. N Lon;
113 deg. 30 min. West and raised the Stars and Stripes amid ex
plosions of gun powder and whiskey according to custom, an
they now wave to the wind in the naked wastes of centra
America a wonderment to the simple savage who can not con
ceive the meaning of so much disturbance. I have now made
farm on the Multnomah on a prairie of about 15 miles long border
ing on the river which is nearly as large as the Ohio surrounded b
beautiful and well assorted timber and watered by a good mil
stream. The soil is beautiful. If some of the things on whic
the minds eye casts a "longing lingering" look where [were] here
might be content to rest from my labors and lay my bones in thi
remote wild.
   I leave here in a few days on a voyage to the interior and sha
establish two more Forts one of which will be near the Great Sal
Lake if I can find any tribe of Indians who can give trad
enough to support it.
   You must excuse my writing short letters I have much to d
in a short time and some things that can not be ommitted
Give my respects to Mr. Norris and family, and be assured o
my best wishes for you and yours

Yr Afte Bro.   Nathl J Wyeth

CCXXXVI.

Columbia River   Oct. 6th   1834

Leond. Jarvis Esq.
   Dear Uncle Since mine of June 21st from
Hams fork I have as I then proposed built a Fort on Snake o
Lewis River in Latt 43 deg. 14 min. N. and Long 113 deg. 30 min
W. which I named Fort Hall from the oldest gentleman in th
concern. We manufactured a magnificent flag from some un
bleached sheeting a little red flannel and a few blue patches, sa
luted it with damaged powder and wet it in vil[l]a[i]nous alcohol
and after all it makes, I do assure you, a very respectable appear
ance amid the dry and desolate regions of centra
America. Its Bastions stand a terror to the sculkin

Indian and a beacon of saf[e]ty to the fugitive hunter. It is man[n]ed by 12 men and has constantly loade[d] in the Bastions 100 guns and rifles. These bastions command both the inside and the outside of the Fort. After building this Fort I sent messengers to the neighboring nations to induce them to come to it to trade, and am now about starting with an equipment of goods for the winter trade. After leaving these at the Fort I shall locate and build two more one of which will be scituated near the Great Salt Lake. I shall return to this place about the 15th May next to see what can be done in the Fishing buisness.

I am now about 75 miles from the mouth of the river, on the South Side. We have built a few buildings for store houses, smiths and Cooper shops, and dwellings. We are near the mouth of the Multnomah. About 40 miles up this river I have begun a farm on a beautiful prairie of about 15 miles long one end touching the river a good mill stream in the center the whole surrounded with good and well assorted timber, of fine soil and mild climate, much game, in fact all that a man ought to have, but still one is tempted to exclaim "Oh solitude, where are the charms that philosophers have seen in Thy face?"

After building Fort Hall as befor[e] stated I proceed[ed] hither and on the 14th ulto. met the Brig then just arrived and coming up the river to find me. She was struck by lightening on the way out which occasioned a delay of about 3 months in consequence of which our fishing season was entirely lost. I shall therefore detain her until another season and then try.

We suffered nothing coming out but lived sometime very short and poor after leaving the Buffaloe country but this is what all who come this way must expect.

I have given a letter of introduction to Capt. William Stewart of the British army to you. He is a gentleman of high family and general attainments and having travelled in the Mountains for upwards of a year past, I thought that you might be pleased to see him.

Now I desire that you will give my best compliments to my aunt and assure her that all the time I have been addressing my self to you I have been thinking of her and her many kindnesses of old times, this is not a country in which I forget the ladies.

I am yrs. &c.   N. J. W.

CCXXXVII.

Copy of note left for Mr. Richardson at the mouth of a fork of the River Des Shutes.

Jany. 7th 1835

Mr Richardson

Sir   In case I return to this place before you I shall leave a note on this pole with directions. I think you had not in any case better stay up this fork more than three weeks, unless the prospect for beaver is very good. At the time you arrive here if you find no note from me, you can either go up the stream in search of beaver, and remain until I send the horses, or send for you, or return to camp as you like. When I go down I shall leave notice at the mouth of each creek in order that you may know my movements, and if you follow me up stream I wish you to leave a notch cut in my poles, one up one down in order that I may know if you are above or below me. Also at each creek that you go up leave a peeled pole and one also on your return.

Yrs   Nathl J Wyeth

CCXXXVIII.

Wappatoo Island   Ap 3d 1835

Friend Weld
          I write, but do not know when I will have an opportunity to send. I am in the mood which you know is always enough for me. If I were at Cambridge the wine would suffer to night and you pretty well know who would be the company. I have had a severe winter of it. All my men have been sick except myself and one man and nothing but pure obstinacy has kept me from being hauled up. It may be interesting to you to know a little of what I am doing. In the first place I got here somehow not worth relating. When here found my Brig not ar[r]ived but outside the bar. Went down the river and met her coming up. This was on the 11th Sept. and entirely after salmon time. Her late arrival was occasioned by having been struck with lightening and being in consequence obliged to put in to Valparaiso to repair. After shaking hands, set about arranging a party to send to a Fort which I have built among the Rocky Mts. This party consisted of Capt. Thing 13 Sandwich Islanders and 8 whites. They proceeded about 200 miles up the Columbia inland at the same time I took a party of 4 Sandwich Islanders and 16 whites and followed inland 150 and got news that Capt Things Islanders had all run away from him. This obliged me to spare all my Islanders, and all but 6 of my whites to enable Capt. Thing to proceed to Fort Hall. With the residue I proceeded to look up the deserters. I struck south thinking that they might have started for California. This was the middle of Nov. During Dec. Jany. and Feb. I got no news from them. About the first of March I heard that some of them were near the Columbia. On this I changed my route and struck that river where I learned from the Inds. that 7 of them had passed down five days before. I followed and overtook them about 80 miles from the mouth of the river 7 in number and took them to Fort William our establishment on Wappatoo Island about 75 miles up the Columbia at the mouth of the Multnomah. Two were

killed by the Indians one was drowned and one froze to death
in the Mts. and two are still unac[c]ounted for as yet. On arriving
here I set about preparing for fishing. Have commenced a
house Boat 70 feet long for a conveyance about to the different
fisherys. Have finished a canoe 60 feet long 3 feet wide 2 ½
deep of one tree which has not a shake or [k]not in it, and this
after cutting off thirty feet of clear stuff from the same tree, and
still this is by no means a large tree here. I think I could find
trees here free from shakes or [k]nots that would square 4 feet one
hundred feet long. It is quite a job to make one of these canoes.
I have heard to day that our Brig has arrived at the mouth of
the river from the Sandwich Islands whither she went last
winter with a cargo of Lumber, and I expect more buisness more
company and more provisions soon the last not the least desirable
of the three. This Wappatoo Island which I have selected for
our establishment is about 15 miles long and about average
of three wide. On one side runs the Columbia on the other the
Multnomah. It consists of woodlands and praire and on it there
is considerable deer and those who could spare time to hunt
might live well but a mortality has carried off to a man its inhabitants and there is nothing to attest that they ever existed except their decaying houses, their graves and their unburied bones
of which there are heaps. So you see as the righteous people of New
England say providence has made room for me and without doing
them more injury than I should if I had made room for myself
viz Killing them off. I often think of the old knot of cronies
about the town with whom I used to spend so much time especi-
al[l]y of an evening.   When I sit down in my lodge on the ground
and contrast the past with the present and wonder if the
future will give as much difference and which way the difference
will be for better or worse?

It has rained almost continually from last Oct. to this time but
still there has been no cold weather except in the mountains at
great elevations.

Now I do not wish this letter published I do hate every thing
in print.

I am yr Friend and Servt.   Nathl. J. Wyeth

CCXXXIX.

Fort William· Sept 6th 1835

Frederic Tudor Esq.

Sir My last was dated Oct. 6th 1834 from this place.
I have not received one letter from the States since I left. A
package came into the Indian country for me but fell into the
hands of another Co. and was detained. Possibly you might have
writ[t]en by that channel.   This buisness has not been successful
in any of its branches therefore it will terminate soon. I shall
not order another equipment to this country until I see again

those concerned with me, and if I know the people they will be the last to go very far in any buisness that commences unprofitably. If I meet with no fatal accident I shall be in Boston by the 1st Nov. 1836 and probably if any opening opens adequate to my wants I shall not after leave it. I need not disguise from you that I must have a living somewhere and that there is no kind of buisness for which I am in any way competent except my original vocation, which I so heartily detest that I will loose my scalp before I will reengage in it, and the Ice buisness, and that in the latter I have no prospect except through yourself. The buisness I am in must be closed not that it might not be made a good one but because those who are now engaged in it are not the men to make it so. The smallest loss makes them "fly the handle" and such can rarely succeed in a new buisness. This your own experience will justify. Personally I have no means to prosecute the buisness further and, however mortifying, must give it up. My intention is to return and if I can obtain any scituation that I am not ashamed of, to remain, if not the woods will alway[s] supply the wants of one who is not lazy and where pride is not concerned wants but little. These things I state in plain language because I for[e]see that when I may arrive in Boston the case will admit of no delay. I have then to make the last election of my course for life and whether such course prove comfortable to myself or not I shall stick to it. I cannot hope after what I have done that you should have so much regard to my wishes as to alter any arrangement that you may have made of your buisness in order to give me a place but I am bound to avail myself of all the chances in my reach to live.

Since writing you last we have lost by drowning, Scalping &c 14 persons none by natural death altho the country is sickly. Loss of property from hostility of Indians has been considerable.

I have taken the liberty to send you a ½ bbl. of plain salted salmon which I hope you will find good. We do not this year send home more than half a cargo.

I am off for the interior about the first next month. The winter will not admit of starting later. I am therefore obliged to trust the putting up of the salmon for my friends at home to Capt. Lambert. Should there be any unsuitableness in it, I ask you to excuse it with the same good feeling you used to overlook more serious failings.

I am Your obt Servt. Nathl. J. Wyeth

CCXL.

Fort William   Sept 6th   1835

Friend Brown
           Doubtless you have observed in your quondam associate some *small* imperfections, and altho he may now have no

temptation, yet the grain may be stil[l] in him. A quotation from
an author you used sometimes to read will do for his creed
>"My son these maxims make a rule,
>And lump them ay the gether;
>The rigid righteous is a fool,
>The rigid wise anither:
>The cleanest corn that e'er was dight
>May hae some pyles o' Chaff in;
>So ne'er a fellow creature *slight*
>For random fits o' daffin.['']

I am disappointed in not having rec[e]ived a single letter from
home since I left the frontier settlements, while others have. I
know it is not reasonable that those who loose but one companion should feel as much as those who loose all. A letter to the
last is in the shape of food to the hungry man. The benevo-
lent bestow in proportion to the want, therefore you should write
me two letters for one. I am not scolding you for your good but
for my own. I am in hopes to make you write either by force or
fraud but whether you do so or not I am determined to continue
the correspondence until you acknowledge me to be as bad as the
old man who rode Sind Bad the Sailor and *perhaps* you may get
rid of me in the same way.

My last was dated Oct. 6th 1834 from this place since which
time there has been the Devils own work in this Country 14 of our
people drowned and killed and much property lost. Personally I
am still happy go lucky with only a broken toe and two or three
upsettings in cold water. This you know I am used to. I expect to come to Boston about Nov. 1st 1836, perhaps to stop. We
this year put up about a half a cargo of Salmon ½ bbl. of which
you will find marked with your name also one for my Father one
for my wife for Leond Jarvis Chas Wyeth Leond I Wyeth. N. J
Wyeth and Frederic Tudor. Any expense please charge to me.

Will you give my sincere respects to your wife and a kiss all the
little ones known and unknown and believe me one of those
whose friendships hold from youth to age who has some ac-
quaintances who are not friends and some friends who are not ac-
quaintances and one who is friend and acquaintance, and only
one.

Yrs &c Nathl. J. Wyeth.

CCXLI.

Columbia River   Sept 20th   1835

Leonard Jarvis Esq.   (Baltimore Md.)

Dear Uncle My last was from this place dated
Oct. 6th 1834. We have had a bad season for salmon. About
half of a cargo only obtained. The salmon part of the buisness
will never do. I have sent ½ a bbl. to you which you will receive through Mr. Brown. Capt. Lambert attends to putting

them up, on the voyage, as there is not time for me to do so before. If there should be any thing wrong you will excuse it on this account. I am now a little better from a severe attack of billious Fever. I did not expect to recover, and am still a wreck. Our sick list has been this summer usually about one third the whole number and the rest much frightened. 13 Deaths have occurred beside some in the interior killed by the Indians. Some property has been lost also by Indians. I leave this in a few days for the interior to winter at Fort Hall. I intend in the spring to return to this place and take up goods then I shall turn my face toward the rising sun, and hope to have the pleasure of seeing you about the last of Oct. 1836. I some think of taking the route by Santi Fee and N. Orleans but hostilities of the Indians render it uncertain what route I may be obliged to take but without serious accident I shall not be far from that time. I am surrounded with difficulties beyond any former period of my life and without the health and spirit requisite to support them. In this scituation you can judge if memory brings to me the warnings of those (wiser and older) who advised a course which must at least have resulted in quietness. Yes memory lends its powers for torment. A few days ago she told me a tale which carried me back to early life, led me through the varying shades of days and years while at every step the tale grew darker and at last delivered me to [the] horrors of the present time. What at that moment they were you may imagine, a buisness scattered over half the deserts of the earth, and myse[l]f a powerless lump of matter in the extremity of mortal pain with little hope of surviving a day and if it could have been said "he never existed" glad to go down with that sun. But with coming health comes also a sense of the obligations that we are under and say to us "Up and be doing."

The above my Dear Uncle are the clouds of sickness they will pass off before I reach the mountains and the clear air of the upper country. I have received no letters from home since leaving. There has been however a great number intercepted by one of the Cos. in the mountains as I have heard. Perhaps you have written by that route. You will remember me to my Aunt desire her to accept that affectionate regard which she deserves from me. That she may pass without vicis[s]itude through life is the wish of at least one of her old pets. I will not presume to wish you any definite good wish but only that all things may tend to complete and fulfil your happiness.

believe me Dr Sir   Yr Affte. Nephew   Nathl. J. Wyeth

CCXLII.

Columbia River   Sept. 22d   1835

Bro Charles (Baltimore)

I am too buisy and too unwell to write

much even to you   It sometimes appears to me that the nearer
the person is to whom I write the less competent is the mode to
the ideas I would wish to express.   However this may be one
thing I know. That to my best friends I always write the short-
est letters in fact I had nearly writ[t]en you as short an epistle as
Caesars to the Senate viz "I am sick dead and buried" and yet I
am not "the Scipper" but the last principle of human life is not
extinct. Hope still maintains her throne and throws the mists of
futurity over the deformities and misfortunes that she cannot
hide.

Our salmon fishing has not succeeded.   Half a cargo only obtained. Our people are sick and dying off like rotten sheep of
billious disorders.   I shall be off by the first next month to the
mountains and winter at Fort Hall.   In the Spring I shall return
here then again to Fort Hall and start about June to see all in
the States, lucky if I get through with all this without accident.

I have sent ½ a bbl. Salmon to you which you will receive
through Mr. Brown.   I hope they will be good but as I cannot
personally attend to putting them up I will not insure it.   Now
Charley may God give you to enjoy life, may the wife be all a
wife should. and may the children be the solace of your age.

I am Yr. afte Bro   Nathl. J. Wyeth.

CCXLIII.

Columbia River   Sept. 22d 1835
Bro. Leonard   (N York)

You often complain of short letters but as I get no
return at all even short ones are enough for you.

Salmon half a cargo one third of our people on the sick list
continually, 17 dead to this date is the amount of the summer.
I am but just alive after having been so bad as to think of writing up my last letters.

I send you ½ a bbl. of Salmon but as I can not attend to putting
them up myself you will excuse any imperfection.   You will receive them through Mr. Brown.   I am off for the Mts. to winter at
Fort Hall in about 6 days.   I hope the winds of the hills will bring
me up.   I intend to return to this place in the Spring then to
Santi Fee thence home by about the last of Oct. 1836.

Please give my compliments to my sister and an affectionate
kiss to all my little nieces and nephew.   My respects also to the
Messrs Osgoods and believe me

yr afte. Bro.   Nathl J Wyeth

CCXLIV.

Columbia River   Sept 22d   1833[5]
Dear Parents

I avail myse[l]f of the last opportunity of writing

you for some time. I expect to be home by the 1st Nov. next
year therefore this will be my last until I see you.
  I have sent you ½ bbl. of Salmon which you will get through Mr.
Brown. I hope they will prove good but I could not put them up myself therefore if they are not quite right lay it to anyone but me. I
have been very sick but have recovered. The season has been
very sickly and we obtained but about a half a cargo of Salmon.
I am off for the mountains in about 6 days. You may be sure
I am much hurried or I would write a longer letter.
                          I am yr afte. Son   Nathl. J. Wyeth.

                          CCXLV.

                          Columbia River   Sept. 22d   1835
Dear Wife
              I have been very sick but have got well and shall be
on my way to the Mts. to winter at Fort Hall in about 6 days. I
expect to be home about 1st Nov. 1836. Mr Nuttall is here and
well. I have sent you ½ bbl. Salmon which I hope will be in
good order, I can not attend to putting them up myself therefore they may not be so good. The season has been very sickly.
We have lost by drowning and disease and warfare 17 persons to
this date and 14 now sick. Keep up good spirits my dear wife for
I expect when I come home to stop there and altho I shall be
poor yet we can always live. I hope to find my trees growing
when I come and all things comfortable. I think this will be
the last until I see you. Give my respects to your mother and
Aunt Rebecca my love to Sister Mary and Bro. Perry if you see
them. And believe me
                          Yr afte Husband   N. J. W.
       For letters after this date see small letter Book.
  [The book referred to has not yet been found.]

JOURNAL OF CAPTAIN NATHANIEL J. WYETH'S

EXPEDITIONS TO THE OREGON COUNTRY.

[The book containing the Journal has been mutilated. There are traces of the removal of four leaves just preceding the page that has the first of the narrative preserved. According to "Wyeth's Oregon Expedition" the Wyeth party on his first expedition left Independence, Mo., May 3rd., 1832. June 6th would thus have been the thirty-fifth day on the route.]

[June 6th, 1832.]
gray and my face like a plumb pudding the skin is entirely bare [?] of skin is entirely off one of my ears On the bluf[f]s the ghnats are equally troublesome but they do not annoy us much except in the day. Geese appear here mated and I have seen some broods of gooselings. Some rain last night. still barren and grass bad our horses about the same our men troubled with the relax toward night found buffaloe killed one which made a scanty meal for all hands for supper made 25 miles

7th Started out hunting killed two antelope about 10 saw a herd of Buffaloe crossing the River waited til they rose the Bank and commenced slaughter killed 3 and wounded many more these afforded a timely supply to the party and we ate heart[il]y. Saw today the first appearance of muskrat since leav-the settlements also Pelicans. Last night in cutting a tree for fuel caught two young grey Eagles one of which we ate and found it tender and good also a Badger saw some rattlesnakes and some other kinds not known to me the men [horses?] appear a little better the men [horses?] about the same Thr. 90 deg. wind S. E. my face so swelled from the musquitoes and ghnats that I can scarce see out of my eyes and aches like the tooth ache

9th I date this the same* on acc of a mistake of a day her[e]-tofore made 30 miles and yesterday 25 arrived at the Chimney or Elk Brick the Indian name this singular object looks like a monument about 200 feet high and is composed of layers of sand and lime stone in layers the sand blowing out lets the lime rock fall down and this action has in time reduced what was once a

---

*"Same" here seems to mean "as I do".

hill to a spire of nearly the same dimensions at top and bottom it
looks like a work of art and the layers like the ranges of stone it
is scituated about 3 miles from the river.   Rain and thunder at
night wind strong S. E. river as muddy as ever   the bluf[f]s for
the last 20 miles have occasionally a few stinted trees apparently
Pitch pine and cedar   the small streams that here empty into the
Platte are frequently dry near the river during the day while
above they are running free while at night there is running water
entirely to the river   Party in better order   Horses about the
same   we now judge ourselves within 4 days march of the Black
Hills
      10th.   28 miles,   2 Buffaloe
      11th   30 miles,   6 Buffaloe
      12th   Nothing remarkeable   crossed Wild Horse Creek coming
in from the S.

      13th   Came   in   sight   of   the   Black   hills   and crossed
Larrimee fork of the Platte   in getting over one of my rafts
broke the tow line   the raft went down stream lodged on a snag
and upset wetting most of the goods on it and loosing two Horse
loads as it lodged in the middle of the river and the stream [being]
very rappid the goods were with difficulty passed ashore   here
an alarm was occasioned by the appearance of 4 men on the bluf[f]s
behind us and an attack was expected every moment which would
have been bad as our party was much scattered in crossing
They However proved to be a part of a party of 19 men in the employ of Gant & Blackwell.   They last winter lost all but 3 of their
animals and in going to Sante Fee got enclosed by snow in the
mountains and nearly starved to Death, and at first they were
hard to tell from Indians or devils   they are now in good health
having felt well for some time   all of them joined Mr. Fitzpatricks
party and proceeded on foot with us to the mountains.   Killed an
antelope

      14th   started late and left the river at which we had en-
camped and proceeded 16 miles   killed one antelope and one elk

      15th   went out for game   killed one antelope, 2 deer 2 Buff-
aloe   made this day 20 miles and passed the first of the Black
hills   the country is now thinly wooded with Box Elder ash
Pitch pine cedar and cotton wood and a variety of small shrubs
among which are the cherry, currant and thorn   wild sage here
almost covers the country and is a plant of many years gro[w]th
      arrived at camp found the company had killed plenty of Buffaloe
and were encamped on a small stream coming in from the S. 20
mile s.

      16th   Warm in mng. cold and rainy in the afternoon a little
hard snow on the Peak of the Black hills   a white Bear was seen
this day   Black ones for some days past.   The lime rock still continues   primitive peb[b]les in the streams and on the knols   the

hills pointed up very sharp from the same cause as the Chimney
the country appears desolate and dreary in the extreme   no one
can conceive of the utter desolation of this region   nevertheless
the earth is decorated with a variety of beautifull flowers and all
unknown to me   hard travelling disenables our botanist to examine them   we have on the whole meat enough but the supply is
too unsteady.   There are here two kinds of Rabbits the largest
weighing about 15 lbs ears 6 inches long   plover and other marsh
birds a[re] common and some 2 or 3 kinds of Gulls.   Struck the
Platte river again   here about 100 yds wide the water high and
rapid   we here find a small kind of Parsnip the blossom yellow
root about 5 inches long ½ inch thick of more than one years
gro[w]th   the men appear better   Horses about the same   made
this day 20 miles

   17th   Wind high N. W.   Ther 40   a drear and cheerless day
made 25 miles   killed 3 Buffaloe 1 antelope 1 Deer   crossed 2
small streams from the Black hills running into the Platte   saw
some rabbits & white bears   Hops.

   18   reached the place for fording the platte

   19th   Passed over my goods during a severe wind without accident

   20th   Mr Subblettee passed over his goods and at night mooved
on about 3 miles

   21st   Made a long march of 30 miles during which one of my
Horses gave out   killed this day 3 Buffaloe and fired at a white
bear   arrived at camp at 11 ock at night.   I have ommitted
one day on the other side of the Platte   I date this right we arrived at Rock Independence at noon after a march of 15 miles

   23*   Yesterday we left the Platte and struck the Sweet water on
which this rock stands   it is scituated in a gorge within 30 feet
of the stream and is granite   today is warm   last night frost and
the two last days cold and disagreable from this time to 2nd July
frost each night and snow once   our course lay in various directions from S. W. to N. W. following the Sweet water and leaving
the first snowy mountains on the right hand   on the 29th we
crossed on to the head waters of the Colorado during all this time
we found abundance of Buffaloe the travelling good but the grass
poor   the streams all fordable but rapid   five streams have been
crossed to this time and we are now encamped on the 6th all
running into the Colorado   trout are found here also some beaver   Some of my men talk of turning back and I give them all
free liberty   many of my horses have given out and the rest are
failing fast and unless we soon come to better grass they will all
die and leave me on foot   the waters running into Lewis river

*The "23" is placed a little above and to the left of the word "left".
From the 21st on the journal was evidently not written up until the evening of July 2nd.

are not more than 8 miles distant, on the creek where we are
there are pine trees in shape lik[e] a Balsam tree leaves like a
pitch pine Bark rough yellowish and scaly The mountains in
this region are not conspicuous are isolated and admitting free
passage between them in any direction the creeks are sufficiently
numerous for watering but feed is poor the 1st [of] July we rested
all the afternoon a respite quite acceptable to our weary legs
Our average during these days about 20 miles but in some cases
quite circuitous White bears are seen but none have been killed.
Wolves and antelopes plenty, King fishers Our hunters have
just brought part of 4 Buffaloe At night encamped on the same
creek that we passed this mng. and soon after were visited by 6
men from Dripps & Fontenelles concern who with 13 others are
encamped 5 miles from this place. This night at about 12 ock.
we were attacked by Indians probably the Blackfoot. They approached within 50 yds. and fired about 40 shots into the camp
and some arrows they wounded three animals got 5 from Mr. Subblette One from an Independent hunter and 4 which I left out
of camp for better feed mine were all poor and sore backed and
useless

3rd Decamped and in company with the men above mentioned proceeded to their camp and passèd on to our route which
lay W. This night encamped on the waters of the Colorado 25
miles

4th Decamped and at noon crossed the divide and drank to
my friends with mingled feelings from the waters of the Columbia
mixed with alcohol and eat of a Buffaloe cow made this day 30
miles and 25 yesterday The snow clad mountains now entirely
surround us the streams this side increase rapidly. One bear
seen this day the grass much better and some fertile land here
the earth in some places was frozen snow yesterday and today.
Three of my men are sick and I have no spare animals for them.

5th We passed along a wooded River and through a very difficult road by its side so steep that one of my Horses loosing his
foothold in the path was rooled down about 100 feet into the river
he was recovered but so much injured as we had to leave him
shortly after. Made this day 20 miles

6th We marched early and at 2 ock stop[p]ed on Lewis river
and within 20 miles of the Trois Tetons three very conspicuous
snow covered mountains visible in all this region this river here
runs nearly S. and is divided over a bottom about 2 miles and into 8 streams very rapid and difficult these we forded which consumed the time until night and encamped after making 18 miles
on the W. bank with no grass. in the morning of the 7th we
proceed[ed] up a small brook coming from a gap of the mountains
due south of the Trois Tetons and passed the range of mountains
of this range without much difficulty it is a good pass for such a
range and fresh animals would have no difficulty in passing

through it On the highest point we had snow accompanied with heavy thunder and being out of meat fed upon the inner bark of the Balsam trees a tree similar if not the same with the Eastern Balsam[?] At Night we encamped at the foot of the pass on the western side and at the commencement of a large valley with several streams running through it into Lewis River surrounded with high and snow clad mountains The weather is here warm in the day time but frost every night the grass is good the land ordinary. On the 8th we proceed[ed] into the plain and after a march of 10 miles arrived at the rendesvous of the hunters of this region here we found about 120 Lodges of the Nez Perces and about 80 of the Flatheads a company of trappers of about 90 under Mr. Dripps of the firm of Dripps & Fontenelle connected with the American Fur Co. Many independent Hunters and about 100·men of the Rocky Mountain Fur Co under Mess Milton Sublette and Mr Frapp. I remained at this encampment until the 17th during which time all my men but 11 left me to these I gave such articles as I could spare from the neces[s]ities of my own Party and let them go. While here I obtained 18 Horses in exchange for those which were worn out and for a few toys such as Beads Bells red and Blue cloth, Powder and Balls fish hooks vermillion old Blanketts We also supplied ourselves with Buffaloe robes we have now a good outfit and here we found plenty of meat which can be had of the Indians for a trifle On the 17th we put out and ste[e]red S. E. in direction to a pass through the same mountains by which we entered the valley these Mts. run E. & W. and the pass I refer to is the next E. of the one refer[r]ed to and through it the waters of this valley reach Lewis River which is on the S. side of this range at night we encamped within about 8 miles of the commencement of the pass. On the 18th we did not leave camp when near starting we observed 2 partys of Indians coming out of the pass about 200 in number with but few horses after securing our camp our riders went out to meet them and soon found them to be Blackfeet a little skirmish ensued one of the Blackfeet was killed and his Blankett and robe brought into camp on this the Indians made for the timber the women and children were seen flying to the mountains at this time only 42 men being the party of Mess Milton Sublette & Frapp mine and a few Independent Hunters were in sight and the Indians were disposed to give us their usual treatment when they meet us in small bodies but while the Indians we[re] making their preparations we sent an express to camp which soon brought out a smart force of Nez Perces Flatheads and whites the Indians finding they were caught fortified themselves in a masterly manner in the wood. We attacked them and continued the attack all day there were probably about 20 of them killed and 32 horses were found dead They decamped during the night leaving most of their utensials lodges &c and many of the dead we have lost

3 whites killed 8 badly wounded among which is Mr Wm. Sublette who was extremely active in the battle about 10 of the Indians were killed or mortally wounded of the Nez Perces and Flatheads in the morning we visited their deserted fort they had dug into the ground to reach water and to secure themselves from our shot   It was a sickening scene of confusion and Blood-[s]head one of our men who was killed inside* their fort we found mutilated in a shocking manner   on the 19th we removed back to our former ground to be near our whole force and to recruit the wounded and bury the dead. We think that 400 lodges or about 600 warriors of the Blackfeet are on the other side of the pass and if they come they must be met with our whole force in which case the contest will be a doubtful one.   We have mad[e] Horse pens and secured our camp in as good a manner as we can and wait the result   this affair will detain us some days.   On 24th we again moved out of the valley in the same direction as at first viz about S. E. and encamped at night in the gorge of it   during the march I visited the scene of our conflict for the first time since the battle   the din of arms was now changed into the noise of the vulture and the howling of masterless dogs   the stench was extreme   most of the men in the fort must have perished   I soon retired from this scene of disgusting butchery   On the 25th we proceeded through the pass which is tolerably good and in a direction of about S. W. by S. and encamped 15 miles on Lewis River (here concentrated into one rapid stream) and about 30 miles S. of where we crossed it in going into the valley   we are now employed in making bull boats in order to cross it   One Buffaloe and some antelope killed today   26 crossed the river in a bull boat without accident in 4 hours and moved on in a westerly direction about 4 miles when we struck into a deep ravine with a little water in it   this ravine is bordered by high presipices on each side and is small   3 miles up this we encamped for the night this stream is called Muddy   as there is several of this name it is requisite to distinguish this by the cognomen of Muddy that falls into [the] "Lewis"

26th   we moved up the Muddy until we found the forks of it then followed the Right hand say 3 miles then took a south direction and struck another stream (small) and running in the opposite direction   this we followed about 5 mil[e]s making 15 this day and encamped

27th.   We moved down the stream until its junction with another called Grays creek   which we crossed and assended a high bluff and travelled an average course of S. W. and encamped on a small creek making 15 miles this day   2 days since I first this side the mountain met with the prickly pear and since leaving

---

*The word "inside" is crossed out with pencil and "near" written above it with pencil.

the valley of the Rendesvous the fruit that was green one day
is ripe the next. The nights are still frosty but the days are very
warm as in N. E. at this time fruits we have 3 kinds [of] currants one of gooseberry all different from those of the U. S. and
Service berrys all the first are sour the latter sweet the country through which we have travelled for these two days past
has a strong volcanic appearance the streams occupy what appear to be but the cra[c]ks of an over heated surface the rocks
are blown up in blubbers like a smiths cinders some rocks ten
feet through are but a shell being hollow. A substance abounds
like bottle glass of about the same weight not so transparent
about as brittle the fracture is smooth and glossy with the exception of the cracks as above the country is tolerably level for
a mountainous country but excessively dry. During our first
days march from Lewis River beside the ravine above mentioned we passed three craters of small volcanoes (as I suppose) and
I am told there is a boiling spring near the same place We here
find buffaloe plenty and fat and entirely different from those met
with in the Spring on the Platte it is preferable to the best beef.
Our party have taken lice from the Indians they are a great
trouble as well as the Musquitoes these last trouble us in the
day but the frost seals their wings at night when the first relieve
them until morning.

On the 28 we moved in a direction about S. W. and during the
march took the bearing of the Trois Tetons which was N. E. by
E. and I think 75 miles we made 7 miles and encamped on a
little stream meandering through a valley of about 100 acres of
fine Black land with the grass as good as the buffaloe and the
cold weather could admit of. Here we found plenty of cows and
more Bulls 13 of the first were killed they were fat and we stopped to make meat these cows were killed by running them down
which is a dangerous method expensive in horses and Requiring
much skill in Riding We of course were obliged to employ help
for none could be got by approaching while they were Running
them

29th We remained all day making meat with a hot sun this
morning sent 3 men down the creek fishing they caught 21 Salmon Trout and returned at 10 this afternoon it rained hard and
during the storm the squaw of one of the party was delivered of
a Boy in the bushes whither she had retired for the purpose it[s]
head was thickly covered with Black hair it was as white as is
usual with the whites in less than an hour afterwards the squaw
made her appearance in camp as well and able for a days travel
as usual it continued raining all night and until 8 of the 30
on which acc. our march was defer[r]ed for the day which was
afterward fine and our meat dried well. 4 Beavers were caught
from about 12 traps last night during this day one of the party
saw an indian which must have been a Blackfoot as otherwise he

would have come to camp yesterday and today we had Thunder
& Hail as well as rain.
     1st. Augt   I date this the 1st. on acc. of having missed a day in
the time past.   This day we made about 15 miles in a S. W.
direction and most of the way in a deep valley and encamped on
a small creek running into one called Blackfoot   this latter is the
second stream we have passed which em[p]ties into S. fork of Lewis
River   the first was called Grays River and is also small (this
since crossing Lewis River) Here we stopped until the 4th to
make meat of which I made enough to eat and no more while the
other two parties who had go[o]d buffaloe Riders and Horses made
considerable   while her[e] we lost one Horse while attempting to
Run Buffaloe by throwing his Rider and Running among the
Buffaloe and going off with them   I sent out a party to get fish
of two men   they Returned with about a peck of craw fish and a
dozen of trout   these average about 1lb and are fine eating.   We
have here the Sandhill Cranes in plenty.   On the 4th we moved
due south and crossed Blackfoot and struck over to a stream emtying into the same as Blackfoot called Portneuf from a man killed near it   18 miles   here we found Buffaloe in the bottom and the
Hunters are now out Running them.   Here we remained this day
and the 5th when the men I had sent out to hunt the horse returned   as I had expected them on the 4th I was much alarmed
for their saf[e]ty being in a dangerous country   while here we
made 7 bales meat   On the 5th. we mooved S. down the valley
3 miles and encamped on a creek running into the valley   on the
7th we made 21 miles   first down the N. side of the valley and
taking the first creek running out of the valley   then in a S. W.
direction and encamped on it   from the valley above mentioned
rises Bear River running into the the Big Salt Lake distant
about S. E.   50 miles   Currants and service berrys are now ripe.
I have been sick from indigestion for some days   more so than I
ever was before.   We have here the Sandhill Crane Turtle dove
Robbin Blackbirds (Crow & Cow) Kingfishers Black & Mallard
Ducks, Ge[e]se.   We find meat making a tedious buisness.   On
the 8th we moved S. W. 15 miles   following the main Portneuf
out of the valley for about 12 miles then took one of its tributaries
for about 3 miles and encamped on the S. W. side of the
val[l]ey in which this branch runs   here we cached 6 Horse loads
of goods and remained on the 9th & 10th & 11th moved on in
a S. W. direction not following any stream but passing the ridge
bordering the valley in a low place near where a small run puts
into the valley from a very rugged pass.   We made this day 15
miles and encamped on a small run going into [the] Portneuf.
     12th   We made in a S. W. direction about 6 miles not follow-
ing any stream but encamped on a very small run with poor grass.
     13   We made 24 miles in a west and by N. direction and met
no water for this distance and encamped on a very small run issu-

ing from a spring a few miles from Lewis River we are here in sight of the River running through an extensive valley in a S. W. direction here are the American falls the place may be known by several high and detached hills arising from the plain the falls at one place [are] 22 feet and the Rapids extend a considerable distance down the River We found here plenty of Buffaloe sign and the Pawnacks come here to winter often on account of the Buffaloe we now find no buffaloe there are here abundance of Service berrys now ripe during a short walk from camp this mng. I saw a buff colored fox with a white tip on his tail. Wolves here serenade us every night making more noise than 50 village dogs and better music for they keep in chord and display more science yesterday we parted from 16 men bound out trapping. We are now in a country which affords no small game and a precarious chance for Buffaloe

14th We made 30 miles in a S. W. direction and encamped on a creek called Casu* River it joins the main River below the Am. falls. This days Ride was through an excessively barren country with no water between the two last camps on the N. side of the Lewis River and about 50 miles distant from it is a range of snowy mounts. [There are]also two or three points in the chain of this side with snow on them.

15th We made along the banks of the Ocassia about 25 miles and encamped on the west bank of it. The valley of the Ocassia is about 4 miles wide and of a rich soil but the excessive cold and drouth of this country prevents vegetation from assuming a fertile character. The air is so dry that percussion caps explode without striking and I am obliged to put the caps on and fire immediately except in the night when we consider it safe to keep the caps on the guns we have in this country a large kind of black crickett 2 inches long said to be used as food by the Indians they are in great numbers and roost on the sage at noonday there are also in the streams abundance of craw-fish we see antelope and old buffaloe sign

16th We made 25 miles up the same side of the Ocassia then crossed it and followed S. W. 3 miles and encamped on a small mountain run making in all 28 miles in a W by S. direction yesterdays march was in a direction W by S.

17th We moved in a W. by S. direction about 15 miles to a creek putting into Lewis River on which we found no beaver of consequence having been trap[p]ed out by the H. B. Co. some years before.

18th We moved out up the creek about 8 miles and still found no beaver saw one Pidgeon Woodpecker this creek runs through what are called cut rocks otherwise volcanic in this region I found one mountain of Mica Slate enclosing garnetts. The Ba-

---

*The name is thus written above "Ocassia" crossed out.

saltic rock appears to be the same formerly and the remains of
the Garnetts are in some cases to be seen.   also I have found
here granite in small blocks   there is also much white sandstone compact   the clefts [cliffs?] on each side of this creek are
high and perpendicular but the bottom affords good grass for this
country.   There is no timber except willow and alder in the bottom and cedar on the hills   this days course about S. along the
creek

    19th   We moved up the creek about 12 miles in a S. W. di-
rection   there was still little beaver   this afternoon I took 2 men
and proceeded from camp about 8 miles about W. following the
creek and slept there   at sunrise on the 20th we moved up about
12 miles in a W direction and while I was engaged in the brook
setting a trap we found three Indians following us   the two men
were on the bank and were seen but myself in the creek was un-
noticed   when they crossed to go to the men I presented my
pistol to the first one who made a precipitate retreat back while I
made mine to my gun having got which I bec[k]oned them to come
to me which they did   we then went to camp which we found
had moved this day about 10 miles in same direction   these Indians were Snakes the first we had seen during the march   the
party passed a hot spring the country still volcanic.

    21st   We followed the creek in a N. W. direction about 5 miles
when we met a village of the Snakes of about 150 persons having
about 75 Horses   they were poorly off for food and clothing but
perfectly friendly   they are diminutive in person and lean.   We
encamped to trade with them but did nothing except getting a
few skins for moccasins   this morning caught my first Beaver a
large one.

    22nd   We followed the same creek about 2 mil[e]s and then
struck into a ravine in a west direction and in about 6 miles came
to a warm spring near a cold one which formed a run which
we followed in a west by S. direction   this we followed about 2
miles and encamped making this day 18 miles

    22nd   We proceed[ed] in a S. W. direction and struck the
same stream on another branch about 2 mils from the junction
about 15 mils this day   these two streams unite and run in a N.
direction through impassable cut rocks   this night caught 2
Beaver and slept out of camp.

    24th   Proceed up the creek in a S. W. by W. direction about
18 miles then in a W. by N. direction about 6 miles.   The last
half of this days travel was through clefts of Scienite rock pretty
well broke to pieces by heat apparently   we have here 2 kinds of
Liz[z]ards the one like that of the United States as far as I could
see   the other shorter and more sluggish   here we find the banks
of the streams lined with Diggers Camps and Trails but they are
shy and can seldom be spoken   and then there is no one who
could understand them and they appear to know little about the

signs which afford other Indians a mode of intelligence from
this region specimens No. 1 are obtained.

25th   We made in a W. direction along the same creek 20
miles.

26th   In a W by N. direction about 20 miles

27th   In a S W direction toward a snowy mountain and leaving the last creek 24 mils and struck one here running S. E.
Country desolate in the extreme   most of the creeks which have
water in them   on   the   mountains dry up   in   the plains of
this region

28th   did not move more than 2 mils up.

29th   About 5 miles in a S. W. Direction to cross a range of
high hills until we struck a creek running in a N. W. direction
which we followed 12 mils and encamped where the creek goes
into the cut rocks   this day we parted from Mr. Sublett[e]s party
with feeling of regrett for this party have treated us with great
kindness which I shall long remember.

30th   We followed the creek in a N. W. direction about 12 mils
through. tremenduous cut rocks I went ahead to look the route I
passed the smoking fires of Indians who had just left 4 of whom I
saw running up the mountain endeavoured by signs to induce them
to come to me but could not   Soon after I came to another camp
I happened to find their plunder   this induced them to come to
me 3 men one boy 4 women   from these Indians I procured fresh
Salmon Spawn which was very encouraging as we are nearly out
of provisions and the country would afford us a scanty subsist-
ence   I gave these Indians a few small presents to convince
them of our friendly disposition.   This day for the first time in
this country saw raspberrys   these Indians gave me a cake made
of service berrys quite good   they had about a Dozen of spotted
fish of a kind I had never seen resembling a Tom-cod.   These
Indians are small about 120 of a good countenance   they are
Snakes or Sosshonees.

30th* We followed the same creek and made about 15 [miles] in a
N. N. W. direction through a continued defile in many places admitting just room for the water through which in many places
we were obliged to make our way The mountains on each side
are about 1000 feet above the creek which has a rapid decent
here are a small fish about 1⁄4 lb. similar to a trout but with large
dark spots.   We meet here plenty of cherrys currants and goose-
berrys the latter sour.   The last of yesterdays and the first of todays route lay through Porphritic Granite rocks in their natural
state   the latter part of to days was through a stratified blue
sandstone untouched by fire for a short distance then assumed a

*The author seems to have lost his bearings with his dates. His uncer-
tainty first appears on the 17th and continues patently through to the 4th
prox.

volcanic appearance. This day we assended the highest mountain in sight and found the exhibit an indescribable chaos the tops of the hills exhibit the same strata as far as the eye can reach and appear to [have] once form[ed] the level of the country and the vall[e]y to be formed by the sinking of the earth rather than the rising of the hills through the deep cracks and chasms thus formed the rivers and creeks of this country creep which renders them of the most difficult character to follow in the brooks we have fresh water clams on which we look with some feeling for the small quantity of Buffaloe meat now remaining admonishes us look for some other means of living game there is little and being obliged to travel prevents our hunting much. from this place the specimen in Bag No. 1 of vitrified quartz was taken.

31st We followed the same creek about 4 miles in a N. direction then took a dry ravine 2 miles in a S. E. then in a N. direction and then followed down another dry ravine about 1 mile when the rocks on each side closed over the top and formed a natural Bridge elevated about 50 feet while the sides approached to within 20 feet of each other and the bottom decended perpendicularly about 60 feet we of course returned on our trail and then ste[e]red a N. E. direction about 4 miles and encamped on a little ravine in which there was only a little water standing in deep places and barely enough for us and our horses. The first half mile of our route lay through the bed of the creek and among rocks from 1 foot to 3 or 4 in diameter this was a very difficult task and several of our horses fell in the water this day we lost two horses which gave out the country still bears the same appearance as for several days past.

2nd Sept. We left our camp in the ravine assended to the height of land which we found to be a high level plain over which we marched in a N. N. W. direction and found during a 10 hours march 2 springs which as the day was warm were acceptable at the end of 30 miles we reached the creek which we left on the 31st We found rabbits plenty on the plain our camp was made surrounded by high and and perpendicular clifts say 800 feet bearing every mark of fire here we found little grass for our horses.

3rd We lay at the same camp and got fish from the brook enough for breakfast after which I took [a] horse and followed the creek down about 1 mile and found another larger joining it a little below which there is a warm spring issuing from the bank about 40 feet above the stream it gives out smoke when it meets the air and discharges a large quantity of water about 2 miles farther down I found a small party of Indians from whom I obtained 8 fish weight about 4lbs each and looking like a salmon for these I gave 4 Hooks they were friendly they advise me to follow the right hand trail but I have determined to take the left and shall perhaps repent it. The left leads N. W. which I think [is] my direction I returned to camp and three of the

Indians with me. One of these Indians had a bad wound on the side of his head and from his signs and appearance was made with a poisoned arrow.

3rd We moved camp in the proposed direction viz N. W. 16 miles During which distance we found stagnant water once and encamped near about 15 Indians diggers 3 of our men we left at the last camp to set their traps at some signs there seen. These Indians are very poor and timid when I approached them alone on a gallop they all began to run but by moderating my pace and making signs the[y] suffered me to come to them they gave me some sweet root to eat for which I gave them 3 Hooks they had a young yellow legged eagle with them and most of the diggers we have met had a small kind of Hawk at their camps these they feed and tame this party also had a young bird tame resembling a King Bird this days travel was on a high plain and good going on an old trail these Indians had with them staves for fish spears so we presume they are going to the river for fish and so think ourselves on the right trail. For three nights passed there has been no frost a thing which has not befor[e] happened for three nights in all since leaving rock Independence. Snow spit we had the 28th Aug. Today a slight sprinkle of Rain being the 2nd time since leaving the Rendesvous.

4th We left the camp early and proceeded over a high and pretty level plain gradually decending to the N. W. in a N. N. W. direction and after 20 mils travel without water came to ravines running E. and dry having gravelly and sandstone (untouched by fire) bluf[fs] and in 5 mils more came to the creek we had left on mng. of the 3rd. [on] the banks of which we found every 20 steps or thereabouts warm or hot springs and the creek tho large and discharging a great quantity [of] water too warm to be palatable Here we found an Indian and family of whom for 2 fish Hooks we bought 7 salmon of about 4 lbs weight each when green. they were split and dried. The two men left behind not having yet come up we intend halting here for them. The creek is here lined with volcanic rock today [we] saw the first fish Hawk in this country.

4th La[y] at camp and repacked our goods and held a smoke with some Indians one of whom we engaged as a guide down the river and to Beaver smoked too much and made myself sick

5th Moved on about 5 mils N. N. W. and again struck the creek and good grass found Beaver sign very plenty and for the first time set all our traps at good sign had a mess of fresh clams for dinner after which 2 Indians came to us with 4 salmon which we bought for 2 Hooks This day heard what we all took for a cannon at about 10 mils distance time will determine whether we were mistaken. In this creek there are a great number of snakes about 3 feet long with a large head and of a brownish grey color about the proportion of the striped snake of N. E.

They Inhabit the water and I saw one catch a small fish within two feet of me while bathing at a warm spring which put into the main stream   The bathing at these warm springs is delicious there are hundreds of them and some large enough to dive in Some gush out of the rocks at an elevation of 40 feet above the stream and discharge enough water for a mill   I can perceive no unusal taste in the water.

6th   Remained at same camp and were visited at 10 ock in the morning by two Indians with whom we held a smoke   we can learn nothing of any white post by these Indians   caught 7 Beaver

7th   Remained at same camp and exchanged two horses with some Pawnack Indians three of whom visited us   also about 10 Sohonees with Salmon of which they have plenty   here we caught a N. England Sucker also a fish a little resembling [a] pike of about 3 lbs weight but without teeth. Caught 3 Beaver. Ravens are here very plenty and tame   the[y] light on the perpendicular sides of the creek waiting for fish   on which they live. Ge[e]se and ducks are also plenty as well as grouse. Some of the Indians have guns but most of them go unarmed   The creek here for about 10 miles runs W. N. W.

8th   Mooved camp down the creek about 12 miles and came to the village under the escort of about 20 Indians on Horseback one of whom by the direction of the chief shewed us the place for our camp where grass and water could be had   here the chief Harangued his people telling them not to come into our lines nor steal from the white people. he sent his squaws with wood for us and also sent salmon for us to eat   I gave him a present of tobacco awls Hooks Powder vermillion knives ect. Here I traded a Beaver skin robe for two knives and six skins with many muskrat which are plenty here   I found these Indians great thieves in the small line   knives ect. Missing mine I went to one of the Sub Chiefs and told him of it   he made enquiry and pointed out the thief who refusing to open his Robe I gently did it for him but inste[a]d of finding the knife found a coat of one of the men which he held upon until I drew a pistol on which he gave it up and caught up what he supposed to [be] one of our guns but it happened to be my covered fishing rod   he was then held by the other Indians and sent to the village and I saw him no more

9th   In [the] morning went to see the Indians catch Salmon which is done by entangling them in their passage up the creek among dams which they erect and spearing them   they catch an immense quanity   the operation commences in the morning at a signal given by their chief. This chief is a good sized man and very intelligent and the President would do well if he could preserve the respect of his subjects as well or maintain as much dignity

10   Mooved down the main river in a S. W. direction which
here runs through moderate banks in a moderate current   We
are told that the next creek has beaver by the chief and that it
is 4 days march   The main river is here full of salmon which
continually jump above the the surface like sturgeon.

10th   Mooved camp along the Bank of the river 3 miles   there
the river diverging to the Northward we left it and followed the
main trail   the river here goes[?] through cut rocks about 30
miles   We made this day 20 mils in all in a W. N. W. Direction and encamped in poor grass on a small creek 1 mile from the
main river   during the march we crossed a small creek up which
about 2 mils is a fine camp.

11th   Moved at 3 A. M. and followed the trail 24 mils in a W.
N. W. Direction and encamped on the bank of the main river
which is here a fine stream about a ⅓ mile or over.   I swam
across it and found it over my head all the way   here we found
Indians and bought Beaver 3 skins for 1 shoe knife and 4
charges powder & lead   we also got salmon of them   the Basalt
here occurs resting on sand and gravel   in some places the rock
is not more than 4 feet thick and appears to have suffered from
intense heat   the country is barren in the extreme   there is usual[l]y a difference of 40 deg. between the day & night the heat at
noonday about 75 to 85 deg.   The Indians here have large nets
made in the European manner of the hemp of the country.   The
trail on the river so far is fine and much used.

12   Moved camp 15 miles on the trail in a W. N. W. direction and following the bank of the river which is here a gentle
stream of about 4 miles and ½ mile wide.   Gnats here trouble
us much and the days are extremely hot about 85 deg. and the
nights warm enough for comfort   The river is full of salmon and
a plenty of them are to be had   of the Indians whom we meet
every few mils fishing on the banks of the stream   Some of the
grass is here so salt that it can be washed in a pot of water and
enough seasoning for boiling obtained   grass is generally poor.
The banks are here generally sand   Many kinds of water fowl
frequent the river here   today we bought a fish of the Indians
dried excessively fat and when alive a large fish, sturgeon
probably

13th   moved camp along the bank of the river and following
the trail 24 miles only deviating from the river about 3 mils
of the last of the travel.   The first 6 miles the river is W. the
next 3 N. W. then S. W. 3 then taking a circular sweep
round to N. by E. which was 9 miles then left the river and in 3
miles struck a creek about as large as Charles River at Water-
town, where we found grass, salmon and Indians and the first
timber we have seen since leaving the Mts. in sight on what appears to be a river coming in from the N. side   this I mean to
ascertain tomorrow and the next day I shall start to explore the

creek for Beaver   This forenoon and yesterday forenoon were cloudy and the first cloudy weather for 2 months except as mentioned before.   We[a]ther still as warm as 80 deg. in day time buy salmon for a hook apiece.

14th   Mooved camp in a N. N. W. Direction 5 miles and encamped on the main river   being out of provisions I sent a man on a mule to buy some salmon   he went up the river about 3 miles and called to some Indians on one of the Islands to bring some   these he bought afterward another Indian came over with some   the man thinking he had got nearly enough offered him a less price   this displeased the Indian who slapped him in the face and at the same time hit the mule a kick which set him out on the run and the Indian ran quick enough to avoid vengeance the man came to camp much displeased having had to walk most of the way and carry his fish   this day also visited by Indians from below with 'salmon

15th   Sent 3 men and 4 animals to examine the small river for beaver   this day a N. W. wind much like the N. E. of the Atlantic with some little rain (at the same camp) this day took a ride down the river to examine for a camp   16th N. W. wind still   took a ride up the river to find a camp where timber, fit for a raft which we propose to build to carry some of the loose baggage and some men who are on foot can be found, found none saw some beaver sign   in trading for some salmon an Indian attempted to sna[t]ch a paper of fish hook[s] from me but he did not make out   returned to camp and sent two men to trap for the beaver   they left their horses and went into the willows to look [for] the sign during which time the Indians none of whom were in sight stole a cloak from Mr. Ball.   They found the beaver had lately been trapped out say within 3 weeks   next morning they returned to camp

17th   Mooved camp N. by W. 16 miles and encamped on a creek about as large as the last near a few lodges of Indians   the main river about two miles to N. E.   This creek appears to run S. W.   The Inds. say there is beaver on it   the main river here makes a considerable detour to the N.   Yesterday had hail and rain & snow and today the Mts. to the Northward are white with it.

18th   With 2 men I went up the creek   this I followed about 50 miles and found its general course about W by N. the first 15 miles S. W. then W. 20 then N. N. W. 15 where the cut rocks begin   This is a large stream when the waters are high in the spring but now is sluggish   here we got a few beaver   It had been trapped by the H. B. 2 years before   we saw no Indians on it during the 9 days I was up.   On the 10th day I returned to where I left the party and feeling in the mood of banter I told the Indians at the mouth of the creek (the party having left) that I had eaten nothing for two days   this to see if they would give

me anything for charity sake. One of them went and looked at
my saddle and pointed to me the fresh blood of a beaver I had
that morning caught and left with the two men   I then bought
2 salmon for one awl afterward I told him I had three children at
home he brought forward three tawny brats and his squaw who
was big   I backed out of story telling with Indians.   I then proceeded on until the moon went down when seeing a light I made
for it   after traveling 5 miles I found it to be an Indian camp on
the other side of the river   I then unsaddled my horse and slept
until 4 ock when I mounted and at 9 ock found where my
party had .camped the same night and a notice in the trail
of their motions   at 11 ock I overtook them with my horse lame
and jaded.   I found an Indian with the party who seems to know
the route to Wallah Wallah and he intends going with us   During my absence the three men sent up the creek above the one I
went up returned without accident, and during the same time Mr.
Sublette with Mr. Frapp & party joined our camp and crossed
by fording to the other side of the river intending to divide into
3 parties and trap up three streams coming in opposite the upper one of which we thought to be salmon river   it proves to be
called Big Woody on account of the timber on it.   They
attempted to come down on the creek above the one I
asscended but after toiling long and wearing down their horses
in a cruel manner they crossed to the one that we decended and
arrived at the Indian village the day after we left it   he left before I returned   I regretted much not seeing this party.   from
Information gained here we suppose that we shall meet no Indians
between this and the fort have threfore provided as much salmon
as we could get and put ourselves on allowance.   Subblette who
went to 2 creeks further than I did saw a large stream running
S. W.   this must either turn and be some large river coming into Lewis below here or be the head water of some river going to
the Gulph of California.   After joining camp we proceed[ed] on
to a creek coming from the N. W. which is our route   the river
here being impracticable and taking a great bend to the N.   and
shall wait here until the two men who went up with me come to
camp The river from where I lef[t] camp runs about N. 20 miles
then west 10 miles then N. again into cut rocks   found the party
all well and the horses much recruited

    29th   We lay at same camp.

    30th   Mooved about 5 miles the creek running about W.

    1 Oct   Mooved camp along same creek about 5 miles still W.

    2nd   At same camp   at this place the bears dung was plenty
but we saw but one.

    3rd   Moved camp about 15 miles   creek still west and trail
good.

    4th   With an Indian and 4 men I left camp in order to explore
this creek the N. W. trail here leaving it   after leaving camp I

proceed[ed] over bad hills about 18 miles and encamped among cut rocks on the same creek it here being W. by S. during the march we observed a range of high snowy mountains to the N. of us but w[h]ether on our side of the river or not could not determine.

5th   Made about 5 miles through intolerable cut rocks   some beaver

6th   At same camp.

7th   5 mils on same creek which bears W. by S   here left it. having sent a messenger to camp with orders to proceed on the route to Wallah Wallah and ste[e]ring north passed some snow clad mounts. which we walked up with bare feet and after 25 mils struck a small run going into the next creek   during this day we passed through an immense forest of pine of different kinds and unknown to us altho very similar to some of ours on these mountains we found unripe service berrys, cherrys and thorn apple all of which are gone on the rivers   it snowed and rained most of the day   many of the pines were 4 feet through

8th   Moved 4 miles to the main creek and laid down cold and hungry and supperless hoping that our traps would give us beaver in the morning

9th   Got 7 beaver and went to eating like good fellows mooved this day 6 miles down   creek here running about N.

10th   Moved N. and down creek about 15 miles and found the rest of the party who had come on the mail trail in an average N. W. direction about 45 miles   This day rain   this creek from where we struck it to this place runs in an extensive plain of fertile soile equal to the best I ever saw of about 5 mils average width   here we raised a great smoke and am told by our Indian that the Nez Perces will see it and come to smoke with us

11th   To the S. W. of us is a range of snow clad Mts.   the Indian says it is 7 days to Wallah Wallah. This creek runs about N. E. by E.

11th   Started at 8 ock and moved about N. N. W. 30 miles over high ground of good soil.

12th   Left the party after killing a horse of the poorest kind for food in order to go ahead to find indians or whites or food The party here remained one day in a valley of about 20 miles long and 15 wide of a very fertile soil   in this valley saw extensive camps of Indians about one month old   here they find salmon in a creek running through it and dig the Kamas root but not an Indian was here at this time   we put out in a N. W. direction and assended the hills which soon became wooded with good timber   our course this day was about N. N. W. and 40 miles   I had with me an Indian and three men and a little horse meat   we camped this night in the woods without water.

13th   Arose early and continued our route until 9 ock and stopped for breakfast of bad Horse meat on a creek of some size where we found the red thorn apple and a few cherries after 3 hours stop we moved across the creek which runs West and is called Ottillah on ascending the opposite bluff we saw a smoke about 20 mils down on it to which we went and found some poor horses in charge of a squaw and some children the men were all out hunting they had no food but rose berrys of which we made our supper they were much fright[en]ed at our approach there having been some Indians of this tribe viz Walla Walla killed by the snakes above, and this family was murdered the night after we left them

In the morning of the 14th we put out about N. and arrived at fort Walla Walla about 5 ock in the evening distance 30 miles near the fort the river Walla Walla was crossed which is about 75 feet wide and about 2 feet deep current moderate the size of the last creek passed I was received in the most hospitable and gentlemanly manner by Peanbron [Pambrun] the agent for this post the fort is of no strength merely sufficient to frighten Indians mounting 2 small cannon having two bastions at the opposite corners of a square enclosure there were 6 whites here. My party arrived on the 18th having fared for food in the same manner as myself but for a longer time. They met a Nez Perce village on the 16th and got a supply of food they passed my trail and went N. of it and struck the main river above the fort they brough[t] in all the horses At the post we saw a bull and cow & calf, hen & cock, punkins, potatoes, corn, all of which looked strange and unnatural and like a dream. They gave me a decent change of cloth[e]s which was very acceptable I took a ride up the river 9 miles to the junction of Lewis River which comes in from the S. E. and soon takes a S. course the Columbia comes here from the N. W.

On the 19th I took leave of my hospitable entertainer in one of the Cos. barges with my party leaving my horses in his charge at the fort and proceeded down the river about 4 mils and s[t]opped to tighten our boat the river forms fine eddies to work up with and about 3 mile current down the 2nd run of fish failed this year in the river and the Indians are picking up the most nauseous dead fish for food the course of the river [is] about S. W.

20th Left the beach at sunrise the River still S. W. and kept on until about noon when a furious wind arose from the S. W. and stopped our further progress the sand flew so as to obscure the air Here we traded a few fish from the natives for Hooks awls powder &c made 10 miles during which we passed some rapids of a bad character at which in times of high water portage is necessary the ge[e]se are numerous seated on the banks of the river. River W. by S. a large snowy mountain S. W. by W. ahead which the river leaves to the left called by the French "Montagne de Neige" made 10 miles

21st   Wind same but more moderate   Put down the river still W by S.   passed a large Island at the lower end of which we stopped for the night.   Ther. 22 deg.   Made 16 miles during the day   our boatman bought a colt which we found fine eating shagg and ge[e]se plenty

22nd   Made 30 miles   wind moderate and no rapids of much dif[f]iculty   stopped at night at a village where was a chief sick to whom our conductor administered some medicine and bled him his eyes were exceeding yellow and his blood after standing a short time was covered with a scum of yellowish green   he gave us a horse to eat of which he had 260 in fine order and of good breed   we found the meat equal to any beaf and quite different from the poor and sick old ones we had eaten.   They here sell Horses for 100 loads am[m]unition 1 Blankett and ¼ lb tobacco.

23rd   The chief much better and we left him   Yesterday our people in search of wood of which there is none but drift here found a pile which they brought to our fire but were soon told by the natives that they had robbed the dead   we will avoid the like mistake in the future   we made this day 28 miles during which distance we passed one bad rapid and the river John Day from a trader of that name.   This river is large but obstructed by rapids and enters from the S.   is 79 miles below Walla Walla no rain as yet but we are informed that the rain is now constant below the falls   we see Indians every few miles who come off to trade what little articles they have sometimes with nothing to beg a chew of tobacco sometimes with a little wood for fuel sometimes with two 3, one or ½ a fish   a few berrys   our conductor appears to have a wife at each stopping place   4 already and how many more sable beauties god only knows   these Indians are tolerably honest but will steal a little.

24th   Started about 9 and after about [6 miles]* passed the grand falls of the Columbia just above which a small river puts into the Columbia about the size of the small rivers above the Wallah [Wallah] for instance   these falls now the water is low are about 25 feet   when the water is high these falls are covered the water not having a sufficient vent below   the water here rises about 40 feet   just before arriving at the falls are considerable rapids   the falls are easily passed in boats at high water   we hired the Indians about 50 for a quid of tobacco each to carry our boat about 1 mile round the falls   the goods we carried ourselves shortly after passing the falls we passed what are called the dalles (small)   or where the river is dam[m]ed up between banks steep and high of not more than 100 feet apart through which the whole waters of the mighty Columbia are forced with much noise and uproar   I passed through with some Indians while my men went round they not being good boatmen enough to trust

*So written but crossed out.

and fright[en]ed withall. We are now camped at the Great Dalles which are still narrower and more formidable than the small having stop[p]ed after making 20 miles the wind being high and unfavorable for passing at the gorge of this pass the water rises[?] by the mark on the rock at least 50 feet forming a complete lock to the falls above the back water covering them entirely. The Indians are thieves but not dangerous before us and apparently in the river rises the most formidable mountain we have seen the country ahead is clothed with forest to the river side which has not been the case before and the western horizon is covered by a dense cloud denoting the region of constant rain during the winter.

25th   Made this day 6 miles and passed the great dalles similar to the small ones which we passed yesterday but still narrower being 75 feet about in width through this pass we went with an unloaded boat at an immense speed the goods and Baggage were carried past on the backs of my men and some Indians hired for that purpose my men not being good boatmen and timorous I hired Indians to work ours through going with them myself to learn the way during part of this day we had a fair wind the river still W. by S. here we saw plenty of grey headed seals we bought some bear meat from the Indians which we found very fine. We encamped for the first time on the river among timber among which I saw a kind of oak and ash. Indians Plenty one chief at whose lodge we stopped a short time gave me some molasses obtained from [the] fort below to eat He had a large stock of dried fish for the winter 4 tons I should think roots &c he was dressed in the English stile Blue frock coat pants. & vest comported himself with much dignity enquired my name particularly and repeated it over many times to impress it on his memory his sister was the squaw of an American of the name of Bache who established a post on the river below the great dalles three years ago last fall and who was drowned in them with 11 others the following spring the remains of the fort I saw as also the grave of the woman who died this fall and was buried in great state with sundry articles such as capeau vest pantaloons shirts &c. A pole with a knob at the top is erected over her remains at the foot of the Dalles is an island called the Isle of the Dead on which there are many sepulchers these Indians usually inter their dead on the Islands in the most romantic scituations where the souls of the dead can feast themselves with the roar of the mighty and eternal waters which in life time aff[f]orded them sustenance and will to all eternity to their posterity.

26   After 30 miles of beautiful navigation with little current and fair strong wind and no rapids we arrived at the Cascade or lower obstruction of the river here it is necessary to carry the boat and the Indians are all dead only two women are left a sad remnant of a large number their houses stripped to their frames

are in view and their half buried dead   this portage will be a hard job   during this day I went ashore to a small lake near the river I killed at one discharge of my double barrelled gun 5 * of them which gave 5 of us a hearty supper   no rain as yet   but constant appearance of it ahead   at these rapids are a great many seal   it is a mystery to me how they assend them.   The direction of the river is here about W by S. and a little snow on some of the highest of the hills   this day we passed the high mountain covered with snow her[e]tofore mentioned   it is on the left of the river and is a more stupendous pile than any of the Rocky Mts.   Always covered with snow and is called the Snowy mountain.

27th   in the morning commenced carrying the boat and goods which we finished at 1 ock. and   making 9 miles in all stopped to repair the boat which was leaky from damage   sustained in carry-ing   rained all this day and saw but two[?] Indians.

28th   With a fair wind and a little rain we decended the river at a great rate   on the route we killed a goose   which dropped in the water   a white headed Eagle from a distance seeing this took occasion to come   he seized it and lifted it into the air a few feet but our near approach fright[en]ed him away   made this day 26 miles and stopped at a saw mill belonging to the H. B. Co. under charge of a Mr. Cawning[?] a gentleman who came here 22 years since with a Mr Hunt   he is in the service of the Co.   We were treated by him with the greatest kindness   he gave us moc-[c]asins and food in plenty.

29th   Started at 10 ock   and arrived   at the fort of Vancouver at 12, 4 miles   Here I was received with the utmost kindness and Hospitality by Doct. McLauchland [McLoughlin] the acting Gov. of the place   Mr McDonald Mr Allen and Mr Mckay gentlemen resi-dent here   Our people were supplied with food and shelter from the rain which is constant   they raise at this fort 6000 bush. of wheat 3 of Barley 1500 potatoes 3000 peas a large quantity of punkins   they have coming on apple trees, peach Do. and grapes.   Sheep, Hogs, Horses, Cows, 600 goats, grist 2, saw mill 2.   24 lb guns powder magazine of stone   the fort is of wood and square   they are building a Sch. of 70 Tons   there are about 8 settlers on the Multnomah   they are the old engages of the Co, who have done trapping.   I find Doct. McLauchland a fine old gentleman truly philanthropic in his Ideas   he is doing much good by introducing fruits into this country which will much facilitate the progress of its settlement (Indian corn 3000 bush) The gentlemen of this Co. do much credit to their country and concern by their education deportment and talents.   I find my-self involved in much difficulty on acc. of my men some of whom wish to leave me and whom the Co. do not wish to engage no[r] to have them in the country without being attached to some Co.

_____

*A word is omitted from the journal.

able to protect them alledging that if any of them are killed they will be obliged to aveng[e] it at an expense of money and amicable relations with the Indians.   And it is disagreeable for me to have men who wish to leave me.   The Co. seem disposed to render me all the assistance they can   they live well at these posts they have 200 acres of land under cultivation   the land is of the finest quality.

30th to 5th. Nov remained at Vancouver and except the last day rain.

6th   started down the river to look with a view to the Salmon buisness   we decended the river at about 4 mils per hour and accomplished the journey in parts of 4 days   the river is full of islands but they are all too low for cultivation being occasionally overflowed as also the praries (what few there are) on the main land   with the exception of these small levells the country is so rough that a great part of the earth must be inhabited before this but the soil is good and the timber is heavy and thick and almost impenetrable from underbrush and fallen trees   the description of Mess. Lewis & Clark and others is fully borne out as to size and more also   the river is so well known at this part of it that I will not insert any observations of my own   there are a great number of fowl on this river at this time and there will be more as they say soon   there are large swan white ge[e]se a goose with a motled breast and yellow bill a trifle smaller than the goose of N. E.   A white goose almost exactly like the domestic goose of N. E. yellow feet and legs as also the former there is another goose like that of N. E. but I think smaller there is the tame duck of N. E. with 19 tail feathers and a fine duck to eat   there is the grey duck of N. E.   green winged teel   Buffle heads Cape Races Dippers of the Sea loons seal deer   I killed one swimming the river   I saw no elk but only tracks   fort George now occupied as a trading post by the H. B. Co. is well scituated on a sloping bank of the river about 2 miles outside of Tongue point and 6 miles inside of Clatsop point   Chinnook point is opposite the latter and inside   Chinnook is a river of small size is also inside Tongue point   above Tongue point about 6 miles are the Cathlametts   they are an archipelago of reedy Islands overflown at high water   Here are ducks innumerable.   the Indians in this part of the river are of late much reduced   they appear good and hosptable as far as an Indian ever is that is they are willing to sell provisions for all they can get for them   they appear to live well and I believe any one may with plenty of powder and lead on this river either as a purchase or to shoot there are no beaver here   We arrived at the Fort of V. on the 15-th Nov having had no rain during this time.   I must here mention the very kind gentlemanly conduct of Mr. Jas. Bernie suprintendent of Ft. G. who assisted me to a boat and pilot for the outer harbor and acted the part of host to perfection   I had much pleasure with a little liquor and a pipe in his company   he has seen much of this country and is of the old N. W. concern   I derived much information from him   on my return to the fort my men came forward and unanimously desired to be released from their engagement with a view of returning home as soon as possible and for that end to remain here and work for a maint[en]ance until an opportunity should occur.   I could not refuse   they had already suffered much and our number was so small that the prospect of remuneration to them was very small   I have therefore now no men   these last were Mr. Ball Woodman Sinclair, Breck, Abbot, Tibbits   they were good men and persevered as long as perseverance would do good   I am now afloat on the great sea of life without stay or support but in good hands i. e. myself and providence and a few of the H. B. Co. who are perfect gentlemen   During my absence Guy Trumbul died on the 7th of Nov. of the Cholic an attack of which he had on the Platte of which he nearly died   in this case he was taken in the evening and died early in the mng.   His funeral was attended by all the Gentlemen at the place and prayers were said accord[ing] to the form of the Church of England for this attention to my affairs in my absense was considerate to my feelings and I hope will be duly appreciated service is here performed on sunday and on the days prescribed by the church of Eng.   our excursion down the river was performed in an Indian canoe which we hired for a 3 ½ point Blankett[?] We found it very kittish but withall a good craft for sailing and easy to paddle but the men were exceedingly awkward.

19th   From this to the 29th I remained at Fort Vancouver eating and drinking the good things to be had there and enjoying much the gentlemanly society of the place.

On the 29th. with Abbot and Woodman in an Indian canoe I started for a journey up the Wallamet or Multonomah River this river which is highest in the winter was so at this time but is not rapid until near the falls   the subjoined scetch will shew its course as I made it   distance by the river by my estimate 27 ½ miles to the falls which are perpendicular about 20 feet   past these we carried our canoe about ¼ mile and launched above the falls   the water though generally more rapid above would admit of the running of a steam boat.   In this river at this time there is more water than in the Missouri and not of a more difficult character to navigate   the tide flows to within 8 miles of the falls below the fall the banks of the river are not suitable for cultivation being overflowed as far as the bottom extends which is not far and beyond these the country rises into rocky hills unfit for tillage but producing very large timber mostly if not all of the pines   On the bottoms there is consid[e]rable oak of a kind not found in the States but of excellent quality for ship building and is

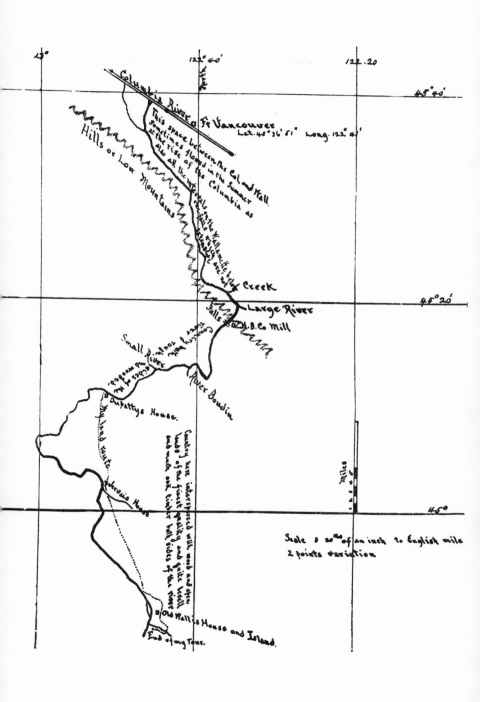

45° | 122°40' | 122.20 | 45°40'

Columbia River Ft Vancouver
Lat. 45°36'51" Long. 122°41'

This space between the Col and Mall
sometimes flows in the summer
at the rise of the Columbia as
also all the

Hills or Low Mountains

Creek

Large River
H.B.Co Mill

Small River not

River Boudin

Dupattys House.

Country here interspersed with wood and open
lands of the finest quality and quite level
no much oak timber both sides of the river

Old Wallis House and Island.

End of my Tour.

Miles

45°20'

45°

Scale of an inch to English mile
2 points variation

the only kind of oak found in the country of the Columbia   I noticed but two streams coming into the river below the falls the river to within 6 mils of its junction with the Columbia runs along the N. E. side of a range of hills or as they would be called in N. E. mountains   at the falls it passes through this range this river has two mouths   the East one is the one I assended the west one follows the range of hills above described to their falling on the Columbia about 3 miles below   the eastern entrance [of] the mouth of this river is in Latt 45 deg. 36 min. 51 sec. Long. 122 deg. 48 min.   Above the falls for 22 mils by estimate the banks of the river are high enough to prevent [over]flowing but timbered and not fertile and rough and the country apparently not valuable except for timber which is here mostly of the pines except a small quantity of cotton wood and alder   the latter is here a tree of sometimes a foot and an half through   at the falls the H. B. Co. are erecting a saw mill to which they contemplate adding a grist mill   the scituation for mill priviledges is beyond any thing I have ever seen   22 mils from the falls are 3 or 4 Canadians settled as farmers   they have now been there one year have Hogs, Horses, Cows, have built barns, Houses, and raised wheat, barely, potatoes, turnips, cab[b]ages, corn, punkins, mellons The country here becomes open, but still wood enough and a much greater proportion of oak   prairies of from 1 to 30 miles in extent bound by a skirting of timber   this country seems a valley between the mountains to the East and West of about 50 miles wide including both sides of the river and is very level   of nearly uniform soil   extremely rich   equal to the best of the Missouri lands.   Accounts vary much as to its southerly extent I have seen it at least 75 mils in a southwardly direction and from all I can learn I think it extends with but little inter[r]uption as far south as the vall[e]y of the Buneventura   which is also of the same description of country.   and I have never seen country of equal beauty except the Kanzas country and I doubt not will one day sustain a large population   10 mils by land above the first settlement and 30 by the river is another by a Mr Jervie which was a very fine beginning of one years standing of the same character and product as the one below   in all about 9 settlers are on this river   if this country is ever colonised this is the point to commence   the river is navigable for canoes to its very sources but as I understand very circuitous   deer abounds in this district and wolves one of which   a large devil I shot   these settlers I found exceeding attentive to my comforts especially Mr Jervai at whose house I slept 2 nights   I was absent from the fort this time 10 days.

To the 4th Jany. the weather was little better than a continual rain not however a hard rain often but a drizzling uncomfortable air   during December there fell 9½ inches rain by a pluviometer   on the 4th the wind came strong to N. N. E. with fair

and cool weather Ther. averaging about 19 Deg.   this continued
to the 8th when there is much floating ice in the river and those
here think that with two days more of this weather the river will
close.   The readiness w[it]h which the river fre[e]zes must arise
from the water getting intensely cold in the upper country.   During this month Mr. McKay gave our room a treat of Buffaloe
meat salted and smoked and this being the first opportunity of
comparing good Buffaloe meat with other good meat was highly
acceptable.   I think it equal to the best meat ever eaten.   Up to
the 4th there was no frost in the ground and ploughing is commonly done all the winter during the latter part of January the
River rose about 4 feet which must have arisen from the rains as
there could be no melting of snow on the Mountains at this season these rains must have I think extended farther back than is
described to be their range viz the falls at which the timbered
country terminates. Carrots are here finer and larger than I have
ever before seen one I think was 3 inches through and of fine
flavor.   There appears much sickness amon[g] the people here especially among the common people which I think arises from low
diet and moist weather for as far as I can observe the gentlemen
who live well are not much subject to disorders.   the main dis-
order is an intearmittent fever which has carried off all or nearly all
the Indians who live even worse than the engages. The Lima which
sailed a month since had not to the 1st Jany. got out of the river.
I have been Informed by Mr Douglas and Mr. Finlesson that vessells have laid off the bar 7 weeks before they could enter.
    11th Jany. The River closed with ice and I am detained here
until it opens. Last winter the river remained frozen 5 weeks
there is yet no snow. Today heard by Mr Hermatinger of the
death of Mr Vande[r]burg killed by the Blackfeet up to this time
the weather continued clear and cold for this country the Ther.
varying from 12 deg. to 20 deg.
    On the 18th at 2 oclock it commenced hailing and at day light
the hail was about 2 inches on the ground the River closed
on the 10th and so remains at present on the 14th I walked
across the Columbia and found the ice about 6 inches thick where
it lay smooth but it was much turned up edge wise afternoon of
the 18th commenced Raining and on the 19th rains still the hail
was at one time from 1½ to 2 inches deep on the 18th.
    19th after raining hard all night there is no snow left it is
warm and showery to day Ther. 54 deg.
    20th Raining stil[l] and Ther. 52 deg. River not yet cleared
ice stationary.
    21st 22nd warm and Rainy.
    23rd The river Broke up still warm Ther. 51 deg. I am
informed by Mr Dav. Douglas that a Mr Woodard whom he
saw in Calafornia was intending to come to the Columbia for Salmon he is a Brother-in-law to Capt. Ebbets and is from New

York   Mr. Douglass saw him in Calafornia in July 1832.   I am informed by Doct J. McGlaucland that he has seen strawberrys ripe here in Dec. and in blossom in Jany.   the weather warm up to the 28th with occasional rains   there is now little ice on the river on the banks the wreck and rubbish of the breaking up of the river.   The H. B. Co. are now making a fort at Nass. to counter-act the Am. vessells on the coast.

28th   Warm still and fair   the Co. are about sending a party under Mr. Manson to make a fort at Milbank Sound.

30th   Today a party sent to enquire after another reported to be cut off beyond the Umquoi or near the Clammat River under a man by the name of Michelle returned having as-certained that one white and two Inds. only of said party had been killed this party I [am informed] was under a man by the name of Duportt   I requested to accompany him but the Gov. would not consent alledging the[y] would conceive that I came to avenge the death of Mr. Smiths party who was cut off by the Umquoi Indians, all which I interpreted into a jealousy of my motives this party brought back 200 skins which they had traded   they did not go beyond the Umquoi, they were gone 2 months lost no men and but 2 horses which Died of fatigue.

31st to the 3rd. Feb. we had warm and wet weather   on the 3rd at 10 ock. we started for Wallah Walla   I had with me two men and am in company with Mr Ermatinger of the H. B. Co. who has in charge 3 boats with 120 pieces of goods and 21 men. I parted with feelings of sorrow from the gentlemen of Fort Van-couver   their unremitted kindness to me while there much en-deared them to me more so than it would seem possible during so short a time   Doct McGlaucland the Gov. of the place is a man distinguished as much for his kindness and humanity as his good sense and information and to whom I am so much indebted as that he will never be forgotten by me   this day we came to the Prarie Du Li[s]   15 miles   raining most of the day.

4th   Left the prairie Du Li[s] on the lower end of it   this prairie is about 3 miles long and through it the River Du Li[s] a small creek enters the Columbia   we made but 2 miles when one of our boats ran foul of a rock and was stove it landed its cargo without wetting much   this accident detained us till ¼ before 12 ock when we started and kept on till 2 ock and stopped 20 minutes to dine then kept on till ½ past 5 ock   making 17 mils this day this River is at medium water   the rivers banks high precipitous and rocky   from the Lea prairie in one place the bank on the N. side rises to 200 feet perpendicular   I saw a hawk light on a pro-jecting crag about half way up which gave me a good idea of the height of the rock   from this rock a small stream casts itself into the Com. w[h]ether a permanent one or not cannot say but should think not   there are here many white headed Eagles   one skunk we saw today   the timber appears much smaller than below   no

rain but cloudy this day   wind west and Ther. about 40 deg.
now at 8 ock at night the full moon is looking down calmly upon us ap[p]arently thinking that the cares of us humble individuals
concern her little.

5th   We left camp at 7 ock and made 4 miles to breakfast and
in 7 mils more the foot of the Cascades   our breakfast was made
on a small island abreast of a rock rising perpendicular from the
bed of the river as I should think 400 feet high   Lewis & Clark
call it I think 700 feet   this rock is nearly surrounded by the
waters of the river

The Cascades occasion a portage of 100 rods   our goods were
carried across this day   the river is here compressed into a very
small place and the bed is full of rocks   I should think the fall
to be about 8 feet in the space of the 60 rods   There are here two
fishing villages   both now deserted as the people here say from
the inmates being all dead of the fever but I suspect some are
dead and the rest and much larger part fright[en]ed away   we
made the portage by the North side on which is one of the above
villages   it is near the river on a little clear spot with a little lake
in the rear   here the Inds were once hostile and great caution was
once used   in passing now but little is requisite it rained all the
latter part of the day and night and morning of the 6th   finished
the portage but our boats were so bruised that the rest of the day
was taken to gum them   took a look about me   the rest of the
day   found that the tripe de roche grew on the rocks here
but small   here there are many petrifactions of wood in a bank of
gravell some of which are perfectly petrified and will not burn in
the fire but others appear only half so and burn and cut freely
they are found bedded in stone composed of rubble of some
former world   the gravel is cemented together by finer gravell
the whole being volcanic and water worn.

7th   At 1 ½ mile above the Cascade is a small river from the
N. and 4 ½ above this a creek from the N.   rained all the 6th
and rains a little today   came in all 27 miles   passed many
Indian habitations on the river and canoes   15 mils above the
Cascades is a Torrent that precipitates itself into the river from
about 60 feet   17 mils from same on same side viz south is a
creek   both small   one between them on the N. side   timber growing gradually thinner.

8th   We found that a Capeau and 2 blanketts had been stolen
by some Inds. from one of our men and went to the village
just below our camp to recover them   they acknowledged the
theft but the thieves had run off   we took two canoes to our camp
and breakfasted   immediately after breakfast the man who had
lost the articles took an ax and broke the worst canoe for which
he was reprimanded by Mr Ermatinger   the other he left and a
little after we left I saw the Ind. come and take it   we made 29
mils to the Dalles which are one mile or thereabouts long and en-

camped   having passed two of the boats   the other owing to
some mistake had she[e]red out and forced the line from those who
were towing and forced one Indian into the stream and was
drowned   he was on a bank about 15 feet high   he swam until
he got into a whirl pool and went down.   Just below the Dalles
the timber ceases   there are here   many Indians Tilky &
Casineau are here the chiefs and very clever ones   all this day we
saw Indians on the banks   the water passes even now at a furious
rate and at high water it is impassible and boats are carried as
much as two mils and all the goods   for assisting through this
place a little tobacco is given the Inds.   we gave the usual
quantity and saw a personal struggle for the division of it.

   9th   Left the Great Dall[e]s and in three miles came to the little dalles which we passed by towing in which we were delayed
by reason of having only two lines one having been lost at the
time the Indian was drowned   in three miles more I arrived at
the Shutes or falls of the Columbia which are not in this stage of
the water more than ten feet perpendicular but much more than
that including the rapids above and below in the immediate vicinity   these falls once during the times the whites have been
here have been sailed up owing as I suppose to the Dalles at such
times affording a slow outlet to the accumulated waters and their
being raised by this circumstance to above the level of the falls
this day got our baggage and goods over at the G. Dalles   I traded one horse which I sent on by Abbot   at the Shutes we found
about 150 to 200 Indians who were very troublesome [having] to
pay for very trifling services   however they stole nothing.

   10th   Passed over and gummed the boats and at ½ past 12
started up the river having traded another horse and sent it on
by Woodman   one mile above the river Aux Rapide comes from
the south   the size of the stream I cannot tell as I only saw the
mouth of it   here on the N. side of the river Abbot came to me
having lost the horse entrusted to him   I took Mr. Woodmans
and gave [left?] Abbot with orders to wait until 10 ock tomorrow
and then to come on whether he got the horse or not   we came
today 9 miles and 6 yesterday   here we have to give a piece of
tobacco for every stick of wood we get   last night was the first
frost I have seen since the river broke   the grass is somewhat
green   this part of the river affords trout in small quantity.

   11th   Started at an early hour and made the mouth of a considerable stream coming from the S. called John Days River
from a hunter of that name formerly in this country   distant
from our last camp 7½ milles   we camped 22½ miles from this
on the North side of the river having had a strong and fair wind
all day   one thing I observed in this part of the River is that the
savages are civil and as much as one in ten has lost an eye as I
suppose from the effects of the fine sand of the river being blown
about or the violent wind for which this part of the river is noted

we found some few roots and little game with the natives the
night was windy and uncomfortabl[e] but no frost but a little rain
    12th At ½ past 6 we started and made 2 miles to breakfast
on the N. side fair wind and clear one boat stove and must
stop to repair and gum found two small logs of drift wood at
10 ock. recommenced our journey with a fair light wind and
made in all this day 17 miles during the day had the satisfaction of seeing Abbot come up but without finding the lost horse.
    13th Calm in mng. but after breakfast had a fair and mid[d]ling
strong wind at 1 ock passed the upper end of Grand Island an
Indian to day brought me a pouch and horn stolen from one of
my men going down but the balls and powder used up which I
redeemed for a little tobacco last night a frost not severe
made this day 25 miles found wood enough for use on the banks
but it is a custom of the Indians to run along the beach and take
possession of the wood there may be and sell it [to] you for
tobacco which appears to be their greatest luxury a quid is pay
for almost anything.
    14th We started at 6 ock and in one mile passed the River
Ottillah one mile above which rapids commence the[se] we
passed one mile long making 3 to breakfast and started at ½
past 10 with a fair and strong wind and reached Wallah Walla
at 5 p. m. just befor[e] reaching this place the cut rocks close into
the river in such a manner that there appears but a small perpendicular sided gap to look through past these and at W. W.
both bank[s] fall down to a nearly levell plain we were again
hospitably received by Mr. P. C. Pambrun we remained at this
post until the 19th. of Feb. the weather mild and clear but high
S. W. winds W. W. is a place noted for high winds a little
frost during the nights only gras[s] just getting green My horses
in tolerable good order and all found eat horse meat all the time
at this post On Sunday took a ride up the river W. W. found its
bottoms good but not extensive and no wood the corn for this
post 150 bushells last year was raised at least 3 miles from the fort
none was stolen by the Indians a good test of their honesty as
they are all most always starving. This place is kept by about
5 men Inds. are freely admitted inside of it about 1200 skins
traded here it is kept up mostly for trading horses and the
saf[e]ty of the communication the course of the Wallah [Wallah]
river is E. by N. near the fort when I saw it.
    19th Just as we were leaving the fort an Indian brought in
the horse which Abbot lost at the Dalles and a short time after
leaving the fort an Indian sent by Mr. P. brought one other
which had strayed from Abbot at this place we made this day 17
miles to a branch of the Wallah [Wallah] river here coming from the
N. the space nearly a plain and barren and sandy but good grass
this branch appears to be about half the Wallah [Wallah] river
encamped a little after sundown and for 12 yards blue clths. 1 Blkt.

2 ½ pt 50 balls & powder　2 knives　1 lb. Tobacco bunch beads, 10 fish Hooks traded a good horse　this appears a fair price here.

20th　We made a late start and after travelling 9 hours without water arrived at the Snake river　here running W.　our course was this day N. by E. 22 ½ miles over a country which would be considered light sandy land with little sage　grass good and in tufts　very level except some trifling roundly swelling hills these make one think of gently swelling breasts of the ladies. Day warm and clear　We in the first of the day followed the branch of the W. W. mentioned yesterday say four miles on which I saw blackbirds which Mr. Pambrun says stay at W. W. all winter.

21st　No frost in morning.　Crossed the river to the mouth of a creek coming into the river from the N. for 10 miles which was the length of our march this day　this creek is through cut rocks of moderate height for this country.　We followed the stream on the east bank.　These banks were about 300 feet high to the levell of the plain if that can be called a plain where the hills rise to an almost equal height and the gullies are abrupt and narrow.　The soil was what would be called in N. E. a poor sandy soil producing good grass but still no wood　Traded two horses this day at the usual rates The people who are most used to this country are so little afraid of the Indians that they either travel without guns or with them unloaded.

22nd　A pretty hard frost in the morning　followed the river one mile on the North side then crossed it and made North 3 miles and crossed a branch of it coming from the N. W.　Our course this day N. by E. and encamped at a little run of water running S. E.　This is inconsiderable　Saw about 20 antelope this day in one herd　at our camp this nigh[t] observed about 2 inches of frost in the ground　this days ride over very rocky country the valleys of which are very good but small otherwise more sandy than common　grass good　Made 22 ½ miles

23d　N. 17 miles over a rough and Rocky country with a few small bottoms which are good land　at 9 miles from last camp passed some of the best specimens of Basaltic colum[n]s which I have seen　They were 5 sided and about 50 feet high　some standing independent others tumbled down to the foot of the wall like demolished Towers　This days march [passed] many small lakes　whether formed by the snow or not I can not say but I think some of them are permanent　none larger than a few acres Camped at a stream coming from the N. and were visited by three Indians who report the road to Colville impassable for snow　a hard frost last night and frost in the ground beside the lakes mostly frozen over but not thick　these made me think of the old buisness of my life.

24th　20 miles N. through timber in the first of which we encamped last night　the stream which we camped on here forks no game except two small prairie hens   passed many little lakes one of which is as large Fresh Pond and one nearly so   the rest smaller   Patches of snow and one third of the trees prostrated last year by southerly gale   their trunks much obstructed the path before us   on the right are snow covered and moderately high Mts.   found good wood at our camp by the light of which I now write   the scene reminds me of my Ice men at work by torch light   not frost enough in the ground to prevent driving tent stakes   the little [rain] and snow made streams [which are] run[ning] Southerly

25th   in a N. direction 15 miles to Spokan River   a stream now about half as large as the Snake River   it is now high from the melting of the snow   its sources are not distant and in a range of Mts. in sight   this Range runs about N. W. which is here the general course of the stream but how far I cannot say as it is visible but a short distance   at this place are the remains of the old Spokan House   one Bastion of which only is now standing which is left by the Indians from respect to the dead   one clerk of the Co. being buried in it   the banks of this river are here rocky and precipitous   I observed among the rocks of its bed Granite Green Stone   Quartz   sandstone Lava or Basalt   the country on approaching this river from the South resembles the pine plains of N. Hampshire near Concord   we passed the divide between the waters of this and the last river about 5 mils from our last nights Camp   striking then after passing the isolated wood in which we had camped and a large plain devoid of wood   a deep valley running N.   Crossed the most of our baggage today

26th Arrived[?] After perusing the enclosed loose papers I proceed*

27th March† due N. E. by N   24 miles we made this day This line cuts the Spokan river   This point we turned but I call the course direct for convenience   this course is through a tolerable fertile prairie   the grass good and flowers plenty on the W. side are low range of rocky hills which are granite and a better development of the broken rock named yesterday   I find it to be volcanic by its being [a word omitted] blending with porous rock on our left   and about half way of the days march   passed a mile distant a little

---

*The loose papers referred to were probably pinned to the preceding leaf of the journal, but have been lost. They no doubt were the journal notes made by Mr. Wyeth while taking a trip from the "Spokan House" to Fort Colville and back.

That Mr. Wyeth took such a trip is evident from the fact that one of the letters bearing the date of March 12th 1833 was written from Fort Colville. The journal of March 28th refers to such a trip and the return to the "Spokan house".

†The word "March" is to be read as part of the date. The trip referred to above seems to have consumed exactly a calendar month.

lake ½ mile across   to the E. by N. of this is a lake 3
miles across from which the Spokan flows   neither of these I
have seen but take this from hearsay   arrived at our camp and
all well and in better order   I have forgot to mention that the
stream that comes into the Spokane near the House brings down
peb[b]les of volcanic rock   also that the streams near our present
camp come from the hills   enter   the   prairie of the Spokan River
and disappear in the ground.

28   Made 18 miles N. through a level and wooded country and
camped with only snow   water and poor grass   the rocks seen to
day are bolders of granite   and   observed that the compass in one
place would not Traverse   this happened   while going to Colville
from Spokan and coming from there back   also observed Today
and yesterday the effects   of some former gale in prostrated trees
direction here S. W.

29   horses missing in mng. and not found till noon   went
N. 9 miles and struck Flat Head River   compass again refused to
traverse   through   deep   snow today and yesterday and thick
young trees and fallen timber   observed here the white pine and
Hemlock   snow and rain all yesterday   found our people at the
river with the boats.

30th   Remained at the   same   place   crossed the river   I here
saw an Indian who was entirely blind   he seemed to be taken
good care of by his relatives   made him a small present for
which he thanked me   parted   company with Mr Ermatinger he
to go on with the goods by water   myself with horses by land
last night the coldest for some time   today warm and pleasant

31st   Moved early N. 7 miles passing a point and two little
streams   Excessively bad going in crossing the point from snow
and brush   E. two mils   along the river   N. N. E. 5 miles to
the Lake then a line to our camp   cutting the lake   5 mils more
N. N. E.   This lake is about three   miles   broad and indeed the
river so far resembles a long lake little or no current and ¾ miles
wide plenty of pa[r]t ridges, ge[e]se, and Duck and some deer meat of
the Indians   all clay country   mountainous   one Horse gave out
and left him   a good lo[d]ge made of Branches of Pine had
almost made me forget   that it had   snowed   and   rained all day
ourselves and goods were wet through   we had no human comfort except meat enough to eat and good.

1st April   E. 2, N 3, E by S. 3, and found that from this spot
the place where I entered on the lake [it?] bore S. W. N. by E. 2,
E. by S. 5 N. 3 and made the traverse of a large peninsular at one
mil[e] E. by N.   struck the head of a creek which after 3 miles
more led us back to the Lake at the entrance into it of the River
Fete Plate. This Lake is a large and fine sheet of water it appears
of a good depth   There looks as if a large   river   entered on the
S. side   at the east end it is widest and there are two Islands   it
is surrounded by lofty and now snowy Mts. but their summits are

timbered yesterday saw nothingbut Granite   today saw Slate and Sandstone   not the least volcanic appearance in this part of the Country.

2nd Made E. S. E. 6 mils through a difficult swamp over a hill and to the main river again during which time we passed two small streams   this swamp had the largest cedars apparently the same as those of the N. E. that I have ever seen   I measured one at my height from the ground of 31 feet circumferance and I presume some were larger   no rocks to day but sandstone and slate   camped on acc. of my horses having had no feed lately the slate is tortuitous and I think mica slate   here my Indian brought me in some onions and two kinds of trout   some of the trout I have bought of the Indians as large as 10 lbs. they are plenty and taken with the hook   there are plenty of ducks and ge[e]se   the Ducks are the [same] as the tame ducks of N. E.

3d   10 mils almost due E. cutting a mountain and through almost impenetrable wo[o]d and deep snow much trouble and delay to keep the trail from the mountain 4 mils from last nights camp saw our last camp on this Lake which bore W. by N. to night we camped without grass but could not go further some of the horses strayed in the trail behind

4th   Started our Indian early to find the strayed horses and started camp ahead 9 mils E. following the river the whole way altho the trail cuts off the point and encamped where the trail again strikes the river at this place there is a considerable [creek] coming from the E. by N. into the river here for the first time since reaching Walla Walla I saw fresh Beaver sign the Indian has not yet come up with the horses and little feed for those we have with us   to day saw a small sized Bear but he was off too soon for a shot

5th   12 mils E. S. E. through deep snow and thick wood most of the way sometimes miry sometimes slippery with ice and always obstructed by the great quantity of fallen wood Last night late the Indian brought up all the lost horses

6th   9 mils E. S. E. trail better slate rock only Camped on the river last night in the mountains.   Yesterday two horses gave out left a man to keep them and bring them up if possible to day one gave out which I will leave at this camp for same man

7th   Arrived at the Flathead post kept by Mr. Rivi and one man after a ride of 17 mils E. S. E. through thick wood not very good trail and a snow storm which loaded the pines in such a manner as to bend them down to the ground frequently load- ing me with the snow as passing I disturbed the branches trees loaded down in this way and frozen so as to be firm constitute much of the difficulty of the route from Flathead or Ponderay Lake to this place want of grass at this time of the year the residue with

some mire rock mica slate this place is scituated on a fine prairie
2 mils long 1 wide and seems pleasant after coming through
thick woods and mountains counting my horses found 32 of
47 with which I started but think I shall recover all but one
left on the Lake having sent men and Indians in search of them
Mr E. came in the boats in 5 days I have now news by four
Indians who came in on the 6th on foot the Nez Perces have lost
all but 4 horses of their band of about 500 stolen by the Blackfeet
The Flatheads expected in about 15 days on the 11th started out to see if there were many beaver in the country with
intention of staying 12 days but was recalled by the arrival of the
buffaloe Indians found few beaver and the country can only be
trapped on foot plenty of pa[r]tridges to be found in this country
arrived again at the post on tho 17th of April my route was
back on the Flathead River.

18th to 20th remained at the post having now found all my
horses started camp 2 miles East up the river and to the upper
end of the prairie on which the house is built at this place is a
large creek coming from the N.

21th rained hard last night and from the 17th to this day have
had one or more slight showers each day the plain is now good
grass we are much an[n]oyed by the dogs of the Indian village
which are numerous they eat all our cords and fur flesh they
can get at in the night this is always a great trouble while travelling with Indians until you get to Buffaloe where they find better food for three nights no frost This valley is the most
romantic place imaginable a level plain of two miles long by
1 wide on the N a range of rocky and snow clad Mts. on
the S. the Flathead river a rapid current and plenty of good fishing running at the immediate base of another lofty Snowy and
Rocky range of Mts. Above and below the vall[e]y the mountains
of each range close upon the river so as apparently to afford no
outlet either way about 200 horses feeding on the green plain and
perhaps 15 Indian Lodges and numerous barking dogs with now
and then a half breed on horseback galloping gracefully with
plenty of gingling bells attached to all parts of himself and horse

it is really a scene for a poet nought but man is wanting to complete it

22nd Moved 8 mils E. N. E. along the river at 6 miles
passed a very bad rock called le Roche Mauvais the mountains
as yet closely follow the river on both sides but seem declining in
height as we stopped early we spent the rest of the day in preparing to prevent the bla[c]k Foot from stealing our horses they
have have never but once passed the bad rock and then the Flatheads gave them such a beating as keeps [them] since in better
order the[y] infest much the country we are now about entering

23d   Moved 8 mils E. N. E. to Horse plain thence N. E.
5 mils cutting a hill and leaving the River which we had her[e]-
tofore followed decending the Mts E. N. E. 6 mils to a large
open vall[e]y in the hills with little timber and much grass opposite to our Camp is a mountain where 200 Flatheads Conterays,
Ponderays and other Inds. were killed by the Blackfoot Inds.
During the first part of the last division of the days march passed
a small lake with many waterfowl and one sand hill crane. We
are now fairly in the dangerous Country through Horse plain
and into the R Flathead is a small brook to day 2 Indians ar-
r[i]ved from the main Flathead Camp at Porte D'enfer with news
that the Blackfoot have made 2 h[a]uls of horses from them the
Flathead Camp consists of men of various tribes
      24   mooved E. by S. down the valley to Flathead river then
4 miles E. following the river then Forded it and made 3 mils E.
by N. and encamped on it at a place where last year a man by
the name of La Couse was [killed] by the Blackfoot Inds. the
river is not now high when so it is not fordable and is here
a good sized stream the salts here whiten in the ground and the
animals are almost crazy after it which makes them bad to drive
      the morning was sult[r]y and I travelled without my coat but in
the afternoon we had a fine [s]hower with some thunder of good
quality the vall[e]y we left today abounds with the finest
Kamas I have yet seen as provisions are scarce in camp the
women dug much of it
      25th   Mooved Camp up the main river 12 mils E ½ N. then up a
large but fordable branch 3 mils E. by S. trail fine grass good
weather beautiful no frost for three nights the Climate appears much as at Baltimore at this season
      26th   made E. along the creek last named 5 miles then crossed
and followed it 4 mils S. E. then recrossed it and followed it E.
S. E. 3 mils crossing a small branch then 2 mils recrossing
the main creek again then followed 1 mile E S. E. and recrossed it and followed a small branch of it S. E. 1 mile crossed the
branch and followed it 2 mils S. E. to Camp clear except 1
shower but only comfortably warm Count[r]y hilly but open
E. lay a heavy pile of snowy Mts. 5 mils distant ap[p]arently
running N. & S. the rocks for a few days have been Sandstone
mica slate this day saw a white bear which we surrounded to
kill but he broke through and escaped earth in some places
whitened with salt which makes the horses bad to drive horses
getting fat grass good as also the bottom lands which are tolerably extensive
      27th   Remained at same camp snowed a little this day the
Inds went hunting and got one Deer
      28th   Abbot brought in one Beaver started Camp 2 mils S. E. 2
S.S.E.2 S.4 S.by W. thus far through woods and a defile crossing the
vide between the creek which we were on and another going to

that branch of the Flathead river to [which] we came this day.
then into open plains   snowy mts on each side   3 mils S. S. E.
then 5 mils S E by E crossing two slews of the Flathead river
and Camped on a third and larger one which we shall be obliged
to raft over   I judge it twice as large as the one we crossed
some days since   the river here runs S. W.   a little snow today
quarrelled and parted with my man Woodman   he appeared to think
that as I had but two he might take libertys   under such circumstances I will never yield an inch   I paid him half as I conceive
he had gone half the route with me   here we met some Inds from
the great Camp which they say is a moderate Camp distant
    29th   Forgot to mention in proper place that I saw Plumb
trees at the place we left W. branch of the Flathead
river   these are said to be good   about [one] inch through   ripe
in Sept. and found nowhere else but at this place   I tried hard to
get some stones but could not   Moved this day S. S. W.   we
crossed by fording   contrary to expectation by loading high
and taking high horses   at 8 miles struck another branch of
same river as large as those already passed   at 4 miles further a
creek from opposite side   ford tolerably good   at 20 miles
came to main Camp of 110 Lodges   Containing upward of 1000
souls with all of which I had to shake hands   the Custom in
meeting these indians is for the Coming party to fire their arms
then the other does the same   then dismount and form single file
both sides and passing each other shake hands with men women and
children a tedious job   buffaloe have come here and even further
but they are killed at once and do not get wonted   her[e] the
racine amani or Spetulum is found   this Camp is on the river
good grass   river direct S. S. W.   six nights since the Blackfoot
stole horses from this Camp here   I found thre[e]
Canadians   one of whom was one who came to us the night before we were fired on on the heads of the Spanish River   this
days march between two parralled ranges of Mts now Snowy   but
I think not always so   there is much kamas in this region   we
find little meat in the Indian Camp and are therefore much short-
[e]ned for food
    30th   went out to collect some flowers for friend Nuttall after-
wards to see the Camp   find 120 lodges of us today some having
arrived   they are collecting to go to the Buffaloe in force to meet
the Blackfeet   looked at their games   one is played by two men
at a time   a level place is made on the ground about 15 feet long
by 3 feet wide with a small log of wood at each end to stop a
small iron ring which one of them rools from one end of the
all[e]y to the other   both following it   each having an arrow
which they endeavor to throw after and under it   so that when
stopped it will rest on one of them   the one on whose arrow it is
wins   at least this is all I understand of the game   the game is
kept by a third by means of placing sticks on one side or the

other another feat much in practice from the smallest to the
largest in Camp is two with some arrows throw them so as to
go as near the first thrown as possible advancing continually untill
all are expended then throwing them back again in same manner
another game is two or more opposite the one side having some
small article in their hand keep changing it from one hand to
the other as swift as possible accompanied by a tune and motion
of body and limbs except feet (for they sit all the time) the get
is for the other party to designate the hand in which it rema[i]ns
at the last this is the most practised game and requires much
dexterity on both sides it is kept with sticks as the first every
morning some important indian addresses either heaven or his
countrymen or both I believe exhorting the one to good conduct
to each other and to the strangers among them and the other to
bestow its blessings he finishes with "I am done['"] the whole
set up an exclamation in concord during the whole time
Sunday there is more parade of prayer as above nothing is done Sunday in the way of trade with these Indians nor in playing games
and they seldom fish or kill game or raise camp while prayers are being said on week days everyone ceases whatever vocation he is about
if on horseback he dismounts and holds his horse on the spot until all is done Theft is a thing almost unknown among them and
is punished by flogging as I am told but have never known an instance of theft among them the least thing even to a bead or
pin is brought you if found and things that we throw away this
is sometimes troublesome I have never seen an Indian get in anger with each other or strangers. I think you would find among
20 whites as many scoundrels as among 1000 of these Indians they
have a mild playful laughing disposition and their qualities are
strongly portrayed in their countenances. They are polite and unob-
trusive and however poor never beg except as pay for services and in
this way they are moderate and faithful but not industrious. they
a re very brave and fight the blackfeet who continually steal their
horses and kill their straglers with great success beating hollow
equal numbers They wear as little clothing as the weather will
permit sometimes nothing on excep[t] a little thing to cover the
privates and sometimes but rare this is ommitted at play but not
when there are women and allways at a race the women are closely covered and chaste never cohabiting promisc[u]ously with the
men the pox is not much and perhaps never known among them
it dies here of itself when brought from the coast where it is rife
   the young women are good looking and with dress and cleanliness
would be lovely today about 100 of them with their root diggers
in their hands in single file went out to get roots they staid about
two hours and returned in the same order each time passing the
chief's lodge it was evidently a ceremony but the import I could
not learn in a lodge or other place when one speaks the rest pay
strict attention When he is done another assents by "yes" or

dissents by "no" and then states his reasons which are heard as attentively it is a practice when a woman has her courses to make a little lodge outside her husbands lodge and there remain until they are finished. The more peaceable dispositions of the Indians than the whites is plainly seen in the children I have never heard an angry word among them nor any quarrelling altho there are here at least 500 of them together and at play the whole time at foot ball bandy and the like sports which give occasion to so many quarrells among white children

May 1st. Same camp the day reminds me of home and its customs it is a fine and almost summer day altho the nights have been frosty of late but the days are warm This morning the squaws left camp with their root diggers singing in good accord the tunes of their country Yesterd[ay] Mr. Ermatinger traded 29 beavers I find an Indian Camp a place of much novelty the Indians appear to enjoy their amusements with more zest than the whites altho they are simple they are great gamblers in proportion to their means bolder than the whites

2nd Moved Camp 2 miles S. E. by E. 4 miles S by E. over a hilly but open country and diverging a little from the main river to the Eastward and Camped on a small river going to the same river the two parallel ranges of Mts. still continue on either side of the river It rained a little of the last night and some this morning the day is cloudy and moderately warm The absence of quarrells in an Indian Camp more and more surprises me when I come and see the various occasions which would give rise to them among the whites the crowding together of from 12 to 1800 horses which have to be driven into Camp at night to stake in mng. to load the starting of horses and turning of loads the seizing of fuel when scarce, often the case, the plays of men and Boys &c. At the Camp yesterday saw the bones of a buffalo bull not old being the first sign of buffaloe yet seen.

3d. Same Camp.

4th Same Camp To day heard a sound like a heavy piece of ordonance and I suppose arising from the fall of some mighty fragment of rock from the mountains The sound seemed to come from the N. I suppose the sound heard in the Snake coun-try arose from the same cause altho then no heavy mountains were in sight but there were cut rocks enough weather some-what smokey but warm and clear A party of hunters who pro-posed to go out for beaver deferred the thing on acc. of the water being too high to set a trap. A Thunder storm in the afternoon with high wind from the S. W. and Rain.

5th. Sunday according to our reconing there is a new great man no[w] getting up in the Camp and like the rest of the w[o]rld [he] covers his designs under the great cloak religion his followers are now dancing to their own vocal music in the plain perhaps 1-5 of the Camp follow him when he gets enough followers he will branch off and be an independent chief he is getting up some new form of religion among the Indians more simple than himself   like others of his class he works with the fools women and children first while he is doing this the men of sense thinking it too foolish to do harm stand by and laugh but they will soon find that women fools and children form so large a majority that with a bad grace they will have to yield. These things make me think of the new lights and revivals of New England rains a little today

6th. Bright and clear found all of my horses three of which had been missing Moved 4 mils S. and encamped on a creek of the main river about 1 ½ mils from the latter

7th. Same Camp cloudy all night and today but warm

8th. Same Camp last night had a false alarm Some Inds. of the camp who were gambling for a gun discharged it before laying [it] on the stakes This though a common occurrence gave the horses a fright and one frightens another in those cases until all are alarmed the running of those that have got loose the snorting stamping and rearing of those who cannot when there are at least 1500 the Howling of dogs men running with guns the contrast of firelights with the darkness of the night make altogether a scene of confusion to be recollected This day hunters went out 2 only one returned sun two hours high with one antelope the other at night with 4 To day a small boy broke his arm but as I understood that the Indians reduce fractures well and as I am quite ignorant I did not meddle with it

9th. Moved S. by E 6 mils and camped on the main river on the march saw two bla[c]kfeet who ran with all the speed of their horses to the mountains a little rain but warm high wind and somewhat dusty The rain does not seem to lay the dust in the least The country covered for the first time with sage and so far the same kind of minerals as near the Ponderay Lake This afternoon came to us a Snake a Nez Perce and a Flat head on foot they came from Salmon River and bring no news except that the Nez Perce Camp is at Salmon river and that they are mostly without horses

10th Mooved 7 mils E. by E. [?] rained a little shower but clear in the afternoon. This moment Chief Guineo is saying the usual afternoon prayers I observe that he first makes a long one which is responded to by the usual note in accord then a short one followed by the same note on horse back the whole time walking about the Camp hat on in an audible voice and directed as though addressing the men below rather than ''him'' above To day 11 Flatheads started on foot to steal horses from the Blackfeet

11th Started out early hunting for the first time this trip We are now short of provisions. The Camp moved 10 mils S. by E. and camped on the river the wide bot[t]om of which is

done it is now jammed in between the hills   during this distance passed two small creeks big enough for beaver only   saw
four antelope killed nothing   saw two olived green snakes about
2 ½ feet long   blunt tail but slender   afternoon clear and warm
    12th   Being Sunday remained at same Camp   the hills here
are of Granite with large bed of quartz.   Mica slate is common
Gneiss also in some places   the same rock as at Kittle falls observed in one place a black mineral like that found at Franconis[?]
covering iron ore   it looks like horse hair in a mass combed
stra.ght   the hills are now well covered with grass   the river is
now at its highest but is fordable   this morning long prayers
in form as usual   at some lodges the Inds. are singing as an
act of devotion
    13th   Went out hunting   killed one N. E. pa[r]tridge only
saw 4 cubs   4 deer   Camp moved 6 mils S. S. E. and
camped on the W. side   we approach the head of this river fast
    14th.   remained at same Camp   snow and sleet all day   An
Indian died in camp to day but I do not think the Camp was delayed on that account   it was a bad day which I think the reason
    his friends are now singing over him according to their custom
    15th   Made 6 miles S. S.E. and crossed the river and camped on
a little creek   crossing two on the W. side all too small at low
water for beaver.   snowed last night and until 8 this mng. altho
as much as 4 inches of snow has fallen it is at 11 oclock all gone
except the hills which are white   grass good   Granite country
and fertile in the bottoms and and on the hills and mountain
sides
    16th   Made 9 mils S. E. following a creek of the main river
    about ⅓ the size of the same   this we crossed 6 times during
the day   this morning 4 inches snow which fell during the night
but all gone at 9 ock   fair at 4 in afternoon   this day finishes
all our provisions   in above distance river crooked .
    17th.   2 miles S. E.   3 E and cutting a high mountain   1
mile S by E. and struck the river again in a large and fertile
plain   here crossed the main branch of it and followed 2 miles a
creek running S by E   at the place where we left the river it
receives a small creek from the S and where we struck it again
another quite small from the N. The main branch appears to run
about E. from the plain   when arrived at Camp finding no meat
I took my traps out to catch beaver when returning saw
the spuaw bringing in moss and roots   when I came in found the
hunters had come in with one bear one Elk and several deer and 5
beaver this makes a timely supply Indians are gone ahead to see
the mountain is passiable   This mountain divides us from the
heads of the Missouri.
    18th   2 miles up the creek S. by E.   then assending the
mountain S. E. 2 more then 2 S by E down the mountain
and struck a little thread of water which during 28 mils

increased gradually to a little river and S. E. to another coming
from the S. and both go off together N.   this is one of the heads
of the Missouri   we crossed it and camped   here we found both
Bulls and cows which makes all merry   this pass is good going
when there is no snow   now there was about one foot   in places
drifted more   we took 8 hours to pass   there is a visible change
in the apppearance   vegetation is not so forward   the trees appear
stinted and small   the land poorer and covered with Sedge
the other side   there is little   on the W. side   all is
granite   as soon as I passed the divide I saw Pudding Stone   we
had showers of snow and rain this day but this I believe is constant in this region at this time of the year   the Mt. is much
higher [on] the W. than [on] the E. side   This I observed also at the
Trois Tetons   The grass is poor and has started but little   the
prairie in some places has snow   The vall[e]y runs N and S. and
is bounded E. and W. by a range of Mts.   this day my horse
keeper left me taking an offence at some misinterpretation about
a horse.   The 16th. Woodman came to camp from his hunt for
beaver tired and famished having eated nothing for three days

   19th   Same Camp   snowed by fits most of the day   being
Sunday the medicine chief had devotional exercises with his followers   he formed them into a ring men women and children and
after an address they danced to a tune   in dancing the[y] keep
the feet in the same position the whole time mer[e]ly jumping up
to the tune   keeping the hands in front of them   at intervals he
addressed them   at night Blackfeet were seen prowling about the
camp   at least so the Indians say   erected myself a lodge for the
first time in the country and paid a treat of rum &c to the whites
in Camp and some of the principal Indians to wet the same as it
is called.

   29th.   Snowing hard in the morning   one horse so lame that
if we move Camp to day he will remain for the Blackfoot or
wolves.   Much the same.   Started at half past 12 found
the horse could be drove a little   got him along about four miles
shall return for him to morrow   this day 9 miles E. S. E. over
a level plain of rich deep soil wet and miry in the extreme   saw
our Indians running buffaloe ahead   At 5 mils crossed a little
brook running N by E and camped on a considerable creek running N. by E.   and all falling in to the same as the creek we left

   At about the junction it doubles round a point of mountains
and apparently takes a north[?]eastwardly course   rain snow and
and sunshine as usual today.   4 hunters left us to day to hunt
beaver in the Blackfoot country, Pellew, Charloi, Narbesse, Rivey.

   21st.   Same Camp sent back and brought the lame horse into
Camp Went out to the mountain to cut log poles   found a
Blackfoot lodge recently occupied   snow as usual   saw the Indians

cooking a root resembling the yellow dock, but not so yellow tasted like parsnip raw, informed by them that it is bad before being cooked suppose it is more or less poisonous

22d Same camp Blue Devils all Day Turned in

23d 6 miles S. S. E. and up the valley 3 S E by S. 3 S. E. This valley is all good land about four miles wide and perhaps 50 long and how much further it goes N. I cannot say. Went out to hunt buffaloe killed one Elk out of a large band mountains with snow each side of valley snowed a little as usual

24th A double portion of the usual weather viz. rain Hail snow wind rain and Thunder into the bargain we are so near where they make weather that they send it as if cost nothing Course S. E. 6 miles up the creek then by N. E. 3 cutting a height of land but low and perfectly good going to the head of another river running S. E. down this two miles and camped hunted today killed one cow saw some hundreds

25th. Followed the creek 5 miles S. S. E. then it turned round a point more eastwardly We continued same course 4 mils and struck a creek going into the same about 2 mils below the point spoken of rain snow & Hail today with sunshine grass better to day had a long ride before sunrise after the lame horse which I brought to Camp.

26th Same Camp A blackfoot Trail discovered in our vicinity a numerous camp of them better weather than usual to day Sunday according to our reconing. At night one of two Indians who started on an express to the Nez Perces Camp returned with three blankets one white shirt and [some] tobacco and powder which articles they found buried with a Blackfoot Indian who was unscalped two bullets through his head and one through his body We apprehend that there has been a battle between the Blackfoot Indians and perhaps the whites.

27th 17 mils S. crossing two small forks of the Missouri and camping on the third of small size near Camp found a red blankett Hat and some small articles but no body. soon after Camp arrived one Indian with news and soon after 2 more and three squaws comprising the only survivor[s] of the battle which happened thus 21 Nez Perces 18 Flathead and two Iroquois and 1 Ponderai started with intent to steal horses from the Blackfeet near the head of Salmon River they saw 4 and some horses these they attacked just at this moment a horse threw one of the Flatheads he seized on one of the horses of the Blackfeet and ran after him up a mountain he looked back and saw a large number of Blackfeet killing his companions not one survived but himself he made the best of his way to the Nez Perce Camp to tell the sad tale to the wives and children of the dead in this Camp [where] the relatives of the deceased Flathead are there is weeping and wailing. Fair all day and comfortably warm. there were 46 lodges of the Blackft. do not know if women were

with it or not   if not it is a much larger Camp than ours,   the
blanketts &c found are accounted for in the practice that the
Blkft. have of cutting a piece of flesh from near the shoulder
tying it to an article and throwing it away to propitiate the
Deity   the circumstance of the flesh being tied with them I did
not at first know.

28th   Moved S. 8 miles following the left branch of the creek
which forks at our last nights camp then S. S. W. 4 miles and
camped on the same creek a little rain just after we came to camp
a band of Buffaloe passed the camp which gave a fine chance to
the Indians to run them one of them they chased into camp and
then killed her a fine cow.

29th   Moved S. by E. 6 miles cutting the divide of waters and
struck a small creek going into Salmon river then 7 miles S by
E. following the creek through high hills of lime rock on which
we found plenty of sheep some of which were killed then
3 miles S. W. and struck Salmon River here a small creek running through a fine open plain valley about 6 miles wide and extending each way as far as the eye could reach the river runs
here about W. by N. On the S. side is a high range of snowy
mountains perhaps not covered the whole year this range is
parrallel with the river. the country I should call for two days
back volcanic flints are found in abundance some of the stones
have a white crust on the outside of them whether of lime or
Epsom salts can not say both abound the lime rock is mostly slate blue but is found in layers of all shades from white to
deep blue and very much contorted and forming frequent caves
and holes. It is the intention of the chiefs to remain at this
camp until the Nez Perces come to us and then to move together.
This morning left my wounded horse.

30th. Same Camp rained all last night and all day Went
up into the mountains to hunt sheep wounded one but a snow
storm coming on his trail was covered and I lost him Saw plenty
it is surprising to view the places where they go no one would
imagine it possible for an animal to climb the rocks they do Got
nothing and hearing a firing hast[en]ed to the top of a hill to see
if the Camp was attacked but found that the Nez Perces had arrived with 9 whites a Mr. Hodgskins at their head. This
party is 16 lodges and only escaped the Blkft. by the latter falling
in with 31 Indians 30 of whom they killed It is supposed the
30 killed about 50 of the Blkft. They mustered about 700 all
men and were sufficient to cut off all our Camps if they would
trade man for man.

31st   Got news that 20 lodges of Blkft. are now camped at our
camp of 21st Inst. and I think likely that these are the same who
killed the 30 Indians and as usual 10 times over rated. This
day moved 7 miles S. E. up the river and following a small creek
near our camp of last night a creek comes in from the S. one

which we followed coming from N. W.   this one fro[m] the S. S. E.   the main river S. E.   went into the mts.   saw antelope   killed nothing in the mountains   heavy thunder with a snow and hail storm and high wind.

June 1st   Same Camp   some snow on Mts.   got wet.

2nd   17 miles S. E.   1 E. by N.   through an open plain nearly level   finished the streams of Salmon river and struck one called little Goddin   it terminates near the three butes in a little lake here goes S. E. through the valley   the mts. appear terminating on both sides   a fair day   the S. r ange comprises much more of a stone which I will call quartz   the same as is found at Kettle falls   there is also lime stone   Blue and without organic remains.

3d   15 miles S. E. through the same vall[e]y   gradually decending   the stream became a rapid and pretty large one   as large as some that pass 300 miles   We camped at a narrow pass formed of low hills   here is between the hills a slough of clay saturated with Epsom salts   the hills are of Basaltic rock in collumns the first I have seen in this region   lime rock is found here in pudding rock   Killed plenty of Buffaloe here

4th.   Moved through the vall[e]y following the river called as I am informed little Goddin in a S. E. by E. 6 miles during which space I found the lower hills of Basalt   the mts. are of lime rock the same as passed her[e]tofor[e]   Wind high   N. W. which brings warm weather here and clear   grass very bad.

5th.   Clear warm day   moved S. E. by E. 8 miles   went in search of Buffaloe   found none   Saw an old Blkft. Camp of 65 fires   half as large as our present camp   Saw several whirlwinds which raised the dust at a distance and appears much like smoke. Saw the three Butes come in sight one by one and then the Trois Tetons   the Butes S. E. by S.   20 mils distant about   so far this river rapid and little brush and no beaver   grass worse and worse.

6th.   Same Camp   last night arrived 3 Kootenays with 25 beaver who left us on Flathead river being on foot the whole time   last night sent out Indians to see in what direction were the most Buffaloe   one came back this mng.   reports cows to the S.

7th   Moved E. N. E. 15 miles and without water the whole route   the Trois Tetons bearing E. perhaps 90 miles distant over a level and dry plain without grass or extremely little   in the afternoon had a gale from the S. W. which blew down the lodges accompanied with a little rain and enough dust to suffocate one on our left there is a range of high hills from which come numerous streams   but they sink in the plain and are warm and muddy   went out this evening to bring in the meat of a cow killed in the forenoon and found a horse extremely fat   it is surprising how fat a horse gets by being left to himself   no grooming that I have ever seen will make a horse appear as beautiful as to be left to his own resources   the Butes bear due S.

8th   5 miles N. following the same creek up which grows larger as we assend   had a fine rain & Hail and Thunder today which is Sunday.   Water very muddy   grass little and but a little.

9th.   10 miles N. and following the creek has some tolerable wild[?] cotton wood and willow on it   wind N.   clear and windy country same   Three Nez Perces arrived at camp   Bring news that Payette is with four Nez Perces Chiefs.   Capt Serrey with 7 is detained by snow   that the Blackfeet village is camped at the spot where we met the Nez Perces.   We find that Payette will meet us at the forks   Capt Serrey has got 31 horses   this day a bull was run into camp which I shot at my lodge door   To day an Indian was running bulls   he turned   the horse stopped and threw him   the bull gored him into his chest so that his breath was made through the apparture   by the help of the women he reached camp.   When Mr. Ermatinger dressed his wound he very composedly made his will by word of mouth   the Indians responding in concord at the end of each sentence.   He appeared not in the least intimidated by the approach of death.   I think the Indians die better than the whites   perhaps they have less superstition in regard to the future   and argue that as the deity makes them happy here he will also hereafter if there is existence for them.

10th.   Same camp   another Indian came to camp who had been looking out for the Blkft.   He was ambuscaded by two of them and narrowly escaped by the goodness of his horse   being wounded slightly in the nose.

11th   Same camp   fresh news of the Blkft.   Made horse pen that my horses might be safe.   I do not apprehend any serious attack but only that they will come suddenly with a great noise of voices and guns and fright[en] the horses   on such occasions horses become wild   one frights another   they run over the lodges this increases the confusion and the yelling firing and runing & snorting of 1200 Indians and 1800 horses is frightfull indeed.   Sometimes a camp with as many horses as the above loose every one   it is commonly whole or none.   Day warm, clear fresh wind W.

12th.   Same camp   warm day   The Blackft camp about 15 mils from this   they are very numerous.

13th.   Same camp   cloudy and cool with high wind from S. E.   Blakft. still near but have attempted nothing yet.   Child died in camp yesterday   remains to bury today.   Find I have missed one day in my journal which has been done   while laying at some camp and accordingly date tomorrow the 15th.

15th   Last night some Blackfoot fired into our camp   a ball passed through a lodge   some straggler disappointed of stealing

horses I suppose.   Moved N. N. E.   5 miles and camped on a
creek now almost dry and soon will be wholly.   There is little
but cotton wood on this creek.

16th.   8 miles N. E. by N. to a small creek which about a
mile below this joins another larger one.   Country nearly level
day windy S. W.   wind cool and cloudy   Trois Tetons bear E.
S. E.   Today saw the Indians carrying the man who was wounded by a Buffaloe   no one could receive more attention, one person
to carry water   he was on a good bed made on poles the
front of which like shafts were carried by a horse led by his wife
the hinder part by 6 men and women on their shoulders   the
camp moved slower than usual for him   these things give a favorable impression of the Indians.

17th.   Same camp   rained very hard all last night and until
noon of today   an alarm of Blkft last night but I believe little of
these things in so large a camp when it is known that there are
Blkft. near   a man straying out of camp is enough to give rise to
a report and a report once raised it gathers like a snow ball.

18th.   Same camp   Severe hail & snow yesterday afternoon and
rain most of last night and until noon today.   Camp about out of
provisions so we are in hopes of moving soon.   Nothing but necessity and that immediate will induce an Indian to do the least
thing, any excuse serves to stop buisness with them and a small
party of whites who are not strong enough to move alone will
find in traveling with them occasion for all the patience they may
have.

19th.   1½ miles to the main rive here going S. W.   this we
found quite deep enough to ford for horses   the mules I was obliged to unload and put the loads on the horses   3[?] miles more
passed

three slews of our stream joining the last river mentioned.   3
miles more camped on another branch of it   making 10½ miles
N. E. by E.   day clear snow in patches in shaded places but the
country green with herbage and mostly in blossom.   All rocks
for some days past volcanic.   This stream looses itself in the
plain.

20th.   Moved 11 miles E. by N. and camped on Kamas River
so called from the abundance of that root   in some spots it is so
abundant as to exclude other vegetation.   This Prairie is very extensive perhaps 15 miles each way and is intersected by numerous
little streams which form one going to the S. and ends in a small
lake on the plain between this and Lewis river   day clear & cool
frost last night   snow on all the high hills   Trois Tetons bear
E.   S. E. I should think about 80 miles distant   found Buffaloe
here the first for 10 days   when we found the last I think at least
100 were killed in one day   42 tongues were given to Mr. E. H.
and myself.

21st.. Late last night arrived 5 hunters Pillew, Nasben, and Churboye and two Indians who left us on the head of the Missouri having seen plenty of recent sign of the Blkfeet but happily saw none   they killed 94 Beaver.   Today went out to hunt   killed one Bull.   forenoon showers and lowery   Kamas in bloom   the Indians are taking large quantities of it   this plain is extensive but about 7 miles across of it only is rich and that is as good as any land I ever saw   the main plain is much of it bare   rock   the surface of which looks like a pan of milk when you push together the cream   evidently it was once a fiery and fluid plain or lake of of lava, probably the whole plain between these mountains and the Trois Tetons   the rock is porous like honey comb   the surface shows plainly the heads of Basaltic colums and in some places the colums stand not perpendicular but at an angle of 5c degrees about, same camp.

22nd.   Same camp   arrived this mng. an express from Bonneville   this express came from the forks in three days   they saw Blkft. by the way   this afternoon Mr. Hodge left to go to Bonneville   day clear and warm   Buffaloe were run into camp.

23rd.   Sunday   Indians singing and dancing as usual   day warm and clear.   These Inds. do nothing on Sunday.

24th.   Moved across the plain 3 miles N. E.   Day warm and clear.

25th.   Yesterday at night some Inds. came in from hunting Buffaloe   reported that they saw two Blkft. and fired on them   at night we saw their fire in the Mts.   Same camp   fine clear warm day   employed in making a saddle.

26th.   Same camp   went out hunting   saw a few Buffaloe but killed nothing but a grouse   as I had some dispute with Mr. David Douglass about the grouse of this country I subjoin a discription; the bird had 10 pointed drab colored, mottled with white. tail feathers   the outer edge of the feathers are only mottled until you approach their end when both sides are mottled   under the tail are 10 or 12 dark brown feathers ⅔ as long as the tail feathers   white at the termination.   The tail feathers are about 8 inches long.   The wing feathers are nearly white underneath and dark drab outside.   From the head of the breast bone to the tail are many black feathers.   On the body under the wings are redish grey feathers   above the breast and nearly on the neck is a place devoid of feathers   of a dirty olive color each side and a little below this is a tuff of short sharp pointed dirty white feathers   they look as if they had been clipped with a shears.   The tail feathers look as though they had been burnt off leaving the stalk of the quill projecting.   The bill is short and curved downwards   above the bare spot on the neck are short mottled feathers cream, white and black.   It is feathered to the toes which are three and a small one behind.   The hinder part of the leg is not feathered from the knee downwards   Toe nails short and obscure, its back pretty uniformly mottled with deep brown dirty white approaching dirty yellow and dun colored   weight 4 ½ lbs.   length from point of tail feathers to tip of bill 25 inches   from tips of wings 3 ½ ft. We were regaled by thunder shower on our return to camp   saw Blkft. trail and a cow recently killed by them.

27th.   Same camp   nothing remarkable.

28th.   Same camp   nothing but lice and dirt.   Cool today.

29th.   Same camp as yesterday   went out to hunt   killed one Buffaloe which fell into the river and had to butcher him   up to my middle in cold water.   Some hunters who went out today came in with news that they had seen the Blkft. camp on Tobacco river   one of the heads of the Missouri   they say it is larger than ours.

30th   Same camp   Sunday   Indians praying, dancing & singing.

1st July.   Moved 2 miles S. and down the creek   clear moderately warm day the first for three days   nights have been frosty   ice made in our pots & pails. Men came from Bonneville in the evening.

2nd.   Moved S. 12 miles and camped on same creek   on the way observed some fine luxuriant clover   grass good   about 9 miles down the creek w[h]ich rapidly increases in size from numerous springs w[h]ich are of fine cold water   we camped in a cluster of large cotton wood   large for this place   about 10 inches through.

3rd.   Last night a Bear made his way into camp among the horses and gave a considerable alarm but was off before guns could be got out.   Today moved 16 miles S. S. W. and camped on same creek with Mr. Bonneville with about 40 men bound for Green river.   I have heretofore forgot to mention that at our camp of 1st July we left about 40 lodges of the Flatheads   country   this days route dry and barren   day warm.

4th.   Same camp   at night saw a band of Blackfeet a little above camp   clear warm day.

5th.   Same camp.

6th.   Same camp   very warm weather.

7th.   This morning our camp forked in three directions Mr. Hodgkin[?] for a trapping excursion with the Nez Perces, Mr. Ermatinger with the Ponderays to go to Flathead river, ourselves East 18 miles to Henrys fork here wooded with narrow leafed cotton wood   our route over a very dry plain   passing at about half the distance some low hills of pure sand with not the least appearance of vegetation.   The party is 26 all told.

8th.   Followed up the river where we were much annoyed by mosquitos about 8 miles N. N. E.   there forded it about belly deep   going E. by S. 5 mils to a large river which must be Lewis fork   here we found Buffaloe   these two rivers form a junction about 15 miles from this point as I believe near two butes but some say not until you get as low as Three Butes   on this river are not many mosquitoes.

9th.   Made this day 22½ miles due East toward the Trois Tetons   at 8 miles struck a small creek with cut rock banks running N. W. and to the river last crossed, which is not Lewis fork, At 20 miles cut a mountain which rises and is wooded to the S W. and diminishes to the plain to the N. E.   We entered Pierre's Hole and camped on the N. W. side of it.   Here we found Buffaloe.

10th.   Moved 12 miles S. E. crossing a difficult swamp and camped about 2 miles from the battle ground of last year with the Gros Ventres   Day warm and a great quantity of grasshoppers for several days past   so much so as to discolor the ground in many places.

11th.   Started early and made 3 miles E. S. E. to the foot of the mountains then 8 miles E. S. E. to the summit then 6 miles E. to Lewis fork and 1 mile E. across it at the same place we crossed last year   found it very high for fording   but succeeded at last.   Wind strong N. W.   clear and moderately warm.   Horses troubled with horse flies on the mountains but not in this plain

found buffaloe in the bottom   also mosquitoes   The river is here much choked up with islands and heaps of drift wood and a great quantity of mud   in coming over the mountains lost one mule and sent a man back for it   he has not returned yet [at] sundown

got a wet jacket in the river trying to find a ford.   There is the trail of about 8 men who have passed through this defile before us   as I think about 14 days   they marked a name on the trees and we suppose that they are men of Dripps & Fontenelle. We as yet see no appearance of the Blkft. except very old forts and lodges.   Lewis fork here runs S. E. about 9 miles then turns S.

12th.   This morning my man came back having been out all night   he found the mule at our last camp.   Made this day 9 miles S. E. along the river then 3 miles E. S. E. to a small creek running into the river.   At this place 9 men under Capt. Stevens were attacked by about 30 Blkft. a little later than this time last year and several of them killed.   Mr. Bonneville informs me that when he passed last year in August their bones were laying about the valley.   I am apprehensive that More, a sick man whom I left in charge of Stevens, must be one of them.   6 miles more over a hilly broken limestone country S. E. to a considerable fork of Lewis river   this stream is strongly impregnated with sulphur. This camp is almost without grass.   In the first place this morning we moved 3 miles and crossed a creek putting into the river. At our camp of to night there is a small branch joining the creek from the S. E.

13th.   East 5 miles   N. E. ½ mile through bad cut rocks on

the N. side of the river   there is also a trail on the S. side   then
½ mile E.   then ¼ mile S. E.   then following a left hand fork
of the river a few rods N. E.   crossed it and made E. 3 miles to
the right hand fork again which we followed E. 2 miles then S.
E. 4 miles to camp   crossing it several times   a good trail most
of the way   one horse of the Indians killed by falling from the
cut rock trail down to the river in the first of the cut rocks   there
is a handsome cave rock lime & sand   a few boulders of granite
seen today as also on the E. side of the mountains of Pierres hole.
The river which we followed this day is rapid and too deep below
the branches to ford   during the last of the route several small
forks from each side.

  14th.   Made 9 miles S. E. to the height of land between this
river and Green river then 5 miles S. S. E. to a creek running into Green river.   there are good trails all the way and to the divide much timber   The creek on which we camped last night just
above the camp divided into three forks.   We followed the most
southwardly for awhile then mounted the hill on the left side of
it.   There has been for two days a high range of Mts. on our left
about 10 miles distant apparently of sand stone and limestone
    these [trend] E. S. E. & N. N. W. and on the divide between this
and Wind river also on our right   there have been a range of Mts.
of same composition about 15 mils distant.   Both ranges have
snow in patches   Many alarms today but still no enemys   killed
plenty of Buffaloe.

  15th.   Made E. S. E. 12 miles to Green river and to Mr. Bonnevilles fort   day clear and fine.   Found here collected Capt.
Walker, Bonneville, Cerry, of one Co. Dripps & Fontenelle of the
Am. Fur Co. Mr. Campbell just from St. Louis, Mess. Fitzpatric,
Gervais, Milton Sublette of the Rocky Mountain Fur Co. and
in all the Cos. about 300 whites and a small village of Snakes
    here I got letters from home.   During the last year among all
the Cos there has been in all about 25 men killed two of my original party with them, viz Mr More & O'Neil. [O'Neal?]

  16th.   Same camp.

  17th. Moved 10 miles down the river S. E.   it is here a large
and rapid stream and to be forded only in a few places.   Here we
were followed by the Snake village   we encamped with the Rocky
Mountain Fur Co.

  18th to the 24 remained at the same camp during which time
the weather was pleasant and warm   for several nights we were
an[n]oyed by mad dogs or wolves which I cannot say but believe
the latter as one was killed.   I think one animal did the whole
mischief as when men were bitten at one camp none were at the
other   about nine persons were bitten at Dripps & Fontenelles
camp and three at ours.   D. & Fs. camp is 4 miles above us on
the same side of the river   we hope he was not mad as no sim-
tons have yet appeared.

24th. Moved E. 12 miles cutting a small divide came to a wide valley parallel with Wind river Mts. in which we crossed 3 large creeks and camped on the 4th. which has much pine timber on it and is called Pine fork they all come into one quite soon by appearance and are not near as large as the main fork on which we first found the whites and which we have now crossed. In coming here it passed to our left that is up stream. Found plenty of Antelope and Bulls.

25th. Crossed the stream and moved E. S. E. 3 miles to a creek the same on which I made a cash last year and crossed at a good ford just below two stony hills then on 7 ½ mile E. S. E. following a branch of the same creek and camped to noon. Buffaloe throwing the dust in the air in every direction and Antelope always in sight. This day a Mr. Worthington in running a bull fell from his horse, the Bull furious ran at the horse and passed him within 3 feet then turned again and passed him he having got up from the ground ran and escaped he killed the bull and found he had but one eye owing to which circumstance he escaped. Afternoon made S. E. 13 miles leaving the last creek of what is called New fork to which all the waters we have passed since leaving rendesvous belong the one we camped on last night heads in a lake about 1 ½ miles over and not far from where we slept. We now struck the west fork of Sandy and camped at an old camp of last year at a place where Ball left his rifle[?] Country covered with Buffaloe.

26th. Made S. E. 9 miles and camped on another fork of Sandy then S. E. by E. 15 miles to Sweet water all the country is granite from rendesvous so far Buffaloe quite plenty also Antelope Today shot a cow with a very young calf the calf ran after our mules for a long way until it found the difference.

27th. Made down the creek 1 ½ miles E. S. E. then E. 8 miles to another branch of Sweet water then 6 miles E. by N. to another branch of same then down this branch S. E. 2 miles and camped. Saw one band of Elk and many Antelope plenty of Buffaloe.

28th. Made E. 2 mils to another Creek running S. by E. crossed made E. 6 miles E. by N. 4 miles at the creek a sort of slate prevailed but soon ran into a red sandstone passed at 11 mils a small pond to our right few Buffaloe today last night Capt. Stewart had some sport with a bear near our camp in the willows which he wounded but did not kill He represented him as large as a mule. In the afternoon made E. by N. 6 miles to Sweet water river then N. E. 3 miles up it and camped. I came ahead and found a white bear in a thickett and after firing a pistol and throwing stones into it started him out he came as though he meant to fight us but I gave him the shot of my rifle through the body He then rushed on us and I ran as fast as I could Mr.

Kamel [Campbell?] snapped at him Mr Sublette ran also being on a
mule

the bear followed us no great distance and turned and ran up
creek   some horsemen followed and killed him after putting 4
more balls into him.

29th.   Same camp, rained all day   two men went out to hunt
and at night one returned alone the other in the morning being
still absent.

30th.   Started out to hunt the man and in about 8 miles came
to the place   hunted the whole country over and found nothing
but a white bear the largest and the whitest I have yet seen   run
him about a mile and fired one shot but could not kill him. After
a long ride returned to camp   found the party had moved on
followed them N. N. W. in 6 miles struck Po[r]poise in a small rapid
thread running through sandstone banks   this we followed N.
W. 3 miles then N. by E. 9 miles more thousands of Buffaloe in
sight and the red bottom of the streams deep and muddy with recent rains and found camp a little after sundown.   The afternoon
of the 29th we found lime rock almost entirely   today sand stone
and a kind of glassy stone resembling Carnelian   a coarse kind
of which I think it is.

31st   N. N. W. 8 miles through a muddy Bottom and little
grass to some large willows   found a party of 4 whites who have
lost their horses and one of them wounded in the head with a Ball
and in the body with an arrow very badly   they suppose the
Snakes did it but I think not.   Little grass.   In the afternoon
moved N. 9 miles to the junction of Great Po[r]poise river which
comes from the S. W.   then N. by E. 4 miles to the junction of
Wind river which comes from the W. turning around as I supose
and running along Wind River Mountains which run N. W.   Altogether they form a large and muddy river but fordable now
which is after a heavy rain.

Aug. 1st.   Same camp find Mr. Bonneville camped a few miles
above us.   On farther inquiry I changed my opinion expressed
above in regard to the Indians who stole the horses   I think they
were 15 Snakes who left our camp at Green river a few days before we left that place.   The case was this.   Mr. Bridger sent 4
men to this river to look for us viz Mr. Smith, Thomson, Charboneau a half breed and Evans.   Two days before it happened 15
Inds came to them (Snakes) and after smoking departed the
second day after they were gone Thompson having been out hunting [hobbled?] his horse to the others and thought he would
sit down by them until it was time to water them and having been
on guard much of the time previous fell asleep   he was waked by
a noise among the horses which he supposed to [be] his comrades
come to water them   raising his head and opening his eyes the
first thing that presented itself to his sight was the muzzle of a
gun in the hands of an Indian   it was immediately discharged

and so near his head that the front piece of his cap alone saved his eyes from being put out by the powder   the Ball entered the head outside of the eye and breaking the cheek bone passing downward and lodged behind the ear in the neck   this stunned him and while insensible an arrow was shot into him on the top of the shoulder downward which entered about 6 inches, the Inds. got 7 horses   all there were.   Charboneau pursued them on foot but wet his gun in crossing a little stream and only snapped twice.

2nd.   Found the river unfordable and assended to west crossing Po[r]poise & Wind river 5 miles up and made thence 20 miles N. E. by N. to a little creek going to Wind now on our right.

3rd.   11 miles N. N. E. to the summit of the mountains which are called little Wind River Mts. and run E. & W.   then N. 5 miles to the river.

4th.   2 miles N. along the river to a clump of sweet cotton wood.

5th.   7 miles N. by W. to the River which between makes a considerable bend to the eastward camped in good grass and some large cotton wood trees   this morning past beautiful camps   afternoon N. by E.   12 miles   3 horses found this day and yesterday probably left by some party of Inds. who have passed this way saw the tracks of several more   we think that when the Crows stole horses of the Snakes last winter they came this route and left their animals on account of giving out for want of food in the snow.   Few Buffaloe and those running indicates Indians near.

6th.   N   10 miles to the River again to noon   found little grass day cool   afternoon 10 miles N. N. E. to the main river again. Since crossing the last Mts.   we crossed a creek the second forenoon   afternoon one   yesterday 2 today   2 all small and I suppose sometimes dry

7th.   12 miles N. N. W and camped on Grey Bull River   here I found a piece of about 5 lbs of Bituminous coal which burned freely   It had in it some substance which I took to be Amber also an impression of wood It looked like and as good as Liverpool Coal.   Its fracture was too perfect to have come far.   20 miles above and on the E. side comes in the River Travelled[?] in afternoon 6 miles N. N. W. and again struck Wind river.   Shell river comes in 3 miles below Grey Bull on the E. side and from the Mts. in the direction E. by N.   Grey Bull is from the S. W. and much the largest stream on this side since Wind river.   For three days have found no Buffaloe and from the nature of the country think it is not often found in abundance along here except in the winter   no antelope   a few Elk and deer.

8th.   W. N. W. 3 miles then 21 miles N. E. toward the right of two considerable Mts. where Wind river passes.   We camped West of these hills on a river larger than Grey Bull called Stinking River coming from the S. W.   This days travel was made between parrallel ridges of broken lime and sand rock some of it appeared calcined and much like fine caked salt. This day picked up some shell they are very numerous also a round concretion which are found also on Cannon Ball River from which the name also a concretion of much the same substance but long pointed at one end with a core in the middle a hole at big end. During this space there was no water to our right there is a range of Mts. running N. W. about 9 miles distant and the other side of Wind River.

9th. 10 miles N. striking a small stream of water This days travel and yesterday was over ground naked of vegetables in which the animals sank near six inches deep at every step perfectly dry and resembling, but of different color, lime in the operation of slacking full of holes down which the waters at the wet season sink the rock is sand and lime stone.

10th. N. 15 miles passing near but not exactly on the river and through rocky hills of no great height. The river here looks tranquil but flows between two perpendicular banks of stone of perhaps 5 to 800 feet high the chasm even at the top of no great width the rock of lime and sand this days march saw Plaster of Paris found for first time this year ripe Service berrys. Killed one mountain sheep which was all the meat killed this day for 48 men short commons. hard rains last night.

11th. Went out hunting killed 2 Cows and 4 Bulls the camp made about a N. course at six miles crossed a small creek at 5 more another probably another branch of the same at 9 more a creek separate from the others but not large all these creeks have high perpendicular banks and are very bad to cross in the course of the day saw 4 Bears white. A fine grass country and a great many Buffaloe.

12th. 4 miles N. E. to Big Horn River this day went out to get Bull Hydes for boat got enough and employed the rest of the day in making a Boat this day followed down a little stream.

13th. Remained at same camp made a Bull Boat day fine.

14th. Same camp day fine.

15th. Made a start in our Bull Boat found it to answer the purpose well large enough runs well leaks a little made 3 miles N. E. stream rapid shoals at places 2 feet. Too much liquor to proceed therefore stopped.

16th. Made a start in our boat found travelling quite pleasant but requires much caution on account of some snaggs and bars. We frequently took one half of the river which dividing again gave too little water for our boat which draws 1½ feet it is quite too much the [boat] ought to have been flatter We grounded about 6 times this forenoon it is surprising how hard a thump these bull Boats will stand ours is made of three skins is 18 feet long and about 5½ wde sharp at both ends round bottom. Have seen on the banks of the river this forenoon 3 grisly bears and some Bulls in

the river and on the banks they stare and wonder much the
direction of this march was as near as I can judge N. by E. we
went from 5 to 11 as I think about 6 miles per hour the indirec-
tion I suppose to be not more than ¼. All feel badly today from
a severe bout of drinking last night. Afternoon made 4 hours at a
good 6 mile rate grounded three times saw a few elk and much
Beaver sign all day there is here the best trapping that I have
ever found on so large a river it is about 100 yards wide when
all together but is much cut into slews which makes the navigation very difficult. The musquitoes have anoyed me much today
  they affect me almost as bad as a rattle snake this afternoons
course about N. N. W. at 6 miles from our noon camp passed a
place where we supposed the Little Horn River came in from the
S. E. at least there is a considerable river at that place but it is
difficult to tell a returning slew from a river this afternoon a
severe thunderstorm which compelled us to put ashore until it
was over
    17th. This day the river made nearly a N. course and we made
about 7 ½ hours at the rate of about 6 miles the river winding
about ¼ of the distance we started at 5 ock. at about 9 ock.
saw several persons ahead on the bank of the river which we at
first supposed to be whites from the fort but soon found to be
Crow Indians they informed us that the whole nation was behind we were anxious to avoid them but could not as the river
afforded us no hiding place they showed us that they meant us
to land very soon by stepping and swimming into the river seeing
this we chose to land without further trouble in this way we
were obliged to make the shore 6 times during the day we arrived at the Yellow Stone which was of clear water and did not
mix with the waters of the Big Horn which was at this time dirty
for some miles about 3 miles below the mouth of the Big Horn
we found Fort Cass one of the Am. F. Co. at which post we traded about 10 packs of Beaver and 150 to 200 pack robes goods
are broug[t] up in boats of about 15 tons burthen 2 of which are
now laying here and one of them preparing to descend in two days
    we were treated with little or no ceremony by Mr. Tullock, who
we found in charge which I attributed to sickness on his part well
knowing that a sick man is never disposed to be over civil to others we therefore pushed on next morning. Just as we arrived
we saw 31 Indians with two American flags come to the other side
of the river they were Gros ventres du Baum the same we
fought with last summer at the Trois Tetons they came to make
peace with the Crows they were treated civily at the Fort and
before night followed the river up to the Crow village where I expect their scalps will be taken for the Crows informed us that not
long since a few Blkft. came and made peace with them shortly
after three Crows went to the Blackfeet two of which they killed
and they were determined to make no more peace with them.

18th.　Started down the river made 3 hours with a hard wind about 4 miles an hour and put up to noon seeing some elk which we were in hopes to get to eat　course about N.　afternoon the river tended more Eastwardly and at last came to E. N. E.　We made at the rate of 5 miles an hour for 3 ½ hours and camped to fish and hunt having no meat on hand　there is along this river pretty bottoms and great quantities of sweet cotton wood which would be fine for winter camps.　We saw some large bands of elk but our hunters were more conceited than good which I have generally found to be the case with the hunters in this country　they are not willing that a new hand should even try, and are far from good shots themselves and commonly have miserable flint guns which snap continually and afford an excuse for not killing. The river sometimes cuts blufs which are mostly of sand stone but the river brings down granite and porphry.　Fort Cass is scituated on the E. bank of the Yellow stone river　is about 130 feet square　made of sapling cotton wood pickets with two bastions at the extreme corners and was erected in the fall of 1832.　The Yellow stone comes from the S. W. till it meets the Big Horn then the two go about N. until they bend to the eastward.

19th.　Made 5 ½ hours in a calm fine day I should think about 6 miles the hour the river going E.N.E. stopped early to try a band of Buffaloe that we see on the left of us, at first we were careful to see if they were really Buffaloe for yesterday we were near approaching a band of Indians which I suppose were the residue of the Blackfeet which I saw at the fort as they appeared coming down from that way.　Nooned in a fine cool place under the shade of a large Cotton wood in a large green bottom　the musquitoes take much from the pleasure of the trip which is otherwise fine but I believe for a party like ours rather dangerous　in afternoon 2 ½ hours about 6 per H.　River E.　stopped on hearing the bellowing of Buffaloe on shore to get meat.　Our hunters as usual having failed went myself and killed a cow　got a good ducking from a shower and returned loaded with meat much fatigued. About 4 miles before we stopped we passed the mouth of Rose Bud　a river coming from S. S. W.

20th.　Started early and made this forenoon 6 hours at the rate of about 5 ½ miles.　River about E. N. E.　last night a smart rain which wet our clothes much　caught just at dusk last night plenty of Blue Catfish and a small one which resembles an Ale wife　soon after starting this morning found an immense herd of Buffaloe close to the river　stopped and killed 2 fat cows and could have killed any number more but this was enough　they keep up a continued grunting night and day now that we have fairly got into them　in the afternoon made 5 ½ hours　current about 6 miles and E. N. E. at 5 hours found bad rapids but at this low stage of the water it is said to be better passing on account of the chanell being more visible　we had a good joke on much as usual during the afternoon we had a good joke on the old hands as they call them selves in distinction to those who have been a short time in the country two bald headed Eagles being perched on a tree on a point and ranged to the other side of the river our motion made them appear moving the old one cried out Les Savvages others of them said on horseback with white scarfs I looked long but not supposing that they meant the eagles I said I saw nothing but the eagles they soon found out their mistake and we had a good laugh at them and a pleasant one as all the Indians we meet here we expect to fight. This day and yesterday whenever the river makes perpendicular banks we saw veins of poor bituminous coal in 5 to 7 veins horizontal from 3 ft. to 6 inches thick and 10 to 15 feet above each other rock sandstone.

21st. Made 5 hours river about E. N. E. passed the mouth of Powder River at 4 hours and half an hour below a bad and rocky rapid but without accident the coal still continues and thousands of Buffaloe day fine stopped to noon a little below the rapids in the afternoon made 5 hours current about 5 miles per hour in about E. N. E. direction no rapids of consequence the blufs have ceased these blufs are a part of the Black hills as I am informed the Black Hills I am also informed make the Falls of Missouri at the Three Forks just on leaving the blufs the coal veins appeared thicker day fine. Buffaloe plenty.

22nd. Made at 5 ½ per hour 6 hours in forenoon using a sail which we found of little advantage and but a little course of the river N. N. E. and from the junction on the E. side of first Rose Bud then Tongue and then Powder Rivers it is of about the color of the Missouri altho the Yellow stone above is of clear water quite so above the junction of the Big Horn. Our boat getting quite rotten in afternoon made 5 hours same course 5 miles per hour river better not so [many] bars and country not mountainous the coal appears to have given out.

23rd. Made in forenoon 4 hours at the [rate] of 5 [miles] per hour river about N. E. Day fine and hot plenty of Elks in herds afternoon made 4 hours N. then 2 ½ hours E. N. E. current about 4 miles per hour saw but little game only 2 Elk river broad and shoal.

24th. Made N. N. E. 2 hours with a heavy head wind about 4 miles per hour then the river turned Westwardly and when it enters the Missouri is running W. by S. this made one hour more when we found the Missouri which we assended N.W. about 5 miles to Fort Union where we arrived about noon and were met with all possible hospitality and politeness by Mr. McKensie the Am. F. Co. agent in this country.

27th. This day at ½ past 10 oclock we took leave our hospitable entertainers and on the experience of a few days with prepossessions highly in their favor we found Mr. McKensie a most polite host I was particularly pleased with a Mr. Hamilton and I am perhaps presumptious in saying that I felt able to appreciate his refined politeness   he is a man of superior education and an Englishman.   I was here supplied with a ·peroque traded from the Blackfeet.   A Mr. Patten shewed me a powder flask which he traded from the Blkft.   I immediately knew it to be one of mine and on examination found No.4 H.G.O.M.graven with a point on it. It was Mores flask who was killed in Little Jackson Hole last year on his return home after rendesvous.   Fort Union is pleasantly scituated on the N. bank of the Missouri   6 miles above the junction of Yellowstone   there is no timber on a high bank above the fort I am told that there is not enough moisture here to raise vegetables potatoes grass ect,   Some corn is traded from the Inds. lower down   the fort is of usual construction about 220 feet square and is better furnished inside than any British fort I have ever seen at Table we have flour Bread Bacon Cheese Butter   they live well I here saw a small sturgeon but they are very rare   Cat fish are good and plenty   they have cows and bulls   milk etc.   I saw lime burning also coal   here they are beginning to distil spirits from corn traded from the Inds. below. This owing to some restrictions on the introduction of the article into the country.   Above this we have met plumbs, grapes, cherrys, Currants, ash, elm. The river being already well laid down shall no longer give the course we left the fort and went 2 hours and stopped for Mr. Sublette who remained behind to finish some business   he came accompanied by the gentlemen of the fort   after leaving us we made 4 hours then supped and made one hour more and found Mr. Wm. L. Sublette at anchor with a large Bull boat   this gentleman we had expected to have found on our arrival at the Missouri   he is come to trade furs in opposition to the Am. F. Co.   he treated us with much politeness   his brother preferred to remain and come to the states with him   we are therefore left without any one who has decended the Missouri but I can go down stream.

28th.   Pulled one hour   put by from wind and to regulate then pulled 6 hours and stopped to supper   the banks continually falling in   after supper we floated through the night 11 hours. Calm

29   While breakfast was preparing went out to hunt   killed one deer and found a severe time in the thick swamp and mosqutoes   pulled 8 ½ hours and drifted 11 hours through the night which exposed me to much rain and wind from two thunder showers.   I had much difficulty to keep the boat from bars and snaggs   ran several times on to Bars all hands being asleep had to jump over board to get [her] off   In the night elk keep up a continual sque[a]lling it being now the commencement of their running season.

30th   Day pulled 9 hours   Saw three white Bears this day and some Elk and a herd of Buffaloe   night floated 8 ½ hours and were stopped by a gale from the S. E. not thinking it expedient to pull with a head wind and in the dark.

31st   Blowing a gale.   Made about 4 hours about the rate of 2 mils per hour and finding it too bad laid by at a considerable river coming from the S. entering by 2 mouths   this I took to be the little Missouri as laid down in the maps.   In this vicinity we find primitive peb[b]les and bo[u]lders   much petryfied wood other al[l]uvial productions   stopped all night on acc. of wind and rain which màde our scituation uncomfortable in the extreme the weather had heretofore been very warm   average as much as 90°   this day cold like an Eastwardly storm.

1st.   At seven the weather having abated a little made a start. At 3 o'clock found some of Sublettes men cutting timber for a fort and learned from them that the upper Mandan was 9 miles ahead   we made it at 6 this day made only about 3 per hour this village was about 1 ½ miles from the river   taking my Indian and a man with me I went to it and was well received by Mr. Dorherty, Mr. Sublet[t]es clerk and the Inds.   Stopped about one hour with him and then pulled 3 hours more   passing 3 villages of Mandans and not seeing the fort and being afraid of passing it stopped for the night.

2nd.   Pulled ½ hour arrived first on a high point at the village then immediately round the point found the fort and was well received by Mr Kipp.   the Am. F. Co. agent for the Mandans Stopped 2 hours   took breakfast   the[y] presented me some dry corn and some roasting ears.   All these villages cultivate còrn peas beans pumpkins ect. At ½ past 7 ock pulled a short distance when we had a good breeze and sailed until 5 ock then stopped to supper   then floated from 6 until 12 ock   then stopped owing to fog with head wind.

3rd.   Floated 2 hours and stopped to Breakfast   having found no game have lived much upon the stores we have taken from the forts above   At the last place we were presented with some green corn which we are now roasting   Makes us think of Old Lang Sine.   We have had for four days rainy cloudy & foggy weather our bed clothes are wet and musty in consequence   after Breakfast pulled 6 hours when I thought best to go on shore to cook I sent a man out to hunt in the meantime   as soon as he assended the high bank he perceived horses on the other side   we after[-wards] counted 21 lodges and from the number of horses I have no doubt there might have been from 75 to 100.   I immediately had the boat put into a little thicket and fortifyed as well as I could then went to fishing and spent the afternoon   caught but two large catfish   as soon as it was dark we proceeded forward with a high wind and a cloudy sky and no Moon   all went well until we were just opposite the village when we perceived lodges and fires on our side also   On seeing this I ste[e]red the boat to the middle of the river but unluckly took ground on a sand bar here we worked hard for some time to get off and had the Indians seen or heard us her[e] we were in distance for shot from both sides and could have made little resistance but they did not and after some time we got off and glad we were. We proceed[ed] in all 4 hours pulled, then stopped for the night these were probably the Aricarey and would have scalped us. I feared much for my Nez Perce for we could not speak to any Indian on the river and all would without explanation have made some fuss and perhaps have killed him.

4th. With almost a gale of wind from the W. pulled 6 hours and then stopped to eat having twice nearly upset in carrying sail and wet all our things after drying and eating started on still blowing fresh and pulled 3 hours then floated through the night 11 hours It was a beautiful still night the stillness interrupted only by the neighing of the Elk the continual low of the Buffaloe which we came to soon after starting the hooting of large owls and the screeching of small ones and occasionally the nearer noise of a beaver gnawing a tree or splashing into the water and even the gong like sound of the swan it was really poetical but sleep at last laid in his claim and I gave the helm to a man. Oak is now plenty in the Bottoms and for a few days past has been seen The upland along the river is here pretty good plumbs we occasionally see and have since we first took water on the Big Horn frequent squalls of rain yesterday.

5th. Pulled 7 hours stopped to eat pulled one more came to a deserted village on the S. bank fired two guns to see if there was any one in it but had no answer pulled one hour more then floated 7 hours more then pulled 3 to Breakfast saw in morning a band of Elk playing like children in the water failed of killing any of them owing to the impatience of one of the men who fired too soon pulled through a dreadful rain 7 hours and camped wet and cold rained all night strong east wind.

6. In the morning made 8 hours pulling seeing an Elk on the sand Bar stopped and killed him very aceptable as we have had nothing to eat since yesterday noon and saved his horns for my best of friends Mr. F. Tudor of Boston pulled 2 hours more and the night being dark and appearance of a storm did not run.

7th. Last night about 11 ock was awakened by the water making a breach over the boat got her off the shore but was obliged to make the shore again on account of some of the men who were so frightened that if I had not they would have jumped overboard laid the rest of the night on a lee shore thundering in a loud strain and raining at no allowance spent a most uncomfortable night an[d] rose in the morning benumbed with cold and all hands as dead as loggs started after eating at 8 ock and pulled until 2 ock when we had a fine breeze which gradual[l]y increased to a gale before which we scudded at a good rate almost despairing of seeing Fort Pier[r]e which we began to think we had pass-

ed   at about sundown we saw people on the hills which we supposed to be Inds.   therefore kept on   they fired but we did not
choose to hear   about an hour after sundown we smelt the flavor
of coal and landed and found people who had just burned a kiln
who informed us that the fort was 3 mils ahead   we though[t] to
go to sleep at the fort but soon found that night and a gale of
wind was a poor time for travelling and also that 3 miles was in
fact 3 leagues   after being near filled by the surf and running
afoul of several sand bars and getting overboard to push off we
concluded to stop for the night which we did cold and tired and
wet   we spent the night as we best could   one comfort plenty of
elk meat   stopped at 10 ock.

8.   Made by sailing 3 miles and found Fort Pier[r]e pleasantly
scituated on the right bank   rather low but withall romantic
were received with all hospitality imaginable by Mr. Laidlow who
is in charge of the Am. F. Co. post here   was much pleased by
the order and regularity apparent about the place   we stopped
here for the day and visited Mr. and Mrs. Sublette who is scituated about one mile below   we here saw melons of two kinds   corn
    pork   cows   horses and stacks of hay.

9th.   Remained at the fort until about 1 ock. when we made
by pulling 2 hours an Island 9 miles below the fort on which the
Co. have about 15 acres of ground under cultivation   here I remained all this day eating and drinking of the good things afforded by the earth and the cellars of the Co.   Found cucumbers
water & musk mellons   beets   carrots   potatoes   onions   corn
and a good cabin and the Company of Mr. Laidlow and Doct.

10th.   At 8 ock. began pulling   the water has within two days
risen about 2 feet in consequence of the rains which so an[n]oyed
me above and the surface of the water is covered with all manner
of drift rubbish and the water as muddy as possible.   Wind ahead
all day but current much improved   stopped at 6 ock at the commencement of the great Bend and remained all night.

11th.   Commenced pulling at ½ past 6 after having sent a
hunter across the foot of the Bend and after 6 hours got past the
Bend and found our hunters who had hid themselves in the brush
being alarmed by seeing Inds. whom we also saw and gave some
amunition to   took them in and in two hours more came to the
agency for the Sioux & Poncas   Mr. Bean agent but not at the
post   we found it a miserable concern only three or four men but
poorly fed and buildings out of order though new and shabbily
built at best   we were hospitably received by the young man in
charge.

12.   Pulled against a severe head wind 9 hours in hopes of
finding White River but camped without seeing it   got plenty of
good plumbs which were an object to stop for as we are about out
of food and the vicinity almost destitute of game.

13th   Pulled against a severe wind 3 ½ hours   finding we did not make much headway. laid by for the day.

14th.   Blowing still fresh ahead   we started and made 15 hours night and day continuing until 12 ock at night   it was dark and we were nearly upset by a snag but our fears of starvation impelled us to haste   did not see an animal all day   during the latter part of the night it rained in torrents and wet all our things and persons.

15th. Commenced pulling at 7 ock.   Still blowing fresh ahead and raining a little   about 3 ock cleared off and stopped to cook during meal time killed a fawn which was very good luck   after supper pulled 5 hours more and found a keel boat of the Am. F. Co. alongside of which we stopped for the night in the morning of

16th.   Put ahead with a fine wind not having been asked on board of her and immediately passed the Ponca village but I believe not in its usual place   saw and delivered a message to Mr. Sublettes agt. here and gave the Chief some tobacco. Made with a wind which as usual soon died away and pulling 13 hours when we ran on a sand bar and was unable in the dark to extricate her and slept all night on it   the musquitoes almost murder us   rained most of the night.

17.   Started at 5 ock.   Pulled this day 10 hours   rained some in the course of the day   saw Powquet the first since leaving the states   also mulberry trees   Bass wood.

18th.   Started early after a rainy night and pulled 10 hours saw wild Turkeys this evening but killed none   nearly out of all kinds of provisions   saw this day a herd of Elk   tryed hard to get some but failed

19th.   Made with a strong and fine wind 12 hours and camped without meat   supped on a little flour boiled in water   Saw during the day 3 deer   looked with folly at them and fired two shots and they ran off.

20th.   Stopped until ½ past 6 to hunt caught one goose which we eat for breakfast   afterward put ashore the hunters for game they were fortunate enough to kill a fat doe on which we feasted right merryly and having lost so much time we concluded to run until the moon went down altho we were before informed that it was not safe   a few hours we got along well enough but at last went over a snagg with limbs above   which taking our mast and the boat swinging broadside she was taking in water at a jolly rate and in a little she would have gone with the suck under the rock   I immediately had the mast cut away just in time to save her   escaped from this I determined to try more   we ran a little and were driven head foremost on a large tree lying across the river   We stopped about midway and lay swinging like a pendulum   with much danger and difficulty we extricated her not being yet discouraged we ran on but soon were driven into a

large drift   we narrowly escaped being carried under and half full
of water and our oar broke we made the shore as soon as possible
resolved to run no more nights, after making 10 ½ hours.

2 1st.   Made 9 hours with a head wind and camped at the old
post of Council Bluffs   it is now grown up with high weeds a
memento of much money spent to little purpose   it is a beautiful
scituation   the magazine and three or four chimneys only remain.

22nd.   After 5 hours in a dead current we arrived at a trading
post of the Am. F. Co. Mr. Josh. Pilcher agent by whom we were
entertained with the utmost hospitality   I had met Mr. P. at St.
Louis on my way out   on this account I had   much pleasure in
stopping   we found a good assortment of vegetables and a supply of such things as we wanted.   Dined with him and made
three hours more and stopped to hunt   Killed a fat deer and
camped for the night.

23rd.   Made 2 hours pulling and passed an agency   ½ mile
farther a trading post of Mess. Dripps & Fontenelle.   Made in all
13 hours and camped   during the day killed one deer from the
Boat   from Council Bluffs to this have found the Hic[k]ory
Shagbark   Sicamore and Coffee Bean   trees not seen above also
Night Shade Brier.   Ducks   Ge[e]se and Pelicans have been very
numerous but shy for about 8 days   stopped at the above trading
post   found only an old negro at home   the rest out cutting wood.

24th.   Made this day 10 ½ hours   Killed one goose   saw
plenty of deer

25th.   Made 11 hours   Killed one Turkey from the boat,   saw
this day the first Pawpau fruit and trees   wounded one deer from
boat and stopped to search for him but without success

26th.   Made 11 hours   at 8 hours came to a trading house of
the Am. F. Co. called Rubideau Fort at the Black Snake hills
and on the N. bank of the river on a little rise of ground in the
rear of a beautiful bottom.   Today saw the Black Locust for the
first time   the lands are here quite fine and the hills as far back
as we can see clothed with timber and verdure of the most luxuriant appearance   the country is one of the most pleasant I have
ever seen

27th.   After 7 hours pulling arrived at the Cantonment Leavenworth   on the route we saw several Indian canoes with Squaws
children ect.   I had no letters of introduction at the fort and
therefore could not expect any great extension of the laws of
hospitality but was received with all the politeness that [could be]
expected   was offered all the stores which I might require by
Leiut. Richardson   the officer of the day.   My boy Baptiste and
the Indian wer[e] vacinated by Doct. Fellows.   It was amusing
to observe the actions of Baptiste and the Indian when I went
from the boat towards the Barracks the Boy followed me until I
was hailed by the sentry   at view of one so strangely attired and
with a knife on the end of his gun he broke like a quarter Nag[?]

crying Pegoni and the Indian was only prevented from taking the run also by being assured that he would not be harmed. I took the two to Doct Fellows quarters to be vaccinated the Docts wife and another lady happened to be present they were really beautiful women but the eyes of the two were riveted on the White Squaws Baptiste who speaks a little English told the other Boys when he returned to the boat that he had seen a white squaw white as snow and so pretty.

28th. Made about 45 miles to Liberty where I found Mr. E. M. Samuel an old acquaintance who received me with all hospitality supplyed me w[it]h money and all that I wanted.

29th. Rained all day did not start

30. Went to the landing after breakfast a boat arrived going to the Garrison and joined her as I shall arrive at St Louis as soon by this means as any other and more comfortably

Shall close memorandum here with Boat I after[ward] returned to Leavenworth and was treated with great politeness by the officers of the garrison especially a Capt. Nichols who invited me to dinner.

Memo of distances on the Columbia according to the estimates of the English Traders.

From Boat encampment to Colville............309 miles
"   Colville to Oakenagen.......... 150   "
"   Oakenagen to Walla Walla.................207   "
"   Walla Walla to Vancouver...................203   "
"   Vancouver to Cape Disappointment.. 80   "

949 [with

pencil]

                    From Ermatinger.

2nd JOURNAL. [With pencil.]

On the 5th of May having crossed the Kanzas at the agency without accident and in one Half of a day and traded as many cuds and apishemas[?] as I wanted and some deer skins for which I paid Bacon. We started with 3 less men 4 having deserted and one new one engaged. Made this day along the Kanzas about 16 miles on a small stream having crossed one called the Lautrelle

6th. Moved along the Kanzas and made about 12 miles to noon and took an observation found the Latt to be 39° 38' made this day about 18 miles

7th Made about 15 miles and camped on Little Vermillion

8th. In the morning Mr Sublette finding that his leg would not bear travelling turned back made this d[a]y about 15 miles This day left Kanzas River

9th. Made about 20 miles and camped on a small river this day our hunter killed our first deer

10th. Made 15 miles to Big Vermillion and then 5 miles more and camped in the praire with but little wood and a little stagnant water

11. Made 9 miles to a small run then lost the trail and crossed a sluggish muddy stream running N[?] and recrossed the same it rounding and heading North and camped at noon this day Latt. 40° 18'. Sent a man to hunt the trail.

12th. Spent the morning mending hobbles and endeavored to get an observation for Long. but it was too cloudy in afternoon started and in about 8 mils found a camp of Sublettes for nooning and marched until dark and camped the horses having had nothing to eat all day did not tie them up at 1. ock at night was awakened by a furious running & snorting of the animals who all broke from their hobbles and left camp running in their course over any thing opposed to them spent the night in looking them up and found all but two about sun one hour high three Otoes came to us who I suppose occasioned the fright and got the two horses.

13. Started and travelled 7 hours and camped on a fork of the Blue and found the Long. to be 96° 7'.

14th. Made W. S. W. 21 miles and struck the main Blue

15th.   Made about W. 9 miles and found our Lat. to be 4c° 17' ·then made 12 mils W. by N. over a very level prairie and again struck the main Blue and camped

16th.   Made 10 miles about W. by N. to Dinner Latt. 40° 23' and 12 more to the Pawnee trail to the head of the Arkanzas and found that a very large party had passed it about 10 days before and a smaller one this morning.

17th.   Made 3 miles up the stream crossing a very small run course W. by N. then struck out N. W. 3 miles and crossed a little run the same as passed in the morning then same course 6 mils and took an observation for Latt and found it to be 40° 22' then 5 mils more same course and got sight of the Platte then W. N. W. 5 mils to the river and camped

18th.   Raining in morning caught some Cat fish found fresh track of Indians a small party

19th.   Rained hard all day moved camp 15 miles to a small grove of timber on the main land found our horses very skittish during the night.

20th.   In the morning had just raised camp when we discovered two Indians who were shy of coming to us but after a while suffered us to approach them they said they were Pawnees but as we did not not know the Pawnees this might be so or not perhaps Ricarees afterward saw several more on the blufs who did not come to us at noon found our Lat. 43° 1' after traveling 13 miles W. N. [?] in the afternoon traveled 13 miles W. and found our Long. to be 98° 30' this night doubled guard.

21st.   Moved camp from the pickett and 12 miles W. to breakfast fine clear weather old Buffaloe sign and antelope after dinner started and soon saw a band of elk one loose horse took fright at them and ran back on our trail there being no person mounted on a swift horse in camp I followed myself after going to a little creek where we nooned they struck out S. 15 miles to the heads of some little streams with timber probably the Blue where I overtook three of them my horse having failed I lost 2 fine horses. After riding about 12 miles found the Platte at our nights camp and followed it to the camp making in all a ride of about 50 miles arrived about midnight camp moved on 11 miles.

22nd.   Moved about N. 10 miles Lat. 40° 33' afternoon 10 miles W. and camped after a little 3 Pawnee Scouts came to us and slept with us in the morning 12 more came and wished to persuade me to go to their camp 1 ½ days travel N. over the river which they forded here they stole some small things from us

23rd.   Moved from the pickett and 15 miles W. about to Latt. ...... just before nooning passed a little creek then West 11 miles and camped.

24th.　20 miles W. to the crossing of the South fork of the Platte about 8 miles above the forks　found Latt. to be 40° 41'

25th.　Crossed without difficulty and made up the N. side of the South Fork about 4 miles W.　then struck N. W. about 1 mile to the North fork which is here the largest　then made about W. by N. about 15 miles and near to some cut blufs which come close to the river

26th.　W. by N. 12 mils　passing another place where the blufs cut the river and here found much cedar on them and camped on the river in a wide bottom found no Buffaloe today killed one antelope. Afternoon 10 miles W. N. W. at night found the variation of the compass 1° 30' west　at midnight our horses took fright　but being strongly picketed and hobbled but few got out of camp.

26th.　I date this the 26th having over noted one day heretofore　in afternoon 12 miles W. N. W. passing some steep cut blufs which cut the river　afternoon made 12 mils and camped still no buffaloe　Latt. 40° 22' at night.

27th.　Made this day 20 mils during a severe gale from the N. N. W.　the sand cut like a knife and it was altogether a most disagreeable day　this day saw a little timber on some hills to the south of the river　about 5 miles distant　also 2 bands of wild horses　killed one Bull so poor as to [be] uneatable.

28th.　Killed Buffaloe plenty today　Came in sight of the chimney about noon　made 22 mils　wind still high　N. N. W. One of our outriders saw six Indians mounted today.

29th.　No[o]ned at the Chimney　Lat. 41° 51'　After travelling this forenoon 11 miles afternoon 10 mils

30th.　Passed through between two high blufs through a pretty good pass and avoided going between one of them and the river where there are bad ravines.　Made this day 22 miles to Horse creek.

31st　Made after crossing Horse creek at starting about 20 miles.

June 1st.　Made 15 miles to Laramies fork　just before coming to which we made a cut off of about 3 miles over and about 5 miles by the river　forded this fork with ease and made 8 miles up the Platte in afternoon.　At the crossing we found 13 of Sublettes men camped for the purpose of building a fort he having gone ahead with his best animals and the residue of his goods he left about 14 loads

2nd.　Made along the river 5 miles　then struck out into the hills about W. N. W. and made 12 miles to a little creek in the afternoon made 13 miles to pretty large creek and camped for the night　the whole course this day about W. N. W.　Left at Noon camp a bull and cow whose feet had worn out.

3rd.　Made 15 miles and nooned on the river　this course N. W. by N. and cut over the hills about ½ the way　the river taking a bend quite to the N. and passing through bad rocks. After-noon made 6 miles cutting two very bad blufs but still following the river and camped on it

4th.   Forded the river and made W. N. W.   17 miles along the river and camped on it   Sublette one day ahead.

5th.   Made along the river   24 miles along the River

6th.   Made along the river 24 miles   W by N.

7th.   Made 12 miles along the river to the red Butes so called and is the place at which the river turns S. W. and we leave to strike for Sweet Water   Sublette 2 days ahead   weather chilly and windy.   Poor grass for several days.

8th.   This morning I had intended to have turned out the horses at 2 ock. and guarded them   but during the night the horses appeared uneasy and appeared to think there were Indians about which induced me to keep them up until sunrise when we started W. S. W. from the Red Butes and made 18 miles to the high ridge of land and then one point more to the South and 12 miles more to a small creek with poor grass   Several of the horses nearly done up for want of grass and from fatigue   this day kill-ed two grisly bears and many Buffaloe   a little shower toward night

9th.   Made S. W. 10 miles and made Rock Independence on which W. L. Sublette had noted that he had arrived on the 6th but I think he could not have done so before the 7th.   I noted my name then made S. W. along the creek 4 ½ miles to a place where the creek puts through cut rocks   each side perpendicular and about 60 feet high   the trail goes through another place on a level and about 100 feet South of the river   the rock interven-ing   then made 6 miles W. S. W. between mountains but on a level and along the creek.

10th.   General courses W. S. W. and along Sweet Water high granite hills on each side   made 25 miles

11th.   W. 10 mils   then N. W. 9 mils to camp on Sweet Water

12th.   S. W. forenoon   a cut off of 10 miles to Sweet Water afternoon S. W. 9 miles along Sweet Water.   Long. 110° 30

13th   3 miles along Sweetwater S. W. then took up a ravine to the W. N. W. about 1 mile   then W. by S. 9 miles to a creek of Sweet Water   run[n]ing into it about 8 miles off and S. E.   then W. by S. 7 miles to another creek of Sweet Water running about S. E. and emtying into it at about 10 miles   Sweet Water appears to run in cut rocks

15th.   Made due West 5 mils   and crossed a small creek of Sweet Water which comes from a point of granite rocks about 2 miles from which we passed   then W. 7 mils to a spring of good cold water and good grass.   Wind river mountains now bear N.

N. W. and a[re] covered with snow about 20 mils distant,   Latt.
42° 44' Afternoon made W. 6 miles to Sweet Water creek
main body going about S. E. and coming out of cut rocks then
W. by S. 16 miles over broken ground to one fork of Sandy running S. by E.   here horses wer[e] tired   Buffaloe plenty.

15th.   W. N. W.   9 miles to Big Sandy where we found Buffaloe plenty   My hunters not yet come in   been out 4 days fearful they have been scalped.

16th.   Made down the Sandy S. W. by W. 15 miles then 4 S.
E. by E and camped on this stream   so far the grass is miserable
and the horses are starving and also at last nights camp they eat
something that has made many of them sick.   the same thing
happened two year since on the next creek west.

17th.   S. S. W.   10 miles down Sandy which makes here a
bend to the right   afternoon S. 9 miles passing at three miles the
mouth of little Sandy and camped without any grass

18th.   12 miles in the forenoon S. S. W. making small cut off
afternoon W. S. W. 7 miles   camped in good grass.

19th.   About S. by W. 8 miles and camped 1 mile above the
mouth of Sandy on Green river or Seckkedee   on the night of the
17th I left camp to hunt Fitzpatric and slept on the prairie in
morning struck Green river and went down to the forks and finding nothing went up again and found rendesvous about 12 miles
up and much to my astonishment the goods which I had contracted to bring up to the Rocky Mountain fur Co. were refused by
those honorable gentlemen.   Latt. 41° 30'.

20th.   Made W. S. W. 8 miles then S. by E. 15 miles to Hams
Fork running here S. E. and a small stream.

21.   Same camp.

22d.   Same camp

27th.   Moved up the river N. W. 10 miles   grass here pretty
good   but little timber and none but willows for the last 6 miles.

To 3rd. July.   Same camp then up Hams Fork 10 miles N. W.
moved up the fork about W. by S. 12 miles   too many Indians
with us for comfort or safety   they let their horses among ours so
that it is impossible to guard any of them.

4th.   Moved up the creek about 1 mile then leaving it made
W. by N. over a divide and by a pass which occurs in the lowest
part of a high range of hills 7 miles   then W. 13 miles down a
ravine which had a little water in it to its junction with another
small run and the two are called Muddy   here we celebrated the
4th   I gave the men too much alcohol for peace took a pretty
hearty spree myself.   At the camp we found Mr. Cerry and Mr.
Walker who were returning to St. Louis with the furs collected
by Mr. Bonnevilles company   about 10 pack and men going down
to whom there is due 10,000$

5th.   Made down Muddy 5 miles W. then N. W. cutting a
divide into a small ravine which has a little water in it 8 miles

then leaving the ravine cutting moderately high land to Bear river 4 miles. Then down Bear river N. by W. 4 miles to camp

6th.   Made down the river N. N. W. 5 miles to Smiths Fork which is a short stream from the N. E. by N. and nearly as large as Bear river   then same course 3 miles more   then N. W.   5 miles here comes in Kamas creek from the N.   then W. N. W. 3 and crossed Bear river   three more and recrossed   then cut over some high hills   same course 8 miles more   and struck the river again   then down the river same course 1 mile to camp   nothing to eat   due south of this camp about 5 miles is the little lake so called which is about 20 miles long.

7th.   Made 3 miles N. N. W. and passed a little creek   the same course 6 miles along the river, then 3 miles N. W. to camp all day fine grass.   During this day a multitude of fine springs coming into the river.   today killed one bull.

8th.   Made N. W. 10 miles   then 10 miles W. N. W. to a place where there is soda spring or I may say 50 of them. These springs throw out lime which deposits and forms little hillocks of a yellowish colored stone   there is also here a warm spring which throws water with a jet which is like Bilge water in taste   there is also here peet beds which sometimes take fire and leave behind a deep light ashes in which animals mire   Killed one Bull today but so poor as to be hardly eatable   having in the course of the day lost a horse will remain here to hunt him up

9th.   Same camp   assended a mountain and from it could see that Bear river took a short turn round sheep rock about 2 miles below the spouting steam and goes south as far as I could see there are in this place many hundreds of mounds of yellowish stone with a crater on top formed by the deposits of the impregnated waters of this place.   Killed one Buffaloe.

10th.   Moved N. by W 3 mils cutting a range of hills   then N. N. W. 17 miles to Blackfoot on which I found Bon[n]eville again and plenty of Buffaloe and killed 3 Grisly Bears during the day passed many small funnel shaped holes in the lava having the appearance of small craters.

11th.   Made W. 6 miles cutting a range of hills then following in a valley formed by these hills and another range   Made W. N. W. 10 miles to a little brook running N. by W. to camp   Buffaloe   today saw one Blackfoot on foot in the hills who ran like a good fellow.

12th.   Made W. 3 miles and came upon a small creek which was said to be Portneuf   it may possibly be the same water as that we camped on last night but running S. by E   crossed this and a high range of hills and struck a stream which is said to be Ross creek   this runs about W.   after 9 miles more camped   saw but few Buffaloe today.

13th.   No Buffaloe   saw elk on Snake River which we struck

after 6 miles   W. by N.   in some small slew saw a great quantity of fine trout about 2 lbs. weight

14th.   Went down the river about 3 miles and found a location
for a fort and succeeded and killed a Buffaloe near the spot

15.   Commenced building the fort and sent out 12 men to hunt
to be gone 12 days and continued at work on the fort a few days
and fell short of provisions and was obliged to knock off in order
to obtain food   sent out some men for Buffaloe   they returned
in two days with plenty.   The 12 returned the 28th day at night.
On the 26th a Frenchman named Kanseau was killed horse racing
and the 27th was buried near the fort   he belonged to Mr. Mc-
Kays camp and his comrades erected a decent tomb for him service
for him was performed by the Canadians in the Catholic form by
Mr. Lee in the Protestant form and by the Indians in their form
as he had Indian family.   he at least was well buried.

30   Mr. McKay left us and Mr Lee and Capt. Stewart with
him

6th.   Having done as much as was requisite for safety to the
Fort and drank a bale of liquor and named it Fort Hall in honor
of the oldest partner of our concern   we left it and with it Mr.
Evans in charge of 11 men and 14 horses and mules and three
cows   we went down the river S.W. 4 miles and found a ford crossed
and made N. W. 7 miles to the head of a spring and camped in
all 29 strong.   Fort Hall is in Latt. 43° 14' Long. 113° 35'

7th.   Started at day light and traveled 10 hours as fast as possible N. W. by W. 30 miles to the Bute.   being the most southwardly one and from it the other two Butes bear N. N. E.   the
farther about 20 miles off   the other midway   the Three Tetons
about 100 miles off and bearing N. E.   the day was hot and we
suffered some for water and found but a small supply on the N.
side of the Bute   a miserable chance for our horses and not a good
one for ourselves

8th.   Started at sunrise and made N. W. 10 miles to Godins
river then crossed it and made in the same direction 12 up the river and camped in fine grass   where we struck the river there is
no grass nor until we camped   above I am told it is fine   found
no appearance of buffaloe

9th.   Made due W. 16 miles striking for the N. side of it a
pretty high hill and struck up the mountains close on the N. side of it
then wound into the mountains in a S. W. course finding water
several times and cutting a divide struck a small thread of water
at 5 mils   this we followed 3 miles N. W. and struck a pretty
large creek which we followed N. N. E. 1 mile and camped just
at starting killed a Bull and separated from Abbot and a small
party of trappers accompanied by Antoine Godin whom I sent
out for Beaver.

10th.   Made 7 mils down the creek N. N. E. to Godins river
the same we left day before yesterday   then N. W. 3 miles then

West 14 miles today saw a large fire in the mountains on our left suppose them to be Diggers keeping for safety in the hills the Blackfeet trouble them even here saw one band of Buffoloe cows today killed one calf the party I parted from viz Antoine and Abbot are before us on this river.

11th. Made W. 9 miles then 18 S W the angle of the two courses occurs at what is called the Spring prairie which is about 10 miles over in the center of which there are three tolerable Butes these Butes when you approach from the East look like three but when from the West show but as two this day killed an old Bull very strong

12th Moved 3 miles up the creek S. W. at which place the creek divides into about equal parts the one going south I took by the advice of one who said he had passed before followed this up one mile and a branch going E. 3 farther another E. 4 miles farther looked so bad camped took a horse to explore the route ½ mile above camp the stream branches the right at small distance heads in an amphitheater of inaccessible mountains followed the left 4 miles S. by E. and this also heads in an amphitheater. We drove 2 Bulls before us which we killed they being unable to pass. I climbed up the clefts an[d] in passing over the snow had liked to have been killed in the following manner passing over some snow and on which the water was running and being afraid of caving in I missed my foothold in a slippery place and went gradually sliding down to a precipice but succeeded at last in averting my progress to destruction by catching the only stone which projected above the icy snow I however reached the summit and looked into another defile running E. like the one I came up. Got to the bottom again and found one of our two mules gone and being in want of meat packed the other with part of one of the Bulls and walked barefoot to camp during the night through an infernal rough rocky prickly Bruisy swampy woody hole.

13th. Moved down creek back to the commencement of the South Fork then took the other about S. W. by W. at two miles up a creek from the N. forming about half of the stream then three miles farther where the rest divides into two parts very small passed the mountain in a south course between these last forks up a gentle fine trail and not more than 1 mile to the top then down by a very steep bad trail. South still along a branch of Malad 5 miles to tolerable grass and camped this last part of the route about the worst road that I ever passed.

14th. After shoeing some horses that were lamed yesterday started and made 9 miles S. S. W. at 2 of which got a small creek from the N. E. at the end of the 9 miles got a fork of about equal size to the one I came down from the S. W. then made S. E. by S. 10 miles and camped got a creek from the N.

E. at 2 miles of it and at 7 one from the S. W. Saw no game today the dusky grouse plenty for three days past. Horses much knocked up with sore feet.

15th. After crossing the stream passed up a ravine S. W. to its head then crossed some low grassy hills and at 12 miles crossed a small creek going S. E. this creek forks at this place then at two miles in all 14 miles S. W. crossed another which we followed two miles S. S. E. then left it on our left and cut a pretty high hill 4 miles S. S. W. and came down to the plain of Snake River then 3 miles W. to a creek with a fine bottom but no water except what remains in little pools, but excellent grass here found two lodges of Snake Indians.

16th. Made 28 miles W. following the main trail which is good perfectly level and distinct except in one place where it crosses several small branches which in the spring I presume are miry which occasions the traveller to go in no particular place during this days march I observed some low hills on the South side of us which gradually approach and at this camp are about 8 miles distant between us and them a little river appears to run to the W. which I am in hopes is Reeds other wise called Big Woody. Today the travelling was fine and many little streams of water cross the trail at this camp which is on a very small thread there commence small irregularities just enough to note the place.

17th. Made 20 miles due West over a country with easy Hills good and distinct trail and often water in very little streams. Country mostly burnt out by the Indians who have passed here lately going up to Buffaloe. Killed some dusky grouse and dug some kamas which assisted our living a little also found some choke cherries and saw one Indian at a distance on Horse back who fled.

18th. Made over a hilly country 12 miles W. until we passed a high stony hill then bending N. W. made 10 miles more over a stony Hilly but distinct trail with not much water saw a track of a Bull made this morning altho there is very little old signs in this section. Camped on a nearly dry creek running W. today lost 2 Horses.

19th. Left the little run on which we camped last night going here N. N. W. on our right and put out as near as I could judge W. 10 miles the first three over a divide of high steep hills then taking a little run followed it out of the worst hills along this run were many little Indian camps we then left it and went W. N. W. 15 miles and struck Woody River in cut rocks at about 7 miles of this last course struck the run on which we camped last night at Woody we saw plenty of Salmon but had no means of catching any of them this day found a colt in the Rush probably left by the Indians on which I mean to Breakfast tomorrow morning being short of provant.

20th. Followed the river down W. by N. 22 miles in the course of the day traded of some Inds. enough salmon for a Lunch and consumed the remaining provisions.

21st. No Breakfast. Feel very much purified [?] in the flesh. 12 miles down the creek W. at noon found Indians of whom we traded enough Salmon with a dead one we picked up in the brook and a few birds for a dinner   afterwards traded 2 Bal[e]s Salmon of the Inds.

22nd. Made 5 miles W.   then the trail cut a point of higher ground of about 2 miles and again struck the river and crossed it made on the other side 7 miles W.   in all this day 15 miles W.

23rd. Made West 9 miles and found a small village of Snakes of whom we could only trade a very few salmon   then 5 more in all 14 miles along the Big Wood W. and arrived at Snake River which we forded by wetting our packs a little   here we found a few lodges of very impudent Pawnacks of whom we traded a half Bale of Salmon   afterward 4 miles N. along the W. side of Snake River and camped near a few lodges of Inds.

24th. 6 miles N. then made a cut off N. N. W. 4 miles to R. Malheur where we found but three or four Indians and consequently got but little Salmon and consequently may starve a little between this and Walla Walla   afternoon 7 miles N. passing not far from the River.   I had forgot to note that on Big Wood River the Indians attempted to steal some of our horses but the horse guards discovered them and they failed.   Scorpions are here quite common   two nights since I was just about laying down when on my Blkt I saw something move   I folded it in the Blkt. and on carrying it to the fire found it to be a very good sized scorpion. This day at noon parted from Richardson and 8 men to go up Malheur and other creeks to trap   there is something melancholy in parting with men with whom one has travelled so far in this uncertain country.   Our party is now 17 boys   Indians literati and all.

25th. This days march was in many different courses but I average them at 23 miles N. W. and camped just before where the trail finally leaves the Snake river and at the same camp where I overtook two years since my men who without orders were leaving the country while I was up Malheur trapping.   Traded this day about 70 salmon which makes a tolerable supply of provisions for the cut to Walla Walla.

26th. Made about 20 miles in about a N. W. direction up Brule   Last night lost two Horses which I think were stolen and today two more gave out.   I now think of leaving two men behind to bring up some of the worst animals otherwise I fear I shall loose many of them.

27th. After leaving Sunsbury and Briggs to bring up the worn out horses I left and making a cut off to the right going up a ravine   across another and down a third came again upon Brule,

at the open Prairie and camped for noon at the upper end of it on
a little run and cashed 24 bars lead and 18 Traps general course
N. W. 14 miles afternoon 9 miles N. W. W. following the little
creek up and camped on a little prairie near the head of it of about
20 acres here there is two trails one N. W. the other N.
the N. W. one I shall try.

28th.   Here taking the left hand trail we followed it 12 miles
N. W. when it disappeared I then took a N. course and at
8 miles came on Powder River which we followed down about 5
miles and camped this afternoon I shall go out to see where the
trail crosses the river.   This day killed an antelope and a Fawn
and saw fresh Elk Track.

29th.   Turned up the creek again and after arriving at where
we first struck the river made 6 miles W. by N. then into cut
rocks then W. N. W. 4 miles more and Nooned on a little water
in a ravine during the forenoon two men whom I had left behind
with the poor animals brough[t] up all but two also during the
forenoon two men got lost and our hunter got lost yesterday all
missing tonight.   Afternoon made 8 miles N. W. and camped in
cut rocks on the main river at a place apparently not frequented
either by Indians or whites but there are Salmon here but we
have no means of catching any without waiting too long.   I think
by the looks there are Beaver here but will ascertain in the morning in order that my trip here may not be entirely lost.

30th.   Made 8 miles up the creek through Cut Rocks during
which time killed one Salmon and Two Otter so much provisions
and Nooned on the Walla Walla trail West Fork the East being
the one I descended on my first Tour afternoon made N. N. W.
on the Trail.   Here plain and good 15 miles at 5 of which
crossed another Fork of Powder River but dry at 5 more a little
water and at camp a little and but a little country rolling and
soil good.   At our camp two lodges of Kiuses

31st.   Made 15 miles N. N. W. good soil and not very hilly
and nooned at the Grand Ronde where I found some Kiuse Indians, Capt Bonneville and two of Mckays men and learned that
Capt. Stewart and Mr. Lee passed two days before.   Afternoon
took the Walla Walla Trail N. N. W. 12 miles and camped at a
very small Prairie with a little stream going N. W.   Killed 5 Hens
today.   On allowance still.

1 Sept.   After about 5 miles de[s]cended a very bad mountain
and followed a dry creek then assended another bad mountain
and nooned without water at 8 miles of very bad going afternoon making along a ridge of mountain 16 miles arrived at the
Ottilla[?] the trail plain the ground stony about N. W. course
but indirect so far from the Three Butes every day has been
thick smoke like fog enveloping the whole country last night
we camped at 10 ock having found no water and the whole coun-

try burnt as black as my Hat   affording as poor a prospect for a
poor sett of Horses as need be.

2nd.   Left camp behind and proceed across the Utalla River to
the N. and up a mountain then took a slight ravine going N. W.
and crossing several trails until the ravine leads to a dry willowed
creek going N. E with a little water in puddles   then N. W. up a
ravine to the height of land which is a gentle slope   then leaving
the trail and going a few Hundred yards to the left followed a Dry
ravine to the Walla Walla River   22 miles in all N. W.   then
down the Walla Walla W. by N. 10 miles to Fort Walla Walla
where I found Mr. Pambrum who did the honors of the Fort in
his usual handsome stile   also found Capt. Stewart and Mess Lees
who arrived two days since.   Mr. Mckay for some reason remained in the mountains.

3rd.   Remained at Walla Walla this day and made arrangements for going down   at night Capt Thing and the residue of
the party came up,

4th.   In morning left Walla Walla in a boat hired by Capt.
Stewart after proceeding 4 miles obliged to come to land to tight-
en the canoe.

5 6 7th.   Down the river and landed to Hire canoes at the
Dalles for the party still behind.

8th.   Waiting at the Dalles for party.

9th.   Waiting at same place   party arrived at night with news
that they drowned one Horse and the Jackass in crossing the
River   I valued him more than 10 horses as a breeder.

10th   At noon having with Difficulty hired three canoes started down the river with three Indians on board.   Wind high and
soon increased to a gale   swamped one of the canoes which fright-
ed the Indians back.   Obliged to lay by with two of the canoes
behind.

11th.   Walked back and brot up the two canoes.   Gale still
furious and finding that my people were not good boatsmen enough
to follow me left the two boats in charge of Capt. Thing and at
noon put ahead   made about 10 miles and swamped the canoe.

12th.   Gale still violent and canoe so leaky as to require one
man to Bail the whole time   kept on until noon and camped until night when it calmed and we put ahead and made to the Cascades   the roar of which warned me to camp.   Here overtook
Capt. Stewart.

13th.   Made our boat a little tighter with some pitch obtained
of Capt. Stewart and made the portage of the Cascade carrying
our things about 1 mile and letting our boat down with ropes
raining hard   made til 9 ock. at night when it rained so hard that
that with the leakage we could keep the boat free of water no
longer and put ashore,

14th.   At 2 ock in morning cleared up a little and we put on
but it kept drizzling   at 9 ock. made the Saw mill above the Fort

and got some breakfast not having eaten since noon the day before   at 12 ock arrived at Fort Vancouver where I found Doct.
McLaughlin in charge who received us in his usual manner   he
he has here power and uses it as a man should to make those
about him and those who come in contact with him comfortable
and happy.

15th.   Early in the morning having hired another canoe put
ahead and in a rainy day at about 12 ock. met the Bg May Dacre
in full sail up the River boarded her and found all well she had
put into Valparaiso having been struck by Lightning and much
damaged.   Capt Lambert was well and brot me 20 Sandwich Is-
landers and 2 Coopers 2 Smiths and a Clerk

16th.   Kept on up the river in order to make Fort Vancouver
and pay my respects to Doct. McLaughlin but the wind failed and
we could not.

17th.   Took the gig and went up to Tea Prairie to see about a
location but found none.

18th.   Came on board and put down the river for Oak point
where we mean to examine for a location.

19th.   Came too at Carneans[?] house and concluded to remain
at least for the winter.

20th.   After setting the forges at work and commencing a coal
kiln houses etc, started up the river Wallammut in a gig the gig
followed the Wallammut 1 mile then took a creek to the right
and after 5 miles came to the farm of Mr. Thomas Mckay. where
I was treated with great kindness by LaBonte his foreman and of
him procured horses and proce[e]ded by land until near night over
hilly wooded country near night came out into large plains of good
lands surrounded with good timber some oak and overtook Mess.
Lees who had started the day before me and camped with them
they are in search of a location.

21st.   Put out in the morning days travell through good lands
rolling sufficient and assorted timber and water. At 3 ock. came
to [and] crossed the Wallamut at Duportes* House and from him got
fresh Horses and proceed up on the E. side of the river to Jervais
10 miles.

22nd.   Not suiting myself as to a farm returned to Duportes
and went to look at a prairie about 3 miles below his place and
concluded to occupy it it is about 15 miles long 7 wide surrounded
with fine timber and a good mill stream on it. 22d Laid out a
farm   afternoon took a canoe and de[s]cended as far as falls.

23rd.   Made the portage of the falls and was taken violently
sick of vomiting and purging   probably caused by having eaten
some Lamprey Eels   recovered toward night and arrived at Fort
Vancouver and finished an arrangement in regard to trade.

24th.   Went down the river to the vessel.

---

* This name is given as "Dupattys" on the map.

25th.　Making preparation for sending out parties

26th.　　　　　Do　　　& sent off Sunsbury to trade Horses at the Dalles.　Sent Stout up the Wallammut with 2 men and implements to commence farm and started myself up to Vancouver on buisness.

28th.　Up the Wallamut with Mr. Nuttall and Townsend and Mr Stout.

29th.　Going up to the falls and went a small distance up the Clackamas River to look at a spot there　found it would not do. Saw there a chalk formation

30th.　Returning down the rivers.

31st.　At night reached the vessell at Carneans　from this time until the 13th Oct. making preparation for a campaign into the Snake country and arrived on the 13th at Vancouver and was received with great attention by all there

14th.　Made up the river 12 miles

15th.　　　"　　"　　"　River 11 miles

16th.　　　"　　"　　"　River 13 miles to the Cascades.

17, 18, 19　Delayed by strong winds and making portage　on the last day at night sent a division off under charge of Capt. Thing

20, 21, 22nd.　Same camp with nothing to eat but what we catch out of the river with our lines not liking to broach our stores for the voyage

23rd.　At sundown our boats arrived from above and I immediately started up the river　we pulled all night except stopping to cook at midnight

24th.　After taking breakfast and giving the Kanackas two hours sleep we put up the river with a head wind　day raw and chill

25th.　Arrived at noon at the Dalles and found all the people well and but one horse traded

26th.　Started Capt. Thing with 12 Kanackas and 6 whites and all the best Horses

27th.　Remained at same camp and traded 5 Horses at about $5.00 of goods each

28th.　Started the boats back and Hubbard down by land with 13 horses for the farm

29th. & 30th.　Same camp　traded 4 Horses.

31st.　Started up the river Kanackas on foot for want of Horses and goods on miserably poor animals　To the 7th Nov. moving slowly up the river during which time and before traded 18 Horses and 600 lbs dried Salmon which I have reserved for provisions after we leave the river when I know we shall get none　and having hired a canoe for Walla Walla dispatched her with this salmon 2 loads of traps　one woman　one Indian and two whites　she sank once but we recovered all and suffered one days delay only to dry the fish　we have lived chiefly on trash and dogs fearing to commence our stock of provisions expecting to get little or nothing all winter and I do not mean to starve except when I cant help it.

8th.   Traded one Horse   a few drops rain today and for more than two thirds of the days since the 1st of the month.   Kept along the river traded 8 dogs today being a 2 days rations.

9th.   Moved along the River Traded 1 dog but no Horses.

10th.   Left camp and went into Walla Walla found Mr. Pambrum well and good natured, and got the news that Capt. Things 12 Kanac[k]as had deserted him and that he had gone in search of them on their trail.

11th.   Went to Capt.   Things camp and learned from Mr Baker that the Kanackas had taken about 2 bales of goods and 12 horses Returned to Walla Walla   on the way met the men who went with Capt. Thing they had not been successfull dispatched an interpreter Mr. Richardson and two other men down the River in a canoe to head the fellows.

12th.   Moved camp up the river a small piece for grass having crossed yesterday no success in trading horses today the Indians appear to think their fortunes are to be made by an opposition but they will find their mistake   today got word that the Kanackas had not touched the Columbia nor passed the Utalla River and that Richardson had got a party of Indians to accompany him and horses and had taken up pursuit on land.

13th.   Richardson stil[l] out   At night dispatched 4 men after two Kanackas that have been seen by the Indians about 15 miles below Walla Walla on the main river.

14th.   Robinson and Richardsons party returned with no success Robinson had seen the track of shod Horses within 5 miles of Walla Walla

15th.   At 10 [o]ck this morning dispatched Richardson and Robinson with two men to trace out the track seen by Robinson.

16th.   An Indian brot in one shod Horse which had been taken by the Kanackas he found it at the Utalla River and brot word that there saw two of the scamps had bot a canoe and gone down leaving on [no?] horse except fat which they [the Indians?] took and one alive which he brot in

17th.   Robinson & Richardson Returned no news yet of the rest

18th.   Finding there is no immediate hope of getting the Kanackas I today dispatched Capt Thing to Fort Hall having 19[?] men viz 4 Kanackas 10 white men and himself a fur[?] man and three Nez Perces 19 in all.   This is a picked up lot and I have great fears they will commit Robbery and desertion to a greater extent than the Kanackas have done but I was obliged to trust to the chance   it is late and the Blue Mounts. are now covered white with snow altho the grass is green here within 30 miles of them.

19th.   Went up the Walla Walla River about 7 mil[e]s and

raised a deposit of goods which I had made in the ground there fearing that some of Capt. Things men who knew where it was might desert and raise it and attempt to go to the Spanish Country. I am now quite sick with a fever but must keep doing,

20th. Spent the day arranging packs for a move Weather clear and cold with much hoar frost and mist.

21st. Deposited the spare goods on hand at Walla Walla fort

22nd. Finished arranging for moving and [have] given up all the Horses still missing viz. 2.

23rd. Moved down the Walla Walla River and camped on the Columbia about 6 miles below the Walla Walla taking leave on the way of Mr. Pambrun the gentleman in charge of the fort Still not well.

24. Moved about 15 miles down the Columbia and camped without wood night quite cold near some bad rapids just above the mouth of the Utalla where I have a cash of traps which I intend to raise.

25. Moved about 15 mil[e]s down the river and camped I had forgot to mention that on the 23rd in the morning when I was about loading the horses I found that Ira Long a sick and as we have supposed crazy Kanacka was missing I then thought that he wou[l]d go at once to Walla Walla but do not hear of him yet I am at a stand to make up my mind w[h]ether he went out of camp and died suddenly or drowned in the river or ran off what he should run off for no one can conceive as no duty had been required of him and he had tea and other luxurys given him on acct. of sickness that no one else had it is a very strange affair to me. To-day I hear that one of the two Kanackas who went down the river in a canoe as per former report has been killed for killing horses by the Indians other reports say a Kanacka has killed an Indian. I also hear that 6 of the runaways are on the heads of John Days River the whole of which storys I take to be lies invented to tell me in the hopes of a small present of tobacco. We live on dogs chiefly good luck traded 4 today.

26th. Made about 12 mils down the river and during the day traded a young fat dog. 27th. Moved about 14 mils down the river traded one poor little dog and 4 dried salmon. We hear such contardictory and impossible accounts from the Indians of the Kanackes that I do not know what to believe.

28th. Moved down the River 15 miles traded nothing all day providentially killed one goose which made supper and breakfast for 5 of us. Snowed a little this day and of course not much comfort for a little cold and wet spoils all the comfort of our camps.

29th. 16 mils down the river killed nothing traded 2 dogs and some little deer meat dried. Snowed all the first part of the day and uncomfortably cold rains tonight very uncomfortable some of us have no coats[?] [tents?] men grumble.

30th.   The rain of last night changed to snow and this morning the Earth is white and the weather cold   made 12 miles and crossed John Days River   then 3 more along the main River and camped with nothing but grass to cook our supper.

31st.   Made today 12 miles   the last of yesterdays and some of todays march pretty bad travelling for the horses owing to cut rocks   camped one mile up the river of falls called by the French "Revieu des Shutes["]. I do not know if from the numerous rapids of this river or its proximity to the great falls of the Columbia which are about 3 miles below its mouth.   There is here a a small villeage of Inds. from whom I understand by signs that the two Kanackes who de[s]cended the river stole horses here or killed Horses and in some wrangle with the chief concerning it one of the Kanackas shot him.   I shall be sorry if this is true as in such case I shall be obliged to make a signal example of him both in order to quiet the Indians and prevent their rising upon the whites and as a terror to the other Kanackas.

Dec. 1st   After trading 4 dogs and a few salmon and roots and ascertained that there was no ford above or near us and that the road lay on the River   we moved camp down to the mouth and and crossed at a rapid and tolerable deep ford   then assended the hill by a ravine and descending again struck a good sized Beaver Creek at 6 miles due South while on the divide could see far ahead of a dreary snowy exposed country without a stick of timder to relieve the eye except far in the distance a black looking mass like a cloud of pine timber.

2nd.   Moved camp early and left the creek on which we camped by a ravine to the right running S. S. W.   followed it to the height of land then down a ravine to the creek on which we camped last night 6 miles   foll[ow]ed this creek 3 miles S. S. W then S. E. to the left of the creek by a ravine 5 more and camped We here find some little oak timber   traded today about 30 lbs. dried deer meat.

3rd.   Made 16 mils to the River des Shutes S. S. E. and camped near about 20 Lodges of Indians   had to buy what little wood we used a thing I mortally detest   last night about 12 sett in to snow   before morning turned to rain which lasted all day the coldest I ever knew and blew a gale in our teeth   this has been a miserable uncomfortable day the first part of it we assended gradually until we reached a high ridge then de[s]cended suddenly to the river   on the ridge considerable snow and the whole country covered with little round cones of earth denoting that the winds blow over this divide continually and strong. Grass is far as I could see pretty good.

4th.   Moved camp S. S. W. 3 miles and camped on the fork of the River coming from timbered hills to the W. N. W.   We hear that the two Kanackas have been followed by the Indians and killed in revenge for killing one of them and their Horses.

5th.   Same camp trying to trade horses   get none yet.
6th.   Same camp
7th.   Same camp
8th.   Same camp
9th.   Same camp During all this time traded but one Horse, but fared well enough for food as we obtained as many dogs as we could eat during the time   Gully my Indian having lost his horse went out to hunt him and as I believe with a determination to quit me he found his horse and sent it to camp by an Indian with word to send his things with some trifling excuse but I kept the Horse and things the Indian whom he sent said he would go and take the Horse for which I gave him a flogging and he went off   during this time we percussioned 3 Rifles our powder being so badly damaged as to render flint locks useless.   In this vicinity there are Elk and Deer as we trade their meat and skins of the Inds. in small quantities the grass here is good and here I cashed some goods our horses being to[o] poor to carry them on.

10th   Moved but without our guide whom I had engaged who was among the missing when we started and I suppose engaged only to get something but without intending to start We took a S. S. W course and crossed the fork on which we had camped for some days past and after mounting the small mountains which range along this fork found an extensive plain beyond which white and high rose a range of mountains disheartening to look at but ahead is the word and the spirit seems to raise with the occasion

this range runs E. & W. made this day 11 miles to the foot of the range along which is a small stream[?]   here we cashed some provisions for our return route and some loads of dry goods which our horses are too weak to carry.

11th.   S. S. W. and mounted the mountains which we found much less formidable than they appeared to be the earth and trees are covered with a heavy hoar frost which at a distance made them look as if covered deep with snow of which there was but little these mountains have scattering groups of pine timber and some oak and the little plains in them have brown[?] cedars similar to those of N. E. but still of a different sort but yet the robins in considerable number feed on the berries which reminded me of old pleasures and home where I have often been out to shoot these birds from the laving[?] but these are too painful to be indulged and the present evil is enough without calling up old joys to enhance it made this day 15 miles and camped on snow water with good pine wood day cloudy wind N. E. and cold Saw the first elk and deer sign for some time they say we cannot cross the divide to Clamat but I will go as far as I can.

12th Engaged an Indian Guide last night but he too it seems has backed out as I cannot find him this morning Made one mile down the ravine in which we camped and came to a small creek running about E. then assended the hills and after 5 mils

came to a larger creek then 3 miles more where the trail gave out then
courses S. S. W then struck S. by E. 3 mils and crossed a small
creek this and the last running E then 3 mils more and camped
on a dry ravine all these last courses S. by E, grass this far pretty
good and country timbered and prettily levell today with small
prairies.   Saw much Elk and Deer signs but killed none.

13th   Made 5 miles S. by E. over level timbered with small
openings country and came to a creek with very bad cut rock
banks at least 400 feet high   we had much difficulty in getting
our horses down to the water and up the opposite bank   but succeeded after laming several of our horses   this creek is rapid tolerably large and runs N. E.   we then made 3 miles S. by E.
and camped   the snow here covers the ground and the horses
have to dig for their food.   Saw today 12 deer and a great quantity of Elk and Deer sign and one bear track   after camping
went out to hunt but could kill nothing   today the first clear day
for four days   the fog lifted a little and enabled us to see a range
of snowy mts on the west side of us and one very high bearing S.
W. distant about 25 miles   should we have any considerable fall
of snow now we should loose all our horses   they could not sub-
sist with much more than there is now   all the dog meat which
we have brot with us from the last Inds. is done
and we have now to look to our guns to supply us
or eat our horses.   We have about 4 bushells of rice
and flour in camp for cases of extremity and a little dog
grease.   Small game there is none   we have but 10 lbs of
powder along and that damaged   Go ahead   very cold for the
4 last days.

14th   Made S. E. 4 miles to a very small creek running in an
immense chasm into which we got and camped the grass being
good and our horses having bad nothing last night except what
they dug up from beneath several inches of snow   saw many deer
today but killed none   sent our hunters out after camping   all
but one returned empty and him I suppose has lost himself in the
forests as I heard a gun late at night and returned several shots
weather still quite foggy and very cold.

15th   S. E. by E. 4 miles and down the ravine the snow growing less and less visibly in this direction   got out of the woods
and saw the country bare of snow   here found a lodge of Indians
who have 32 Horses   traded one of them and have the promise of
trading two more in the morning   the man missing last nigh[t]
came [in] thi[s] mng.

16th.   Traded the two horses one of which cost 82½ cents of
beads first cost.   Made E. down the ravine 2 mils then struck a
good trail crossing the ravine and going off S. S. W. which I followed over rocky high land 8 mils and came to a very large creek
I should think it must be at least one-half of the River Des
Shutes at least running in an immense chasm into which we de-

[s]cended and camped in good grass and plenty of dry wood which makes us very comfortable for the night is very cold during the march over the high land saw a chain of mts on our left and the other side of the river white with snow and partly wooded.

17th.   Went up the creek W. S. W. 2 miles when it turned south and we forded it at a deep ford   horses suffered much from the coldness of the water   then wound S. E. up the opposite bank of the river very high and precipitous 2 miles more   here saw many deer killed none after attaining the heigh[t] made 8 miles S. S. W. through timber and snow then S. S. E. 4 miles also through timber   saw several places where deer had been killed by the wolves which are here numerous and very large   camped at a little grass the first seen today where the horses can dig up a little food.   The country ahead appears more open   we have now a little rice to eat and no meat   begin to look at the horses   still cold.

18th.   Made S. S. E. 12 miles to a small creek   during this days march a snowy range of high mts. in points lay along our right and front stretching so that our course today just doubles their eastwardly termination at a place where probably a fork of the river Des Shutes passes   this range runs N. E. & S. W. still farther on our left and apparently on the other side of the same river there is another range running N. by S.   today saw a very great amt. of sign and deer and have concluded to stop and hunt tomorrow and rest the horses   tonight a little snow squall.

19th.   Same camp   Went out hunting killed 2 deer and several wolves   this day came to us 5 Walla Walla Inds. who are out hunting   they camp with us tonight   they say that the game comes down from the mts. in the winter on account of the snows which is the occasion of its being so plenty at this time   one man out of camp tonight probably lost   shall wait tomorrow for him if he does not come in the meantime and take another hunt for meat which is now quite a luxury.

20th.   Same camp   killed one deer   found the lost man

21st.   Made S. S. E. 15 miles toward the eastwardly termination of the range of mts which has for some time been visible on our right   at this point we can see no mts. but a little farther on the left they commence again apparently the same range which we have seen for some time ranging on the E. side of the river. Killed no game today but saw plenty.

22nd.   S. E. by E. 10 miles and struck a small creek which though very rapid was so hard frozen over that we crossed it on the ice then N. E. 1½ mil[e]s and came to a very large creek which I take to be the main river   it is about as large as the other fork which we crossed on the 17th inst.   country a little more broken   deer plenty but killed none today   a little warmer than usual.

23rd.   Started up the river E. S. E. and gradually in 4 mil[e]s

travel rounded to a S. S. W. course and made 12 more the last 6
of which the snow increased in such a manner that tonight we
find no grass for our Horses and being afraid to advance with
them another days march I have determined to send them back
and with 3 men I propose to build canoes and assend as far as I
can and ascertain if it is possible to get the horses through and
if so to send back for them and if not to ascertain if there is beaver
and if so trap it   if not further advance [in] this quarter is useless.
Tonight set in to snow hard but soon turned to rain.

24th.   Snowed and rained all last [night] and still snowing
with a gale of wind from S. S. W. nearly all the horses gone
astray about 12   having found all but one killed a poor Horse
for food and sent the party all but three back to find grass for
the horses   cut down two large pines and commenced two canoes
gale all day with occasional snow and rain.

25th.   Same camp   gale S. S. W.   Snow and rain all day a
miserable Christmas   worked what little we could on the canoes.

26th.   Day fair and calm   warm   go ahead making canoes

27th.   Day fair calm and warm   still at the canoes

28th.   day fair calm and warm   still at the canoes and eating
horse meat

29th.   Fair weather and mild.

30th.   Fair weather and mild.   Sick with indigestion

31st.   Fair weather and mild   all so far South wind   myself
better and finished the canoes and horse meat at the same time
viz;   this evening at supper   the men have called our two boats
Black Snake & Triton.

1835 Jany 1st,   Started in the morning in the canoes about 5
miles by the river about 2½ miles due south and came to a rapid
in attempting to assend which got filled with water and afterward
in towing with the line she broke loose and went down stream
we recovered her after a long run and assended again to the rapid
and it being near night camped   killed today one fine fat goose
warm south wind rain   snow deeper as we proceed and is now about
2 feet   country rough and covered with pines   set 4 traps for
beaver today and am in hopes to have one for breakfast.

2nd.   Went to my traps   found nothing   then made snow
shoes and set out with one man to explore the river   took a due
south course and in 3 or 4 miles came unexpectedly to the river
there running smooth.   I was happy to see it as I was entirely
tired of this mode of travelling my shoes were too small and I
frequently sunk into the snow and [it] bothered me much to get
out again   sometimes I would tread on my shoes and fall down
and on the whole I though[t] I could get along better without
them   returned to camp   killed three ducks for four of us   small
allowance with our men   took our boat up to the rapids and
spent the residue of the day in getting our canoe past the rapid
most of the time up to my middle in this cold water   had to make

a portage at last of about ¼ of a mile the river here makes a detour to the E. and around S to west to the place where we take our things across.

3rd. Raised my traps and found one beaver caught the largest I ever saw I think he weighed 65 lbs. and killed one duck a very seasonable supply of food the residue of the day finished making the portage and sett 8 traps the other Boat also got setting above Snow today and rained hard last night nearly all night. Wind Strong N. W. the first wind beside S. since 10 days.

4th. Found but one beaver in our traps took a jaunt up the river at about 6 miles straight line S. the river forks into two apparently equal streams followed the left one about 2 mils S. by E. and returned to camp tired enough having found only sign enough in this distance to set 3 traps the river winds so that we have to paddle twice the real distance rained and snowed some during the day. Saw for the first time on this route swans they appear plenty here country still timbered but much more level.

5th. Caught 3 Beaver rained and snowed hard all last night and part of today raised camp and camped about 2 miles below the forks mentioned yesterday one of the beaver caught today would weigh I should think 70 lbs. and our fries look finely with sundry roasting sticks around full of meat the beaver are fat and we live finely again. Wind strong and south.

6th Rained all the forenoon and hail and snow all the afternoon caught no beaver saw very little sign heard a rapid or fall ahead killed 2 swans so fat that we could not eat all the grease a rare thing in this country to be troubled with fat Seems good to live well after poor horse meat and short supply Shall lay down the course tomorrow when I get it more accurately today being too thick to see and the river more winding than ever timber less plenty and very small and but little of the large kind of pine country as far as we can see very level with here and there a round conical mountain.

7th Started up the river to sett traps found sign for but one and returned to camp at the same place as last night killed one swan which would weigh I should think 35 lbs. too fat to eat one we eat yesterday yielded nearly 2 qts. of oil more than we could eat with it. These birds are delicious it is strange that one only does two of us two meals that is to say a day. They dont eat so in the states day pretty cold wind S. W. strong little snow today and some sun out the bed of the river is a soft white stone or hard clay the same as found on the Clacamas I think it is of the chalk formation.

8th Remained all day at same camp on account of a severe snow storm it snowed all day and fell about one foot Blew strong from the South which is almost constant wind here.

9th went down the river and raised some traps we had set there and returned to same camp The river from the last place[to] which I brought it runs S. E. 1 mile at which point a fork coming from the Eastward but it was frozen up so we could not assend it   then south 5 miles to this camp.

10th   Snowed and rained all last night hard and today so we are blessed with about 8 inches of slush   makes every thing very uncomfortable   did not move camp.

11th,   Last night grew cold and set in for a hard snow storm with a gale of wind from the W. S. W. which continued without intermission until sunset today so we did not move camp   the cracking of the falling trees and the howling of the blast was more grand than comfortable   it makes two individuals feel their insignificance in the creation to be seated under a blankett with a fire in front and 3 ½ feet of snow about them and more coming and no telling when it will stop.   tonight tis calm and nearly full moon   it seems to shine with as much indifference as the storms blow and w[h]ether for weal or woe, we two poor wretches seem to be little considered in the matter.   The thoughts that have run through my brain while I have been lying here in the snow would fill a volume and of such matter as was never put into one, my infancy, my youth, and its friends and faults, my manhoods troubled stream, its vagaries, its aloes mixed with the gall of bitterness and its results viz under a blankett hundreds perhaps thousands of miles from a friend, the Blast howling about, and smothered in snow, poor, in debt, doing nothing to get out of it, despised for a visionary, nearly naked, but there is one good thing plenty to eat   health and heart.

12th.   Started up stream and made S. 6 miles at which point there is a considerable creek coming in from W. S. W.   water as warm as the main river and not frozen up.   Then 3 miles S. S. E. and camped.   Saw but little beaver sign today   river not very rapid but winding   saw only two swans   could not kill them caught one yearling beaver   spit snow all day   at night set in to snow hard   moderately cold wind S. but moderate.

13th   6 miles W. by N.   creek very winding and more rapid than usual and camped just below a severe rapid   fine sun in the forenoon but cloudy and snow spits in the afternoon and this evening.

14th   Snowed about 4 inches last night.   Today pretty cold passed the rapid on the south side of the south channel there being a small island at this place   just above the island there is a raft of drift timber which extends across the whole river   this we made a portage of for about 6 rods   at the rapid I hauled the canoe wading in the water about waste deep and remaining in it about 3 hours and got quite numb but at last got through with it

we then assended the river 3 miles more in good water but very winding S. W.   to make which I think we paddled 8 miles to another rapid not severe   finding that it would take some time and being obliged to return to camp soon concluded not to pass this rapid and returned to the first rapid and set 6 traps day windy from S. W. and some snow and sunshine.

15th. Last night excessively cold the cracking of the trees kept me awake part of the night and night before I was kept up most of the night by a fever arising from indigestion today cold calm and clear as the sun got high it was extremely pleasant and this is the only day I have seen that would pass for a pleasant one in a good climate this winter went to the traps found nothing decended the rapid after another cold job in the water and returned to our camp of the 13th inst on the way down saw 5 swan the first since the 12th but killed nothing but 3 ducks We are getting short of provisions again at evening very cold again.

16th Started down the stream and made the portage of the falls about one hour after sunset last night the ther. must have been 10 below zero and the river scum over with drift ice which made us make haste for if we should get frozen up here it would be hard times for food the water fowl and beaver would be done and other game there is absolutely none and to travel would be almost impossible there is four feet of snow however we could try snow shoes. Killed 4 ducks and one swan today the latter would weigh at least 45 lbs. a very seasonable supply as all our food gave out this morning. Day calm sunny not very cold tonight strong south wind and rain.

17th Moved camp down stream about a mile and found our other boat with Mr. Richardson & Rob[in]son the latter during the severe cold had frozen his toes and fingers and the former was unwell with a numbness in his hips they reported to me that the beaver on this creek had made them sick probably this was what was the matter with me there is plenty of wild parsnip here they raised camp with us and we stopped the canoes where we built them and made a portage of ¼ of a mile this severe work in deep snow we then decended about 3 miles and came to rapids part of which we let our boats over by the line in about ½ mile more came to worse rapids and made a portage of about ⅛ mile then immediately let the boats down further rapids about 100 rods to do which I had to remain in the water the whole time it was after dark when I got through the other boat got nearly through and gave it up and I suppose have camped without fire or food. The river falls at each of these carrying places at least 50 feet Rained most all day.

18th. Went up above the last rapid to see the other boat found them comfortably camped they made a portage of their things and I attempted to run their boat empty just as I took the Shute the bow struck a rock I did not see she swung round filled at once and commenced whirling over like a top I hung to her and passed without further damage than mashing both of my feet severely between the boat and a rock was in much pain

all this day but not very lame   we run by the river about two
miles and passed some bad rapids then made a portage of about a
¼ mile into a slew of the river which we followed about ¼ mile
further   then were forced to make a bad portage up a steep bank
of lava about 100 feet   this portage about ¼ mile   we then ran
about two miles further and camped   snow here not so deep as
above and apparently diminishing fast   men much tired and discouraged and wish to abandon the canoes   which I do not mean
to do until I am obliged to   cashed at the first portage today 22
traps   good weather today.

19th.   Started down stream and ran a continuous rapid for
about 2 miles   we let our boats down about ¼ mile then crossed
the river and let the boats down a few rods and finding the river
was pretty much all rapids and falls concluded to abandon the
boats   cashed all but our blankets books amunition axe and ket-
tles and took it on foot with about 60 lbs each on our backs and
1 foot of hard snow into which we sank sometimes and sometimes
not   it however diminished as we proceeded   we made about 6
miles and saw plenty of deer and camped   killed one which was
just in time as a little piece of swan was all the meat left in camp.

I am very tired [and] hungry but the deer will cure all this there is
little snow at this place   our camp I think can not be far off   on
the other side of the river I can see a grassy plain of about 30
miles long and about 5 wide bare of snow   snowed a little this
morning   day fine   tonight freezing a little.

20th   Started late   sore footed but with a full belly and an addition of about 20 lbs meat each   we made about 6 miles and passed our camp of the 22nd and 23rd ult.   about 1 mile further we
crossed a small fork   the one we before crossed on the ice   then
S. 2 miles and camped and tried hard for a deer but could not get
one altho we saw a great many   day fine   this evening cool
grass not much covered with snow   see no sign of camp yet.

21st.   Made 2 miles N. to the river and camped   took a turn
down the river about 5 miles to look for some sign of our camp
found a little Indian sign of about the same age but nothing of
our people.   Afternoon went out to a high hill to the W. and
made a large pile of brush and after dark set fire to it in order
that if our people are near that they may see it and come to us
sent a man over the river to look but he could not cross but he
saw one of their camps shall go tomorrow and ascertain if it so
killed nothing today so we shall have no breakfast in the morning
day fine   tolerable cool   1 inch of snow last night which went
off today.

22nd.   Snowed part of last night and rained the residue and
the forenoon of today   snow the rest and part of the night in
morning our hunter went out and wounded a deer which the
wolves ran down but before he could find him they had eaten up
all but enough for 2 meals   this morning breakfasted on two beav-

er tails which I had laid by and forgotten so we have not yet on
this trip lost a meal as yet   myself in the morning made a raft
and endeavored to cross the river but found I had selected a bad
place and could not do it   went above   found a better place
made another raft and succeeded   found one of our camps so we
now have some clew to camp and shall push for it after getting a
small supply of meat beforehand   wind strong southwardly camped this night in a cave of the rocks   one mile S. of last nights
camp.

23rd   Moved down to camp of 22nd inst and went out to hunt
killed nothing myself but Mr Richardson killed. a fawn so we
have 2 meals ahead besides two nights supper   Mr R. is sick of a
bad cold in his chest and some biles on his neck and cannot carry
his pack   Rained steady all day.

24th   Made 12 miles N. by W. and using what looked like a
fine ford I tried to wade the river but at first failed   went a little
lower and succeeded and got back safe but benumbed with cold
and after warming myself at a fire which the rest had built took
my things across and built a roaring fire to warm   the others as
they came over   here found some beaver cuttings   saw but little
deer or sign today   cold wind W.   cloudy   snow nearly gone.

25th   Made 10 miles N. and seeing a little deer sign stopped
and our hunter went out   during the march we heard a gun on
the west side of the river   we fired guns and were answered
toward night a little Snake Indian came to us and induced us to
go to their camp which was among the cedars about 5 miles N.
E.   we found them without meat but we bought of them a lean
dog of which we made supper and enough left for breakfast so tis
rub and go.   there were three lodges   they had no guns but had
killed much deer as proved by the number of skins they had
last night and this forenoon snowed about 5 inches   today rained and
melted most of it   no water except snow and that dirty at this
camp.

26th   Under the guidance of a Snake Indian we struck N. W.
to the river 7 miles and forded it at a rapid and waist deep ford
then W. by N. 4 miles and came to 8 lodges of Snakes   here our
guide I suppose heard that our camp had moved and backed out
of his job by running away   we then struck N. W. 8 miles and
came to the small river on which we [camped] the 18th 19th and
20th ulto   here we saw one Indian who ran from us who appeared to be a Snake.   while we were debating which course to pursue
we espied 4 Indians on the opposite side of the creek   these we
spoke and they Informed us where our camp was and one of them
took my pack to it   they had killed several deer but we thought
to get to camp and did not take any   we made from the creek N.
N. W. up a very steep high hill 5 miles and coming very dark we
camped for the first time this trip without supper and me without
blanketts and tired enough.

27th   Got up and having no breakfast to cook or eat started the earlier and moved N. N. W. 2 miles and the rest refused to go further   preferring to wait until some chance Indian should come along hunting to take them the right way to camp   I having no pack started in quest of it and passing the N. N. W. course in 1 ½ mile found it on a little thread of water running N. and deep snow   during the time we had been gone they had killed 20 deer and had not starved   the Walla Walla Indians are here hunting. They go out on their horses and run them and as the deer get tired the Inds. get good shots at them   but the number wounded is much greater than that killed   on these the wolves feast at night and keep up a continual howl   after these last comes the ravens for their share   I found missing from yesterday 6 horses among which was my two fine riding horses and three others which have been stolen by the Snakes who are up to this kind of dealing   today sent men to look for the 6 and they brot but one day fine for any country and warm   tonight freezing cold.

28th   Sent out two men again for the 5 missing horses and after finding the residue which not until noon started N. by W. and after 12 miles struck the old trail on which I came up about 6 miles from our camp of 16 & 17   day very fine   nothing to eat tonight but a little flour   camped on a little stream made by the thawing of the snow.

29th   Rose early and without any breakfast started down the valley on which we camped last night which joins a large fork of the Des Shutes in about 3 miles from this and leaving the old trail on which I came up to the left   made N. N. E. 2 miles then leaving the valley to the left made 1 ½ miles N. E.   then going down a very steep and high cut rock bank E. 1 mile   crossed the large fork of the Des Shutes about 2 miles below my camp of the 16th and 17th ulto.   this ford is deeper and more rapid than the one I made before   possibly the stream is higher on account of the thawing of the snow   We are camped with about 12 lodges of Walla Wallas   they have at this moment a good supply of meat deer which they are drying   I presume they have not often so much on hand as they seem to value it highly   on my arrival I made the chief a good present to induce him to influence his people to trade but as yet have traded of root and meat but about 3 days supply   I intend waiting here three nights in order that they make another hunt and then perhaps I may get a sufficient supply to take me down.   Tomorrow is Sunday and there will be neither trading nor hunting in this camp   this is my birthday but I have forgotten how old I am

30th   This unless my reconing is wrong is Sunday at day dawn the chief called the Inds. to prayers   which consist of a short recitation followed by a tune in which all join without words after which a note in accord to wind off   this is repeated several times on Sunday and is a dayly practice   at daylight to-

day the two men sent for the horses came in and brought 4   2 of
which were my riding horses   this day warm as June in   N.
E. and no snow in this valley.

31st   The Inds. commence their meal with religious ceremonys
and then come and beg a smoke   the day is also closed with
religious ceremonies traded about 2 days provisions of the Indians
day fine as summer and the grass begins to start a little

Feb. 1st   Started [from?] camp early and made 8 miles N. by E.
over a trail which we followed the latter part of the 16 ulto. I then
laid the course S. S. W. to make our camp of the 16 & 17 which
was about 1 mile above our last nights camp   traded today about
2 days provisions   looked at the rocks a little and as the country
has been the same as far as I have been a description of the bluffs
here will answer for the whole. There are some cut blufs of
Basalt in its original position but they are chiefly a very coarse
sand stone of an ash color in layers   some of which are finer and
some coarser   it is soft and is composed of rubble stone of lava
and primitive rocks it sometimes contains organic remains   bones
I have taken out of it in a fos[s]il state   a small piece of which I
have preserved   Today cloudy and on the high land over which
we came today it was quite chilly but in the valley of the Small
creek on which we are camped it is warm   latter part of the day
sunny.

2nd   Moved camp N. by E. 8 miles over a plain and pretty
good trail leaving entirely the route which I followed coming up
the Indians killed some deer   grass appears better   day cloudy
or foggy until about noon when the sun came out like April in
N. E.

3rd   This day the Indians concluded not to move camp   I
therefore requested the chief to call on his people to come and
trade meat   they traded about 6 days provisions and I left them
following the trail N. by E. 8 miles to a creek wnich we crossed
in our march of the 12th u[l]to. the Banks of this creek is of
fine deep red clay and at this camp there is a hot spring   too hot
to bear the hand in long and smoking like a coal pit   it tastes of
sulphur and iron and deposits a whitish substance on the pebbles
as it dries away   we hear for the first time this season the croak-
ing of the frogs   trail good, grass good, day cloudy and chill.
Ther in spring 191°

4th. Early in mng. took my thermometer to ascertain the
heat of the spring found it to be 134° and took a good bath by
going a little distance down the stream to find a suitable tempera-
ture and this first time for a long while feel myself pretty clean.
rose camp and crossed the little stream on which we camped and
leaving the Indian trail struck N. N. E. and in 6 miles came to
the main river Des Shutes along which we found a small trail
we made 4 miles N. and camped   during this distance the river
could be run by a good boatman but it is almost a continued rapid

the rocks of this march appear to be all shades between green and red similar to the earth   it appears by being porous to be volcanic   the first course of the march very miry   the last firm and pretty good, grass improving, day cloudy in morning   sunny this afternoon.   Saw much Big Horn and deer sign by the way.

5th   Made along the river 1 mile N.   then west 2 miles up a mountain   then N. 1 mile and down a ravine   then E. N. E. 2 miles to the main river again and down a ravine   then 7 miles N. by E. along the main river and camped   trail plain all the way but very hilly and stony   grass good, day at first cloudy and on the mountain much hoar frost   in afternoon sunny   the upper part of the mountain was of mica slate very much twisted   this afternoon the rock was volcanic and in some places underlaid with green clay   Saw today small bolders of a blackrock which from its fracture I took to be bituminous coal but its weight was about that of hornblende   perhaps it might be Obsidian but I think was heavier than any I have ever seen   river all this days march might be run if there is no bad place where I cut the mountain   saw Big Horn trails but not the game.

6th   Made along the river 4 miles N. by W. during which space saw nothing that might not be passed by a good boatman then mounted the W. bank of the river and came to a large cedar plain 3 miles N. by W.   then N. by E. over the plain 6 miles more to tinkers camp   in crossing at this camp wet my cases with all my papers by a horse falling in the river while fording   day cloudy with a little snow   found this branch some higher than when I passed up   here we found and raised a small cash which I made on my way up and during the march sent two men to raise another which I made at the next camp above   from these Indians I hear that [of] my runaway Kanackas   10 took the trail over the Blue   one was drowned in crossing some ford   one froze in the upper country   that the residue rafted the Snake river   one more died somehow about the falls   that 7 are gone down to Vancouver   tonight traded 8 dogs for their fat to kill the lice on my horses.

7th   Early in the day the two men sent to raise the cash came in with its contents undamaged   exchanged at this camp a poor little, lame, mare for a tolerable horse in pretty good order   traded for a knife each 6 dogs today   used the grease of these dogs to kill the lice on my horses that are nearly covered with them day cloudy but not cold in the valley   Mount Hood bears ½ point N. of N. W.   sick myself of a bowell complaint   cashed at this camp 1 ⅓ bales corn and 7 setts shoes and nails.

8th   N. N. W. 16 miles   in the first place 2 miles to the top of an elevated range of woodless hills which skirt the west side of the creek on which we camped   then down the slope of these hills 4 miles more   during this space much snow   then struck into a little creek which we followed 6 miles then up the left bank of this creek to another and larger fork of the same 4 miles and camped in good grass　This creek comes from the S. W. and is now as large as the small creek on which I camped the first night after leaving the mouth of the river Des Shutes on my way　up there are several Indians with me who say that once there was much beaver on this creek but that the British Cos have trapped it out　day cloudy　a few drops of rain.

　　9th　Moved camp early on a plain and good trail N. N. W. 10 miles to the Dalls　after following on this trail 3 miles we came to a small creek coming from the W. S. W. and joining the one on which we camped last night and at 5 miles more another which either joins the same very near the Columbia or goes into the Columbia　found Soaptilly[?] and a few more Chinooks at the river of whom I traded one horse and a canoe　they report 7 Canackas gone down and that one was drowned at the falls and one froze in the mountains leaving one unaccounted for　rained a little today.

　　10th　Started early in a very leaky canoe which kept us bailing all the time and made 8 miles N. W.　5 W. and 3. S. W. 1 west and on account of high wind camped about noon　a little rain as usual.

　　11th　At about sunsett last night the wind lulled a little and we made a start but the wind continued high and about 2 ock we arrived at the Cascades a little above which we camped　this morning went to the Cascades and there found Mr Ermatinger with a brigade of 3 boats taking up the outfits for the upper forts　also Capt. Stewart Mr Ray and one more gentleman　made the portage and in 12 hours made the saw mill.

　　12th　In the morning made to Vancouver and found there a polite reception and to my great astonishment Mr Hall J. Kell[e]y he came in Co. with Mr Young from Monte El Rey and it is said stole between them a bunch of Horses　Kell[e]y is not received at the Fort on this account as a gentleman　a house is given him and food sent him from the Gov. Table but he is not suffered to mess here　I also found 7 of my runaway Kanackas　they appear to be very sick of their job so I have concluded not to be severe with them　I hear also that Fort Hall has traded 300 skins up to what time do not know or how true　also that Tom Bule & Harry two more of the runaways are with some of McKays men on Snake River　they will probably fall in at Fort Hall.

　　13th　Went down to the station at Carneaus[?] and found all well and doing pretty well.　This is Sunday and I have lost 3 days somewhere.　During the residue of this month sent Mr Richardson to the Dalles with supplies for the party which I left above trapping　he had tempestuous weather and was gone 13 days　myself took a trip up the Wallamut to look after the farm and my taylor who had deserted me during the winter　after

Richardson had gone I took a small canoe and proceeded up the Columbia and in my progress got filled with the violence of the wind and quantity of rain   I arrived at Vancouver in the morning 23rd Feb. and met a reception such as one loves to find in such a country as this

24th   Started down the Columbia to the mouth of the Wallamut up which about 4 miles to the head of Wappatoo Islands here finding the canoe to deep to proceed against the rapid current of this river now very high   we put down the west slew and crossed over the first bank of the river into the waters back and went to the Farm of Mr Thomas McKay and procured horses and went by land   this took us all of the 25 & 26 both of which days it rained hard   all the little streams made us swim our horses and some of the open prairies were swimming and much of them wading   at night of the 26th arrived at Sandy camp   just above which I had begun a farm.

27th   Went to the farm and found the Taylor and Sloat the foreman gone down to see me they having heard of my return

during the day went up to Mr Lees place in order to get Babtiste to school with him in which I succeeded

28th   returned to Camp Sandy   rain today

29th   Started for McKay Farm during a hard rain and snow

30th   Arrived at McKays farm

31st   Back to station at Carneaus [?] place and here found my runaway Taylor

March 1st   From this time until the 8th employed him in getting out coopers stuff and timber for a house boat which I intend to build.

Apl 13th   Sunday I suppose   employed in getting out stuff for the house boat in cutting 8000 hoop poles and in building a canoe 60 feet long wide and deep enough to chamber barrells of which she will take 25   she is clean of knotts shakes and almost of sap and 27 feet cut off the same tree of the same kind of stuff

the whole tree was 242 feet long and this by no means the largest tree on Wappatoo Island   this is of the Spruce kind today I am on my way down to Fort William where the Brig lay to regulate matters there   I have just parted from Mr McLaughlin Esq. on his way to view the Fallatten [Tualatin]plains I suppose with some idea of making him a farm there some day   I have now out of 21 people 7 sick and little work can be done after deducting from the remaining 14 a provision boat to trade food and enough to take care of the sick   up to the first of this month it rained continually and about ¼ of the time since   I find the plows which I brought from the States of no use in the new lands here   no news as yet from Bg. or Capt Thing   So far with much exertion we provided ourselves with food but the whites in this country are exhausted of all kinds.

COPY OF A LETTER AND A STATEMENT OF FACTS
PERTAINING TO A CLAIM BASED UPON
OPERATIONS INVOLVED IN THE
TWO EXPEDITIONS.

Camb. Dec 13th 1847

Dear Sir,

    The papers herewith enclosed are in continuation of
of the subject brought to your notice in my letter of the 5th of
April last which was accompanied by copy of statements relating
to claims of John McLoughlin Esq., formerly chief Factor in charge
of the H. B. Co's western district comprising all the territories occupied by that Co west of the Rocky Mts. but who has since retired from their service, and resides at Oregon City. This statement or memorial was dated previous to the late treaty of boundary with Great Britian, and under the impression that his rights
would be subjected to the capricious justice of the new settlers
who had then formed a provisional government. I conceive that
the said treaty fully secures his rights, or should they not be
secured by the treaty, you will oblige me by securing them so far
as in your power. I have placed the copy of his memorial as
above stated in your hands for this purpose. At this time I shall
confine myself to my own interests in Oregon.

    Having gone to Oregon in march 1832 for purposes recognized
by the convention then existing between the U. S. & G. B.
having formed establishments there of the same character and for
the same purposes, as those formed previously by the N. W. &
Hudson's Bay Cos. having maintained one of the same through
tenant to the present time, and having after two expeditions, accompanied by much suffering and expenditure of five years time,
and more than $20,000 in money, established the nucleus of the
present American settlement in these regions, I ask the American
government to place my interests in that country on as favorable
a basis, as the treaty of boundary places those of British subjects
whose pos[s]essions are of the same character. The recommendation
of the President would benefit only actual settlers, and would entirely exclude me. It seems to me a law might be passed consistent with justice, granting a preemption to all Americans who have
ever resided in Oregon, and who occupied land there, and continued to hold the same either directly or by agents or tenants, to

the absolute extent of the property so occupied, as it was at the period of the organization of the provisional government of Oregon. And to all Americans actual settlers, occupying lands after the organization of said provisional government, and until the extension of the laws of the U. S. over the territory, a preemption to all the lands so occupied not exceeding one square mile.

I do not believe a law mainly such as proposed above would benefit a single American except myself. I do not know one other who has occupied more than a mile square, while there are several British subjects who have done so, and whose claims are all secured by the treaty whether large or small. And unless some such law is passed it appears to me that I am to be stripped of all my rights, and that the great sacrifices I have made will inure to the the benefit of all concerned except myself. That you may better understand why I desire some protection from the government I here with send a statement of facts No. 1, and a petition to Congress No 2. I remain Very Respectfully

Yr' obt Svt.
Nathl J. Wyeth.

To Hon. J. G. Palfrey, M. C.

(Statement of facts No. 1)

On the 10th day of March 1832 I left Boston in a vessel with 20 men for Baltimore where I was joined by four more, and on the 27th left by Rail Road for Frederic Md from thence to Brownsville we marched on foot, and took passage from that place to Liberty Mo. on various steamboats, which place we left for the prairies on the 12th of May with 21 men, three having deserted, and on the 27th of May three more deserted. On the 8th of July we reached Pierre's Hole at the head of Lewis River where was then a rendezvous of Trappers and Indians. We remained at this place until the 17th at which time my party had been reduced by desertion and dismissial to 11 men, and then started for the Columbia arriving at Cape Disappointment on the 8th Nov. 1832, one man having died on the route. There I learned that a vessel on which I relied for supplies had been wrecked at the Society Islands. This intelligence discouraged the party so much that all but two requested a discharge. Of the 8 who then left me 5 returned to the U. S. by sea, one died there in 1834 and two remained as settlers. In the Spring of 1833 I commenced my return to the states with the two remaining men. When I reached the mouth of the Yellowstone one left me to remain with some of the trappers until I should return. With the other I reached the States, and soon after fitted out a vessel for the Columbia, and on the 7th Feb. 1834 left Boston for St. Louis where I organised a party of 70 men for the overland trip arriving at the head waters of the Snake or Lewis river in July 1834, and on the 15th of that month commenced to build Fort Hall, and after placing it in a defensive condition left it on the 7th August following for the mouth of the Columbia. On the 15th of Sept. I reached Oak Point 75 miles from its mouth where I met my vessel just arrived after a voyage of 8 ½ months, having been struck by lightening at sea and so injured as to be obliged to go into Valparaiso to repair. This vessel was fitted for the salmon fishing of that season. Her late arrival caused me to detain her until the following year. During the winter of 1835 this vessel went to the Sandwich Islands with timber & card returned in the Spring with cattle sheep goats & hogs which were placed on Wappatoo Island where in the mean time I had built an establishment called Fort William on the southwesterly side of the island and about 8 miles from the H. B. Co's post of Vancouver. At this post we grazed all the animals obtained from the Islands California and from the Indians, planted wheat corn potatoes peas beans turnips, grafted & planted apples and other fruits, built dwelling house and shops for working iron and wood, and in fact made a permanent location which has never been abandoned. I made this my personal residence during the Winter and Summer of 1835. In the autumn of that year I proceeded to Fort Hall with supplies, having sent some previous to that time. During the winter of 1836 I resided at my post of Fort Hall, and in the Spring of that year returned to Fort William of Wappatoo Island whence I carried more supplies to Fort Hall arriving there the 18th June, and on the 25th left for the U. S. by way of Taos and the Arkansas river and arrived home early in the Autumn of 1836. The commercial distress of that time precluded the further prosecution of our enterprise, that so far had yielded little but misfortunes. It remained only to close the active business which was done by paying every debt, and returning every man who desired, to the place whence he was taken, and disposing of the property to the best advantage. All the property in the interior including Fort Hall was sold, it being necessary in order to retain that post, to keep up a garrison for its defense against the Indians, and to forward annual supplies to it, an operation at that time beyond our means. Fort William at Wappatoo Island requiring nothing of that kind was retained, and the gentleman then in charge Mr C. M. Walker was directed to lease it to some trusty person for 15 years unless sooner reclaimed. Nothing having been heard from Mr Walker for a long time I sent a request to John McLaughlin Esq. for the same purpose and also to have the island entered in my name at the land office established by the provisional government. That the original enterprise contemplated a permanent occupation is clearly shown by the instructions to the master of the brig Capt Lambert When I arrived on the lower Columbia in the Autumn of 1832 as her[e]in before stated there were no Americans there nor any one having an American feeling.　So far as I know there had not been since Mr. Astor retired from the coast.　Of the 11 men which I had then with me three remained until I again arrived in the Autumn of 1834 and 19 of those who then accompanied me including the missionaries remained permanently in the country.

Nath 1 J. Wyeth

INDEX.

I

Ice business, 10, 34, 83, 108, 111, 118, 133, 143, 150
Independence Rock, 157, 224
Indian boys, 59, 105 (See Baptiste)

J

Jackson, 38, 74
Jarvis, Leonard, assistance offered by him to Wyeth, 7, 8, 10; letter to containing request for assistance and giving considerations affecting the advisability of the enterprise undertaken by the author, 31-3; fragment of letter to expressing thanks for favors, 52; fragment of letter to outlining plans for returning, 55; letter to stating conditions of carrying on fur trade and requesting that Jarvis conduct negotiations with the H. B. Co., 66-7; letter to asking for advice in the treatment of certain calumnies, 81-2; letter to in which author vindicates himself against aspersions in Bell's letters and John Wyeth's book, 85-9; letter to reporting adverse conditions in his affairs, 135; letter to in which the author reviews his situation, 151-2
Jervais, 74
Journal, proposed disposition of 48, 97

K

"Kanackas" (Hawaiians), 234, 240, 250
Kansas river, 22
Kelley, Hall J., addressed as general agent for the Oregon Colonization Society, 1; petition to congress, 17-8; his means for moving and likelihood of his going, 30; probability of his party starting, 36; letter to in which Wyeth gives reasons for not going with him, 39; letter to in which Wyeth declares his resolution to proceed without delaying for Kelley's colony, 43; letter to expressing willingness to take charge of some emigrants, 50; letter to indicating disposition towards colonizing the Columbia region, 51; 90, 250
Ken (See Can)

L

Laidlow, 79

Lambert, Capt., 61, 150, 151, 233
Lansing, E. E., letter to implying that he contemplates joining the first expedition, 45; Leonard Wyeth instructed to write to him, 46
Laramie fork, 156, 223
Latitude and longitude, process of calculating, 101-2
Lawrence, Josiah & Co., agent for Wyeth at Cincinnati, 112, 116, 121
Lee, Jason, letter to giving date of leaving for St. Louis, 111, 128, 227, 231
Livermore, Solmon K., letter to pertaining to his son's wish to join the first expedition, 16, 17; letter to in which the matter of his son's joining the expedition is discussed, 25-6; letter to on the right to trade with Indians in the Oregon country, 30-1; letter to relative to history and prospects of trade in the Oregon country, 38-9, 80, 81, 85-9, 90
Livermore, Thomas, (See in above references)

M

McFarlan, Leonard Wyeth instructed to write to him, 46
McGill, (See Von Phull & McGill)
McKay, 180, 227, 231, 251
McKenzie, 79
McLoughlin, Dr. John, his hospitality 53; letter to expressing obligations to Ermatinger and offering services, 68, 79, 140, 176-7, 181, 233, 251, 253
McNeil, Capt., 61
March, E. E., letter to received from Leonard Wyeth, 46; to be entrusted with papers, 67
Marshall, Josiah, 38
Men for expedition, 94-5, 103
Men of the first expedition, 178
Metcalf, E. W., letter to, 115, 137
Missionaries, (See Jason Lee)

N

Neil, Col. J. W., letter to containing inquiries regarding the contemplated expedition of the Oregon Colonization Society, 3
News, given to Ermatinger, 69
Noah, Cousin, letter to pertaining to communication with Ball, 105
Note, protested, 70, 71
Norris & Co., letter to containing inquiries for traps, 33

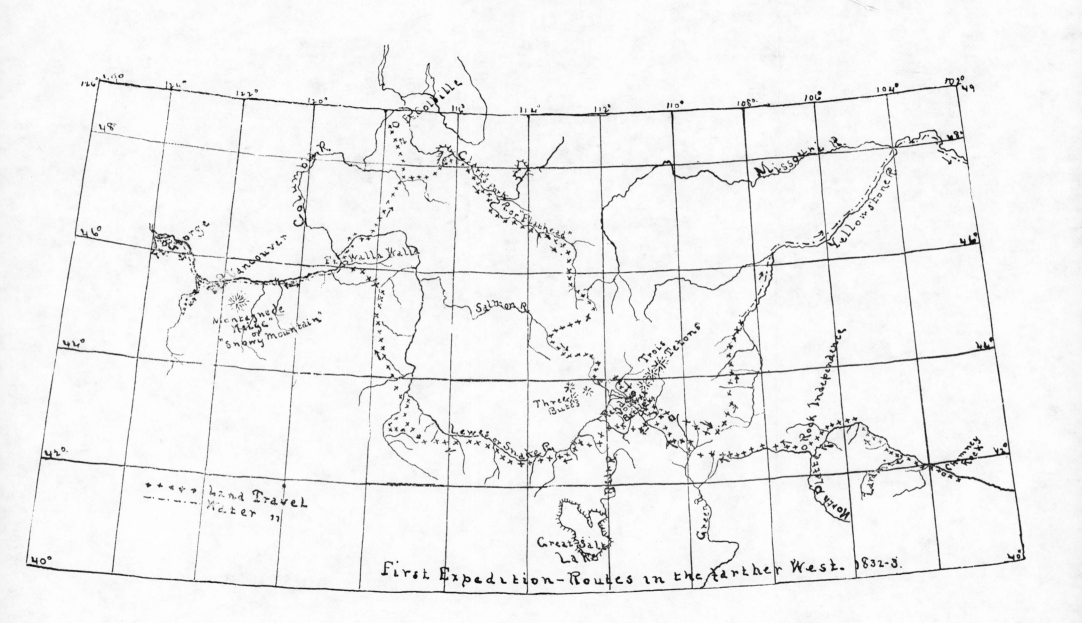

First Expedition-Routes in the farther West. 1832-3.

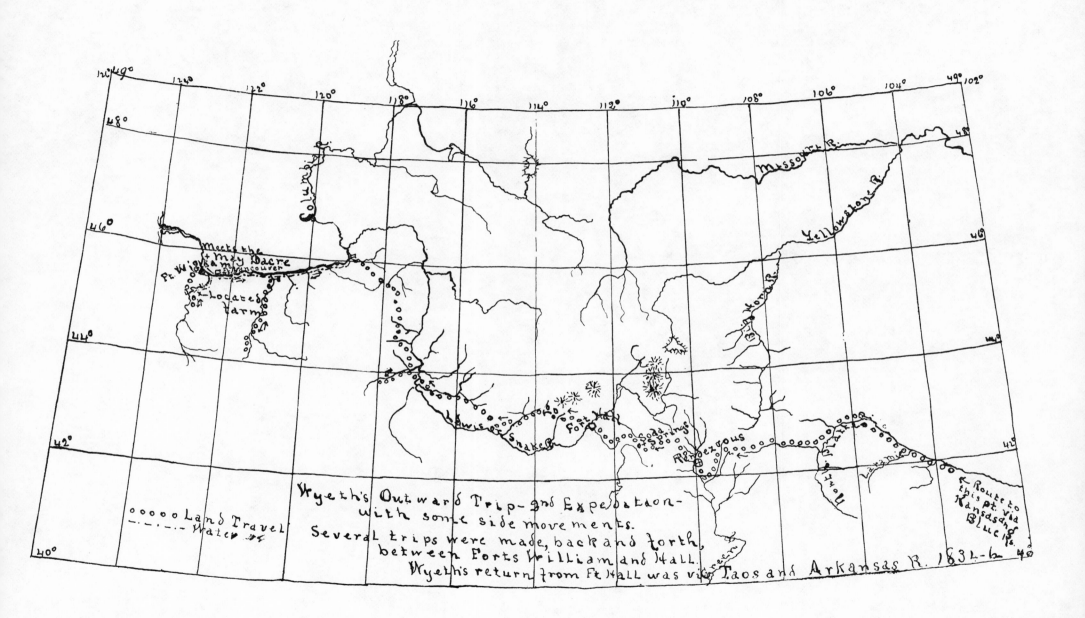

Wyeth's Outward Trip – 2nd Expedition –
with some side movements.
Several trips were made, back and forth,
between Forts William and Hall.
Wyeth's return from Ft Hall was via Taos and Arkansas R. 1834-6

The Far Western Frontier

An Arno Press Collection

[Angel, Myron, editor]. **History of Nevada.** 1881.

Barnes, Demas. **From the Atlantic to the Pacific, Overland.** 1866.

Beadle, J[ohn] H[anson]. **The Undeveloped West; Or, Five Years in the Territories.** [1873].

Bidwell, John. **Echoes of the Past:** An Account of the First Emigrant Train to California. [1914].

Bowles, Samuel. **Our New West.** 1869.

Browne, J[ohn] Ross. **Adventures in the Apache Country.** 1871.

Browne, J[ohn] Ross. **Report of the Debates in the Convention of California, on the Formation of the State Constitution.** 1850.

Byers, W[illiam] N. and J[ohn] H. Kellom. **Hand Book to the Gold Fields of Nebraska and Kansas.** 1859.

Carvalho, S[olomon] N. **Incidents of Travel and Adventure in the Far West; with Col. Fremont's Last Expedition Across the Rocky Mountains.** 1857.

Clayton, William. **William Clayton's Journal.** 1921.

Cooke, P[hilip] St. G[eorge]. **Scenes and Adventures in the Army.** 1857.

Cornwallis, Kinahan. **The New El Dorado; Or, British Columbia.** 1858.

Davis, W[illiam] W. H. **El Gringo; Or, New Mexico and Her People.** 1857.

De Quille, Dan. (William Wright). **A History of the Comstock Silver Lode & Mines.** 1889.

Delano, A[lonzo]. **Life on the Plains and Among the Diggings;** Being Scenes and Adventures of an Overland Journey to California. 1854.

Ferguson, Charles D. **The Experiences of a Forty-niner in California.** (Originally published as *The Experiences of a Forty-niner During Thirty-four Years' Residence in California and Australia*). 1888.

Forbes, Alexander. **California:** A History of Upper and Lower California. 1839.

Fossett, Frank. **Colorado:** Its Gold and Silver Mines, Farms and Stock Ranges, and Health and Pleasure Resorts. 1879.

The Gold Mines of California: Two Guidebooks. 1973.

Gray, W[illiam] H[enry]. **A History of Oregon, 1792–1849.** 1870.

Green, Thomas J. **Journal of the Texian Expedition Against Mier.** 1845.

Henry, W[illiam] S[eaton]. **Campaign Sketches of the War with Mexico.** 1847.

[Hildreth, James]. **Dragoon Campaigns to the Rocky Mountains.** 1836.

Hines, Gustavus. **Oregon:** Its History, Condition and Prospects. 1851.

Holley, Mary Austin. **Texas:** Observations, Historical, Geographical and Descriptive. 1833.

Hollister, Ovando J[ames]. **The Mines of Colorado.** 1867.

Hughes, John T. **Doniphan's Expedition.** 1847.

Johnston, W[illiam] G. **Experiences of a Forty-niner.** 1892.

Jones, Anson. **Memoranda and Official Correspondence Relating to the Republic of Texas, Its History and Annexation.** 1859.

Kelly, William. **An Excursion to California Over the Prairie, Rocky Mountains, and Great Sierra Nevada.** 1851. 2 Volumes in 1.

Lee, D[aniel] and J[oseph] H. Frost. **Ten Years in Oregon.** 1844.

Macfie, Matthew. **Vancouver Island and British Columbia.** 1865.

Marsh, James B. **Four Years in the Rockies; Or, the Adventures of Isaac P. Rose.** 1884.

Mowry, Sylvester. **Arizona and Sonora:** The Geography, History, and Resources of the Silver Region of North America. 1864.

Mullan, John. **Miners and Travelers' Guide to Oregon, Washington, Idaho, Montana, Wyoming, and Colorado.** 1865.

Newell, C[hester]. **History of the Revolution in Texas.** 1838.

Parker, A[mos] A[ndrew]. **Trip to the West and Texas.** 1835.

Pattie, James O[hio]. **The Personal Narrative of James O. Pattie, of Kentucky.** 1831.

Rae, W[illiam] F[raser]. **Westward by Rail:** The New Route to the East. 1871.

Ryan, William Redmond. **Personal Adventures in Upper and Lower California, in 1848–9.** 1850/1851. 2 Volumes in 1.

Shaw, William. **Golden Dreams and Waking Realities:** Being the Adventures of a Gold-Seeker in California and the Pacific Islands. 1851.

Stuart, Granville. **Montana As It Is:** Being a General Description of its Resources. 1865.

Texas in 1840, Or the Emigrant's Guide to the New Republic. 1840.

Thornton, J. Quinn. **Oregon and California in 1848.** 1849. 2 Volumes in 1.

Upham, Samuel C. **Notes of a Voyage to California via Cape Horn, Together with Scenes in El Dorado, in the Years 1849–'50.** 1878.

Woods, Daniel B. **Sixteen Months at the Gold Diggings.** 1851.

Young, F[rank] G., editor. **The Correspondence and Journals of Captain Nathaniel J. Wyeth, 1831–6.** 1899.